Palgrave Studies in Green Criminology

Series Editors
Angus Nurse
Department of Criminology and Sociology
Middlesex University, London, United Kingdom

Rob White
Department of Criminology
University of Tasmania, Hobart, Tasmania, Australia

Melissa Jarrell
Texas A&M University, Corpus Christi
Corpus Christi, Texas, USA

Criminologists have increasingly become involved and interested in environmental issues to the extent that the term Green Criminology is now recognised as a distinct subgenre of criminology. Within this unique area of scholarly activity, researchers consider not just harms to the environment, but also the links between green crimes and other forms of crime, including organised crime's movement into the illegal trade in wildlife or the links between domestic animal abuse and spousal abuse and more serious forms of offending such as serial killing. This series will provide a forum for new works and new ideas in green criminology for both academics and practitioners working in the field, with two primary aims: to provide contemporary theoretical and practice-based analysis of green criminology and environmental issues relating to the development of and enforcement of environmental laws, environmental criminality, policy relating to environmental harms and harms committed against non-human animals and situating environmental harms within the context of wider social harms; and to explore and debate new contemporary issues in green criminology including ecological, environmental and species justice concerns and the better integration of a green criminological approach within mainstream criminal justice. The series will reflect the range and depth of high-quality research and scholarship in this burgeoning area, combining contributions from established scholars wishing to explore new topics and recent entrants who are breaking new ground.

More information about this series at
http://www.springer.com/series/14622

Ragnhild Sollund • Christoph H. Stefes • Anna Rita Germani
Editors

Fighting Environmental Crime in Europe and Beyond

The Role of the EU and Its Member States

palgrave
macmillan

Editors
Ragnhild Sollund
University of Oslo
Oslo, Norway

Christoph H. Stefes
Department of Political Science
University of Colorado Denver
Denver, United States

Anna Rita Germani
Sapienza University of Rome
Rome, Italy

Palgrave Studies in Green Criminology
ISBN 978-1-349-95084-3
ISBN 978-1-349-95085-0 (eBook)
DOI 10.1057/978-1-349-95085-0

Library of Congress Control Number: 2016948408

Cover illustration: Niall Benvie / Alamy Stock Photo

Printed on acid-free paper

This Palgrave Macmillan imprint is published by Springer Nature
The registered company is Macmillan Publishers Ltd.
The registered company address is: The Campus, 4 Crinan Street, London, N1 9XW, United Kingdom

Foreword

This volume was compiled as part of the research project European Action to Fight Environmental Crime (EFFACE) which was funded by the 7th Framework Programme for Research of the EU Commission. The 40-month project brought together researchers from 11 European universities and think tanks and from a range of disciplines including law, political science, economics, and criminology.

In the main, this book presents case studies conducted by EFFACE researchers, but in addition, several other elements of the research were also central to EFFACE's work:

First, EFFACE facilitated an analysis of existing instruments, actors, and institutions that play a role in combating environmental crime. This included country reports on several EU Member States as well as the mainly legal analysis of European legislation and international treaties relevant for environmental crime, such as the EU's Environmental Crime Directive and a number of multilateral environmental agreements. The analysis also demonstrated that the ineffectiveness of the EU's efforts in addressing environmental crime was predominantly a result of the lax enforcement of existing rules rather than major flaws in the regulatory framework.

A second main aspect of the EFFACE research agenda concerned the availability of qualitative and quantitative data on the impact of EU-related environmental crime as well as the possibility to develop monetary estimates of such impacts. Having looked at data availability for various types of environmental crime, researchers concluded that data availability varied. There were some, but not many EU-level databases available (e.g. on forest fires), and existing data from Member States frequently lacked in internal coherence and comparing data from different Member States was difficult. Moreover, there were large gaps in data availability. While methods for determining the monetary impacts of environmental crime were discussed, the analysis also showed the difficulties and the value judgments entailed in doing so.

Third, EFFACE addressed the strengths, weaknesses, threats, and opportunities (SWOT) of the current EU and Member State approaches to environmental crime. This analysis was undertaken for nine different, but related aspects: data and information management, further harmonization of substantive environmental criminal law at the EU level, the system of sanctions (administrative, criminal, or civil proceedings), the functioning of enforcement institutions and cooperation between them, the role of environmental crime victims and civil society in addressing environmental crime, the environmental crime and the EU's external relations, the use of environmental liability to address environmental crime, organized environmental crime, as well as corporate responsibility and liability in relation to environmental crime.

Fourth, and building on the SWOT analysis as well as other results of EFFACE, including the case studies, EFFACE researchers jointly developed policy recommendations. These were discussed with experts and practitioners at a workshop and met with significant support. Some of the core recommendations of EFFACE are the following:

- The fact that environmental crime has been committed in the context of organized crime should be considered an aggravating circumstance in the Environmental Crime Directive.
- Rules on the confiscation and forfeiture of the proceeds of environmental crime should be adopted at the EU level.
- An obligation should be imposed on Member States to provide data on the number of violations of national provisions implementing European environmental law (commonly referred to as the environmental

acquis) as well as the number of prosecutions of and sanctions imposed for these violations.

- Member States should promote effective sanctions, including civil and administrative sanctions (also fines).
- Member States should introduce and use complementary sanctions and measures, in addition to the classic criminal sanctions, that is, prison sentences and fines.
- Non-binding guidelines concerning prosecution and sentencing policies should be developed that can be applied throughout the EU. Ideally, these guidelines should be developed bottom-up by networks of practitioners from various EU Member States.
- Environmental crime should be made a priority at both the EU and Member State level.
- Member States should provide for specialization of prosecution and adjudication.
- The EU should set minimum criteria for environmental inspections and monitoring.
- The role of Eurojust, the European Public Prosecutor's Office, environmental enforcement networks, and Europol should be enhanced, and networking at the domestic level should be stimulated.
- In international forums, the EU should take a leading role in advocating for a tougher approach to environmental crime.
- The EU and its various agencies involved in the fight against environmental crime should seek close cooperation with national and international environmental and police agencies to coordinate the fight against environmental crime across borders.

The most important overall results are summarized in the EFFACE synthesis report, addressed to policy makers and a non-academic audience.

Throughout the project, the EFFACE consortium sought extensive interaction with experts and practitioners on the topic of environmental crime, notably through a series of nine workshops. The EFFACE Advisory Board comprising renowned academic experts as well as two prosecutors working on environmental crime, also played an important role in providing feedback on research results. EFFACE was aimed at making a real impact, not the least through keeping environmental crime as a topic on the political agenda of the EU and its Member States and by developing recommendations on how it can be addressed more effectively. Therefore, EFFACE undertook significant efforts in disseminating its work to policy makers and enforcement practitioners. As a result, EFFACE studies have been quoted in current policy documents of the EU, notably in the context of the preparation of the EU's recent Action Plan against Wildlife Trafficking. They also constituted the basis for a briefing and study compiled for the European Parliament's ENVI Committee and were presented to policy makers and enforcement practitioners, for example, at the European Parliament and conferences of environmental enforcement networks such as IMPEL.

The present book, *Fighting Environmental Crime in Europe and Beyond: The Role of the EU and Its Member States,* is an integral component of EFFACE's dissemination of scientific work. I trust its chapters will provide readers with many valuable insights into the causes of and actors involved in committing environmental crime and efforts to combat it. I wish to thank the editors for their excellent work and effort in compiling this volume. Given the range of disciplines the editors represent, this is truly an interdisciplinary work. Interdisciplinary work always requires a substantial investment in time and commitment to engage with others in meaningful conversations.

Senior Fellow, Ecologic Institute,
EFFACE coordinator

Christiane Gerstetter

Preface and Acknowledgments

This book reflects parts of the work that was conducted during the EFFACE project. It has been roughly 3 years of learning, inspiration, and building friendships. The members of the consortium have, despite flight carbon emissions, met for project meetings in many interesting places in Europe, such as Berlin, Brussels, Granada, and Rome. These meetings and professional encounters represent interdisciplinary academic exchange which taught us about the specific environmental problems of different geographical locations in Europe and beyond, the importance of bringing different academic perspectives to the battle against environmental crimes, and the value of interpersonal cooperation. To cooperate, it is necessary to meet, talk, and get to know each other. To have concluded the project is sentimental, but there's also a real sense of satisfaction because of the project's achievements.

The work has been challenging but fruitful, and in this anthology we are happy to present to the public the result of important case studies from the EFFACE project. We have aimed at not excluding any potential readers through complicated disciplinary or technical terms, and hope our readers will learn as much from this work as we have. Most importantly, we hope that the results presented in this book will be used to improve the situation concerning the various environmental crimes that are addressed in the book.

Finally, as editors, we wish to thank the European Commission for the funding provided and Ecologic Institute and the general coordinator of the EFFACE research project, Christiane Gerstetter, for the support which made the book possible. We would also like to thank the editors of the Palgrave Studies in Green Criminology, Rob White and Angus Nurse, for agreeing to publish this volume in the series, as well as Kerry Fast for copy editing and improving our work.

Oslo, Norway — Ragnhild Sollund
Denver, United States — Christoph H. Stefes
Rome, Italy — Anna Rita Germani

Contents

List of Figures

List of Tables

List of Boxes

1

Introduction

Ragnhild Sollund

The chapters in this anthology are based on the fourth work package of the European Union Action to Fight Environmental Crime (EFFACE) project, consisting of case studies covering a range of environmental crimes in different locations in the European Union (EU) and in places linked to the EU. They show that environmental crimes are indeed transnational, eco-global crimes (White 2011).

This book includes an overview of the legal framework concerning environmental crimes in the EU and the EU's action plan to protect the environment and combat environmental crimes. The chapters also cover environmental crime in a broad range of geographical areas (the EU, Colombia, Brazil, UK, Norway, Kosovo, Armenia, Spain, Italy, and China) as well as a broad range of environmental crimes such as industrial pollution, illegal waste dumping, illegal and unregulated fishing, wildlife trafficking, illegal e-waste shipments, and pollution caused

R. Sollund (✉)
University of Oslo, Oslo, Norway
e-mail: ragnhild.sollund@jus.uio.no

R. Sollund et al. (eds.), *Fighting Environmental Crime in Europe and Beyond,* Palgrave Studies in Green Criminology,
DOI 10.1057/978-1-349-95085-0_1

by mining). This book's case studies include both EU member states and non-EU states. Despite EFFACE being focused principally on environmental crime in the EU, we look at non-EU states because they have extensive political, social, and/or economic ties with the EU and, therefore, environmental crime in these countries directly and indirectly affects the EU. The chapters exemplify different kinds of environmental crimes, the difficulties new EU member states or states moving in that direction, for example, Kosovo, have in complying with EU standards for environmental protection like those set by the EU environmental crime directive, and how environmental laws and regulations have been enforced or not enforced. Further, they illustrate the transborder nature of environmental crime; environmental crimes that are initiated in one geographical location are not contained by borders, but the harms they cause migrate to other, disadvantaged parts of the world where environmental standards have been underprioritized in order to advance economic progress.

The case studies address the following research questions: what are the environmental crimes in question? Are they 'crimes' from a legal perspective, and what does the legal EU framework look like? What causes these crimes to be committed, and do they take place across borders and in organized ways? Who are the offenders responsible for the harms/crimes in question? What motivates them and facilitates their action? Who are the victims and how are they victimized? If at all, how are these crimes controlled, enforced, and prevented?

This anthology exemplifies the value of interdisciplinary research because the different perspectives in it add different foci and nuances to the study of environmental crimes, for example, a focus on legal structures, state actors, or offenders and victims. The various chapters clearly show that the concept of environmental crime is not clear-cut because the harms done to the environment may be equally harmful whether the acts are criminalized or not. Legal scholars will usually rely on legal definitions to determine whether an act is an environmental crime. As noted in the EFFACE analytical framework, the terms 'breach,' 'infringement,' and 'violation' generally refer to a breach of a legal rule, regardless of whether that rule is criminal law, administrative law, or civil law (EFFACE analytical framework). A further distinction could be drawn between a mere 'offence' that might be subject to certain sanctions such as a fine, and actions that result in sanctions imposed by criminal law. Legal scholars, therefore, often do not question the definition of an environmental crime but take the definitions, as given and defined by means of laws and regulations, as the point of departure. For criminologists, the definition of environmental crime is more open to debate. Within green criminology, a field that includes 'the study of those harms against humanity, against the environment including space, and against nonhuman animals committed both by powerful institutions (e.g., governments, transnational corporations, military apparatuses) and also by ordinary people' (Beirne & South 2007 p. xiii), the concept of crime has been expanded beyond its legal definition. It encompasses even those harmful acts that are not legally defined as criminal, but yet are as harmful as any breach of a law or regulation (Beirne & South 2007; Lynch & Stretesky 2014; Sollund 2008; South 2008, 2014; Stretesky *et al.* 2013; Walters 2010; White 2007, 2013, p. 8).

When the concept of crime includes acts that are not criminalized, a normative message is conveyed. It can be perceived in light of the distinction Sykes and Matza (1957) make between crimes that are *mal in se* and those that are *mal prohibita.* In green criminology, it is acknowledged that acts that are criminalized in a legal sense are often, but not always, *mal in se*, but it is also acknowledged that harms that are not currently criminalized—thus *mal prohibita*—but which may *become* criminalized in the near future because of their harmful effects are also *mal in se*. It is also acknowledged that actions that are *mal in se* can be criminalized on some occasions but not on others, for example, when economic interests or stakeholders' abuse of power take precedence (Lynch & Stretesky 2014; Sollund 2015b). While a legal approach has the advantage of a certain clarity and predictability about which acts are regarded as environmental crimes—although this will be subject to interpretation and discretion by the judicial system, not least, judges—it does not characterize acts per se.

As will be shown in this book, harms are perpetrated by states, yet it is nation-states that define what is criminal, corrupt, or unjust (White 2013, p. 24). Therefore, and as stated by White, there is a need to develop the definition of crime and criteria to measure harms that are more universal, incorporating human rights, environmental rights, and animal rights.

For economists, the harms of environmental crimes will often be assessed in economic terms.

From a purely economic perspective, nature is not regarded as valuable per se, but by what it provides for humans. Nature is thus a means to an end:

> The benefits that nature provides to human society are known as *ecosystem services*. These include provisioning services, regulating services, supporting services, and cultural services. They contribute to our social and economic wellbeing—consisting of security, the basic materials for a viable livelihood, freedom and choice, good health, and good social-cultural relations—by providing us with food, natural fibers, a steady supply of clean water, regulation of pests and diseases, medicinal substances, recreation, and protection from natural hazards. (Millennium Assessment quoted in EFFACE Analytical framework, p. 24)

Economic estimations can also successfully be applied to assess dispersal of victimization, that is, the number of victims involved and the ways in which they are affected.

White (2013) argues for a broader and ecology-based analysis of wrongdoing because that will provide a different picture of harm than an economic analysis. This means that ecosystems and the natural environment cannot be perceived merely as ecoservice providers—being there *for* humans—and their value estimated in economic terms (Vetlesen 2015). There is no doubt that environmental crimes, illegal fishing and fishing by unregulated measures as an example, have both economic and an ecological impact. Trawls may severely harm not only fish stocks and ecosystems but also the economy, as people with the legal right to live by these fisheries suffer the consequences of depleted fish stocks and destroyed ecosystems, as in Nova Scotia (Frank *et al.* 2005).

Another approach is typological, listing different forms of environmental harms, for example, those types of environmental crimes that are also 'transnational environmental crimes (. . .) undertaken by persons acting across national borders including *illegal logging* and *timber smuggling, species smuggling*, the black market in *ozone depleting substances*, the *illegal movement of toxic and hazardous waste and other prohibited chemicals* etc.' (UNEP 2013 quoted in EFFACE Analytical framework p. 13). Environmental crimes can also be divided into subcategories: '"Brown" issues tend to be defined in terms of urban life and pollution (e.g., air quality), "green" issues mainly relate to wilderness areas and conservation matters (e.g., logging practices), and "white" issues refer to science laboratories and the impact of new technologies (e.g., genetically modified organisms)' (White 2013, p. 38).

A legal approach within the area of environmental crime will often be anthropocentric; it is human interests that determine whether an act is criminalized or not, and most often human interests are also considered more important than the interests of other species or of the natural environment itself (Boyle 2006). What are usually taken into consideration are environmental justice and environmental rights as a continuation of human rights. Thus, the focus is on differences within human populations; social justice demands access to healthy and safe environments for all, no matter where, and for future generations. Environmental rights as a further development of human rights were established in the Declaration of the United Nations Conference on the Human Environment and the Aarhus Convention:

> adequate protection of the environment is essential to human wellbeing and the enjoyment of basic human rights, including the right to life itself'.... 'every person has the right to live in an environment adequate to his or her health and well-being, and the duty, both individually and in association with others, to protect and improve the environment for the benefit of present and future generations.' (here in Boyle 2006, p. 6)

In these statements, laws are seen to protect the environment because it is in humans' interest, whereas ecological justice (where the main focus is on the environment and on conserving and protecting ecological well-being, for example, forests because it is intrinsically worthwhile) is downplayed. Exceptions to this are the constitutions of Ecuador and Bolivia where Mother Earth—*Pachamama*—is granted rights (Zaffaroni 2011). Species justice, where the main focus is on ensuring the well-being of species as a whole *and* individual animals, is usually not taken into consideration in environmental legislation. When legislation concerns wild animals, such as national legislation that supports the Convention on International Trades in Endangered Species (CITES) and the Bern Convention, they are not usually afforded intrinsic value. They are either preserved for the sake of biodiversity or to ensure humans' interests in exploiting them, or they are granted protection only to the extent that species survival does not threaten humans' interests (Sollund 2011, 2015a). Consequently, environmental crimes are often referred to as victimless crimes, even though innumerous nonhuman and human animals may suffer and die, whether from pollution, loss of habitat, as in the case caused by palm oil production in Indonesia and Colombia (Boekhout van Solinge 2008; Mol 2013), or other environmental devastation. In actuality, more than being a victimless crime, environmental crime affects victims who cannot articulate their cause because they do not speak human languages or they are vulnerable victims, indigenous women and children (Gaarder 2013). Very often, the interests that are protected in regard to environmental protection and criminalization (or lack thereof) are those of powerful corporations and states (Lynch & Stretesky 2014). Not only do such commercial interests perpetuate century-long colonialism through corporate interests, human colonization of nature and the environment parallels this exploitation (Mol 2013). Destroyed are the natural habitats of indigenous peoples (as in the Chevron case in Ecuador [Kimberling 2005]) and the ecosystems that animals depend on to survive. We are therefore confronted with a three-fold victimization: the absence of environmental justice, species justice, and ecojustice.

Obviously, not all forms of environmental crimes, whether legally defined or not, can be covered in this anthology. Yet the chapters exemplify the difficulties connected to protecting the environment through environmental law and law enforcement alone and are concrete in describing the problems of environmental crimes and what should be done about them. This book addresses what White (2013) refers to as 'brown' and 'green' issues, while 'white' issues, for example, biopiracy (Goyes & South 2016), will not be covered.

1.1 Outline of the Chapters

Chapter 2, 'A Paradigm Shift in Environmental Criminal Law' by Michael Faure, provides an overview of EU legislation and how it is implemented on national levels. Faure shows how legislators, beginning in 1980, perceived environmental crime, how, consequently, environmental crime was defined in legislation, and how this has changed dramatically in the past 30 years. He analyzes this evolution and discusses how the changes entailed by it have been influenced by various legal doctrinal shifts concerning the previously strong relationship between administrative and criminal law, even a dependence of environmental criminal law upon administrative law and concerning a strong tendency toward criminalization of any violation of environmental law, hence the absence of a toolbox approach. Central in his analysis is the way in which environmental crime is currently described in legislation. He explores whether the 2008 EU directive on environmental crime is a response to doctrinal changes, and how legislation concerning environmental crime is dealt with in relation to other enforcement systems. The changes observed also entail support for the tool box approach caused by the doctrinal change, thus relying on various measures to control and enforce environmental crimes. He argues that criminal law should be reserved for the most serious infringements, whereas other infringements could be dealt with by other means such as civil or administrative penalties.

Chapter 3, '"Victims in the Land of Fires": Illegal Waste Disposal in the Campania Region, Italy' by Anna Rita Germani, Giacomo D'Alisa, Pasquale M. Falcone, and Piergiuseppe Morone, addresses the environmental crime of toxic waste dumping. This chapter reveals who commits these crimes and who and what are harmed by them. From a legal perspective, the authors discuss how the Italian authorities respond, or fail to respond, to these crimes. While for a long time mafia groups have been responsible for these crimes, in this case, legal enterprises are also involved, and the crimes are committed as an extension of legal activities, thus making them corporate crimes. The issue of environmental rights is central in the chapter as the consequences of the polluting activities are that communities in the vicinity of the dump locations suffer physical harm in the form of diseases caused by the toxic waste.

The illegal disposal of toxic waste can take different forms: dumping it directly in the countryside, dumping it in illegal quarries and construction sites of public infrastructure works, burning it in the countryside and along low-traffic roads, and mixing toxic with domestic waste for disposal in legal landfills and incinerators. The chapter is based on a rich empirical study including interviews with victims and network analysis and reveals how the victims interacted over time with different associations. The authors identify a strong degree of victim empowerment through which the victims strengthened their relationships with local associations in their networks and begin to play an important role in reinforcing their sociopolitical and judicial actions to combat the illegal practices that have seriously affected their lives.

Chapter 4, 'Tackling Illegal Fisheries: The Role of Rights-based Management' by Stephanie Newman and Andrew Farmer, focuses on the causes, motives, and incentives for committing illegal fishing. Based on a literature review, it considers the role of rights-based fisheries management systems in incentivizing or disincentivizing illegal behavior in relation to illegal, unreported, and unregulated fishing (IUU). The authors provide an overview of the regulations and enforcement practices in regards to IUU in the EU and argue that rights-based management is a potential tool in the delivery of better fisheries management that moves away from mere enforcement of regulations, as fisheries are notoriously difficult to control. Much IUU takes part as a prolongation of legal activities; quotas are exceeded, or the wrong species are caught, but fishing per se is legal. The fishers, the offenders of this particular crime, therefore, need to have an incentive to not abuse their legal rights and comply with EU regulations despite the opportunities that IUU offers. Rather than regarding these incentives as purely economic, in a Gary Becker sense, the authors argue, based on other studies, that the adoption of rights-based management could lead to better compliance with fishery requirements due to the interest rights holders have, for example, their ability to lease extra quotas. When fishers are rights holders to fish quotas, they will feel responsible for what they regard as their own resource; they will self-regulate more than when they are competing for the fish. Newman and Farmer conclude that equitable distribution of rights in relation to fisheries might be an appropriate mechanism to better manage those resources and a possible mechanism to reduce this kind of environmental crime. This is important because by regarding fish as a resource, they can be protected for the benefit of the ecosystems they inhabit and the survival of their species, and because it will ensure the viability of the resource for the local communities and others who depend on it.

Chapter 5, 'Wildlife Trafficking: Harms and Victimization' by Jenny Maher and Ragnhild Sollund, is based on a case study of illegal wildlife trade in UK, Norway, Colombia, and Brazil. The chapter sheds light on the questions, *What are the characteristics of wildlife trafficking? (What consumer practices are driving forces, and why?) How are animals (and humans) victimized? What are the common features of how these crimes are enforced in case study locations?* This empirical work establishes that wildlife trade is largely based on consumer practices, such as the purchase of luxury products such as caviar and traditional Asian medicine, and pet keeping, parrots and reptiles being the most popular. The demand for and the economic value of the trade make it an attractive crime for actors of the trafficking chain, although the economic values increase the longer the chain gets. As a result, offenders are everywhere from purchasing a wildlife product on eBay to smuggling ivory from tourist destinations. The case studies reveal that illegal trade in wildlife is not prioritized and poorly resourced in relation to control and enforcement; the enforcement response is often uninformed and uncoordinated, while legislation is complex and disjointed leading to uncertainty and leniency in punishment. The chapter adopts a green criminology harm perspective that acknowledges that the animals who are killed and trafficked and who are often also revictimized, when are killed by the authorities in Norway as a means to enforce CITES, they are the principal and direct victims of the environmental crime of trafficking. The chapter concludes with recommendations on how to prevent this harm: responses to the trade of wildlife require a multifaceted and multi-agency approach, focused on reducing demand, enhancing awareness and compliance, increasing political will, fostering trust between and within agencies (nationally and internationally with all stakeholders), developing a targeted approach, and utilizing the resources and strategies used in fighting other organized crimes.

Chapter 6, 'Illegal Shipments of E-waste from the EU to China' by Andrea Illés and Kristof Geeraerts, concerns an increasing problem of electronic waste and the ways in which this waste is trafficked, usually, from western industrialized economies to the south. Stricter rules for handling e-waste in the EU resulted in an increase in the costs of dismantling and recycling e-waste, thus leading actors to illegally ship e-waste to China, where dismantling and recycling techniques of the informal sector are rudimental compared to the formal sector and do not comply with health and environmental safety standards. The chapter provides estimates for the amounts of e-waste that are trafficked to China. It also highlights the thin line between legal and illegal activities, the problem with parallel legal and illegal markets, and the concealment of these crimes as a continuation of legal activities. The chapter illustrates the modus operandi of the actors involved in the crime, for example, by not warning authorities and means of fraud, and highlights the environmental and health dangers resulting from this crime. The first direct victims are the workers, often poor, rural migrant women and children, who are exposed to hazardous waste. They also carry the toxins with them to their homes, thus endangering themselves, their families, and their neighbors in surroundings that should be safe. Indirectly, victims are harmed when the poison enters surface and ground water, which also harms ecosystems. In terms of control and enforcement, the chapter concludes that the recently introduced amendments to the EU waste shipment regulation and the Waste Electrical and Electronic Equipment (WEEE) Directive have the potential to improve inspection and enforcement, but that this will greatly depend on whether national policymakers will see the fight against transnational e-waste crime as a priority and whether the individual EU member states will be willing to provide the necessary resources to implement the new requirements.

Chapter 7, 'The EU Action to Protect the Environment in Kosovo and to Fight Environmental Crime' by Teresa Fajardo del Castillo, addresses environmental crime in Kosovo, showing the EU efforts to introduce environmental protection in the negotiations that led to the signature of the Stabilisation and Association Agreement of 2015 with Kosovo. Taking a legal perspective, Fajardo Castillo shows how the postwar Kosovo legal order, as well as its political, economic, and human context, poses innumerable challenges in protecting the environment. As do previous chapters, this chapter shows that environmental crime concerns not only traditional criminals, but the state itself acts criminally through lack of control and enforcement and corruption. Nor do environmental crimes concern only easily identifiable victims; its victims are both human and nonhuman.

Illegal practices are openly carried on in most of the territory of Kosovo; illegal logging, illegal hunting, and illegal waste management are examples of such crimes, which are driven by consumer interests and needs, for example, when forests are cut to provide logs for heating, but also by organized crime groups at a wider scale. The lack of regulation in the mining industry is a serious hazard to the environment in Kosovo. Outdated coal plants are so polluting that resettling entire villages has been considered. The poverty-driven environmental crimes in Kosovo cause victimization of the environment, human beings, and animals, who face the loss of their habitat and are also killed in illegal hunts. Although there is adequate legislation in Kosovo, law enforcement agencies lack the resources to adequately build the capacity to ensure compliance, implementation, and enforcement. Fajardo Castillo concludes that a carte blanche to invest is offered that does not include measures to cope with pollution, jeopardizing future investment and the care of the environment.

Chapter 8, 'Environmental Crime in Armenia: A Case Study on Mining' by Christoph H. Stefes and Pete Theodoratos, focuses on the harms caused by the mining industry in Armenia, which in several ways resembles the situation in Kosovo. As a member of the European Neighbourhood Policy, Armenia is politically and economically linked to the EU. As a former Soviet republic, Armenia has inherited a host of environmental problems. Since independence, Armenia has done little to address these problems despite the country's willingness to sign and ratify numerous international environmental treaties and conventions. Environmental destruction is especially apparent in the mining sector, one of Armenia's few thriving economic sectors. Domestic laws and enforcement are wholly insufficient to regulate the country's mining industry, which pollutes the soil, water, and air and devastates Armenia's pristine nature. Most environmentally harmful behavior is legal under Armenian domestic law, although some of these acts are illegal. Lax environmental legislation is the result of collusion between powerful economic players and the government. The country's oligarchs, who are politically well connected, dominate the mining sector, which consists of mostly foreign (including European) companies and their Armenian subsidiaries. This widespread corruption, in addition to insufficient law enforcement and adjudication, contributes to an atmosphere of impunity. Since corruption and collusion prevent the passing of more stringent environmental legislation, it is questionable if a narrow legal approach to environmental crime in Armenia's mining sector suffices to analyze, understand, and address the problem.

The main victims of these environmental crimes are the people living close to the hundreds of mining sites in the country. Pollution also affects Armenians further away and citizens of Armenia's neighboring countries due to transborder water and air pollution and the contamination of agricultural products. Tourism and other economic sectors also suffer because of pollution.

Mining in Armenia is an important driver of the economy at the moment. Yet, the sector is wholly unsustainable economically. Environmental nongovernmental organizations and citizen movements are the only viable actors in Armenia that have had some success in limiting harmful mining activities. Their principal means are the naming and shaming of politicians and business people. Their attempts to use local courts to stop mining activities have, however, largely failed.

The Armenian government is in clear violation of several international treaties it signed, one being the Aarhus Convention. This is an arena in which the EU and its member states could exert some leverage. They could remind the Armenian government of its international obligations and put some diplomatic and economic pressure on it. They could support the country's environmental groups through technical training, financial resources, and diplomatic support. So far, European actors have largely failed to do so.

The conclusion, Chap. 9, Summary of Findings and the Way Forward' by Christoph Stefes and Anna Rita Germani, summarizes the findings of the case studies by focusing on the variegated answers the authors find to the central research questions of this book. Beyond the summary of the research findings, the authors suggest further steps the EU and its member states could undertake to fight environmental crime more effectively within the borders of the EU and beyond.

References

Beirne, P., & South, N. (eds.) (2007). *Issues in green criminology*. Devon: Willan.

Boekhout van Solinge, T. (2008). The land of the orangutan and the bird of paradise under threat. In R. Sollund (Ed.), *Global harms: Ecological crime and speciesism* (pp. 51–71). New York: Nova Science Publishers.

Boyle, A. (2006). Human rights or environmental rights: A reassessment. *Fordham Environmental Law Review*, *18*, 471.

Europa (2012). EUR-Lex *charter of fundamental rights of the European Union* 2012/C 326/02, http://eur-lex.europa.eu/legal-content/EN/TXT/?uri=CELEX:12012P/TXT.

EFFACE Analytical framework (2013/2016). Internal work document for EFFACE. http://efface.eu/wp1-establishing-analytical-framework.

Frank, K.T., Petrie, B., Choi, J.S., Leggett, W.C. (2005). Trophic cascades in a formerly cod-dominated ecosystem. *Science*, *308*(5728), 1621–1623.

Gaarder, E. (2013). Evading responsibility for green harm: State-corporate exploitation of race, class, and gender inequality. In N. South & A. Brisman (Eds.), *Routledge international handbook of green criminology* (pp. 272–282). London: Routledge.

Goyes, D.R., & South, N. (2016). Land-grabs, biopiracy and the inversion of justice in Colombia. *British Journal of Criminology*, *56*(3), 558–577.

Kimberling, J. (2005). Indigenous peoples and the oil frontier in Amazonia: The case of Ecuador, ChevronTexaco, and Aguinda versus Texaco. *NYUJ of International Law and Politics*, *38*, 413.

Lynch, M.J., & Stretesky, P.B. (2014). *Exploring green criminology: Toward a green criminological revolution*. Farnham: Ashgate.

Mol, H. (2013). "A gift from the tropics to the world": Power, harm, and palm oil. In D.S. Westerhuis, R. Walters, T. Wyatt (Eds.), *Emerging issues in green criminology* (pp. 242–261). Basingstoke: Palgrave Macmillan.

Sollund, R. (2008). Introduction: Towards a greener criminology. In R. Sollund (Ed.), *Global harms: Ecological crime and speciesism* (pp. 1–13). New York: Nova Science Publishers.

Sollund, R. (2011). Expressions of speciesism: The effects of keeping companion animals on animal abuse, animal trafficking and species decline. *Crime, Law and Social Change, 55*(5), 437–451.

Sollund, R. (2015a). With or without a License to Kill: Human-predator conflicts and theriocide in Norway. In A. Brisman, N. South, R. White (Eds.), *Environmental crime and social conflict: Contemporary and emerging issues* (pp. 95–125). Aldershot: Ashgate.

Sollund, R. (2015b). Introduction: Critical green criminology: An agenda for change. In R. Sollund (Ed.), *Green harms and crimes: Critical criminology in a changing world* (pp. 1–27). Basingstoke: Palgrave Macmillan.

South, N. (2008). Nature, difference and the rejection of harm: Expanding the Agenda for green criminology. In R. Sollund (Ed.), *Global harms: Ecological crime and speciesism* (pp. 187–201). New York: Nova Science Publishers.

South, N. (2014). Green criminology: Reflections, connections and harms. *International Journal for Crime, Justice and Social Democracy, 3*(2), 6–21.

Stretesky, P.B., Long, M.A., Lynch, M.J. (2013). *The treadmill of crime: Political economy and green criminology.* London: Routledge.

Sykes, G.M., & Matza, D. (1957). Techniques of neutralization: A theory of delinquency. *American Sociological Review, 22*(6), 664–670.

Vetlesen, J. (2015). *The denial of nature: Environmental philosophy in the era of global capitalism.* London and New York: Routledge.

Walters, R. (2010). Toxic atmospheres air pollution, trade and the politics of regulation. *Critical Criminology, 18*(4), 307–323.

White, R. (2007). Green criminology and the pursuit of social and ecological justice. In P. Beirne & N. South (Eds.), *Issues in green criminology* (pp. 32–54). Devon: Willan.

White, R. (2011). *Transnational environmental crime: Toward an eco-global criminology.* New York: Routledge.

White, R. (2013). *Crimes against nature: Environmental criminology and ecological justice.* London: Routledge.

Zaffaroni, E.R. (2011). *La Pachamama y el humano* [Pachamama and the human]. Buenos Aires: Ediciones Madres de Plaza de Mayo.

Dr. Ragnhild Sollund is a professor in criminology at the University of Oslo. She has authored, edited, and co-edited 10 books, of which five in the field of green criminology, including *Global Harms: Ecological crime and speciesism*, Nova science publishers (2008); *Eco-global crimes: contemporary problems and future challenges*, Ashgate (2012); and *Green harms and crimes: Critical criminology in a changing world,* Palgrave (2015). Her main research interest is currently legal and illegal wildlife harms; including wildlife trafficking and the illegal killing of protected predators. Before turning her research interest to environmental crimes, she did extensive research within the fields of migration, especially the situation for female migrants, and police racial profiling. She teaches criminology at the University of Oslo at BA/MA level, and is also supervising students at all levels.

2

A Paradigm Shift in Environmental Criminal Law

Michael G. Faure

2.1 Introduction

In many European Union (EU) countries, during the last 30 years, the way in which environmental crime is described in legislation has undergone important shifts during the last 30 years. Environmental law itself, in fact, only emerged in most EU countries in the 1970s. A first feature of environmental criminal law at that time was that the role that criminal law played in most of this legislation was relatively modest. Initially, environmental laws were primarily administrative in nature, for example, requiring operators to apply for permits and run operations as stipulated in the permits. Criminal provisions would be added only at the end of a particular law, stating that those who act in disobedience of this particular administrative law will be subject to criminal sanctions.

M.G. Faure (✉)
Maastricht University, METRO, Faculty of Law,
Maastricht, The Netherlands
e-mail: michael.faure@maastrichtuniversity.nl

R. Sollund et al. (eds.), *Fighting Environmental Crime in Europe and Beyond*, Palgrave Studies in Green Criminology,
DOI 10.1057/978-1-349-95085-0_2

This phenomenon has been characterized as the administrative dependence of environmental criminal law. Environmental crime in domestic legislation was not defined in an independent manner, for example, taking into account the nature of the danger caused by a particular behaviour to the environment.

Second, the fact that environmental crime was simply placed by the legislator as a kind of appendix to administrative laws gave it a low priority in enforcement policy. Most enforcement authorities, particularly prosecutors, would view the crimes incorporated in the penal code as the most important offences; as a result, the prosecution of crimes embedded in special administrative laws could receive lower priority.

A third feature of this traditional environmental criminal law, as it emerged in the 1980s, was that in most European countries, criminal law was basically the only instrument available to enforce these administrative environmental laws.[1] Other penalties that aimed at deterrence, such as administrative fines, were not available in most legal systems. Prosecutors did—as mentioned above—not prioritize crimes included in laws that were otherwise oriented towards administrative stipulations. As a result, in many countries environmental crimes were never prosecuted, and many violations were dismissed.

This account of environmental criminal law may initially seem to be a generalization (Conceivably, there may have been individual countries who incorporated environmental crimes into the penal code and prosecuted them more frequently.). However, when considering environmental crime as a system that is dependent on administrative environmental law, it is an accurate portrayal for the majority of European legal systems at the time.

In this chapter, I argue that the way in which legislators have viewed environmental crime, that is, the way environmental crime has been defined in legislation, has dramatically changed in the past 30 years. I explore two key examples in which this development was largely influenced by various crucial doctrinal moves. The first involves a German legal doctrine that emerged in the 1980s which addressed the legal dogmatic

[1] Germany with its *Ordnungswidrigkeitengesetz* constitutes an important exception.

foundations of environmental criminal law. A more recent instance is found in the UK where scholars (and increasingly policymakers) argue that in addition to the criminal law, administrative fine systems should be added to the available enforcement tools. Such doctrinal moves have had a marked, albeit implicit, effect on policy change that can be observed in the way environmental crime is now articulated in legislation, particularly as it relates to other enforcement systems.

2.2 Traditional Enforcement Approach

The following features characterized traditional approaches to environmental criminal law when it first emerged (in the 1970s–1980s for most countries): environmental criminal law could be found in administrative laws (Sect. 2.1); there was a strong administrative dependence of environmental criminal law (Sect. 2.2); and criminal law seemed to be the primary tool to enforce environmental law, as there were not many alternatives available (Sect. 2.3).

2.2.1 The Place of Environmental Criminal Law

Criminal law aiming at the protection of the environment usually came as an appendix to legislation having largely an administrative character. As an example of this approach, Article 2 of the Belgian (Federal) Surface Water Protection Act of 1971 prohibited the emission of substances, polluting or polluted liquids or gases into the surface waters. A stipulated exception to this rule allowed for the discharge of wastewater for which a licence was granted in accordance with the provisions of this Act (Faure 1992, 77–83). Article 5 subsequently held that all discharge of wastewater be submitted to a licence. The remainder of the Act specified which administrative authority could provide the discharge permit and which conditions could be imposed in such a permit (Surface Water Protection Act, OJ of Belgium, 1 May 1971).

The criminal law could be found in Article 41, which among other things punished anyone who violated the provisions of this Act itself or the executive orders given based on it, particularly anyone who discharged wastewater into surface water without a permit, violating the permit conditions of Article 5.[2]

The structure of this criminal provision shows a strong relationship between administrative law and environmental criminal law, and unlike other criminal provisions, the description of environmental crime cannot be found either in a specific environmental code or in the penal code itself. Belgium was not the only country where environmental crime could be found in environmental statutes of an administrative nature. In France, for example, the major provisions concerning environmental crime emerged in the 1970s, in an Act of 15 July 1975 concerning the elimination of waste[3] and in an Act on Classified Installations of 19 July 1976.[4] Article 18 of this Act, inter alia, punished anyone who would operate an installation without the required licence.

Although in the 1980s, environmental criminal law in most European countries was still in its infancy, some countries did incorporate environmental crime into their penal codes. A striking example in this respect is Germany. As a result of the entry into force of the eighteenth *Strafrechtsänderungsgesetz* (Criminal Law Reform Act) on 1 July 1980, provisions concerning environmental crime were incorporated in sections 324 and following of the German *Strafgesetzbuch* (penal code). According to German legal doctrine, the incorporation of environmental crimes into the penal code had an important symbolic effect and was supposed to serve the general preventive effect of the criminal law and to facilitate prosecution (Tiedemann 1980, p. 18).

Another example is represented by the Netherlands, where provisions aiming at the protection of surface waters could be found in its penal code as early as an Act of 13 November 1969 aiming at the protection of surface waters (Heemskerk and Ubachs 2001, pp. 9–11). In 1989, those

[2] Article 41 also provided other prohibitions that were criminalized, but that is not material for this discussion. For more details see Mandiberg and Faure (2009, p. 453).

[3] Loi No. 75-633 of 15 July 1975 Relatif à l'élimination de déchets et la récupération des matériaux, published in Faure and Heine (2000, pp. 128–130).

[4] Loi No. 76-663 of 19 July 1976 Relatif aux installations classées pour la protection de l'environnement, published in Faure and Heine (2000, pp. 133–136).

provisions were changed into Articles 173a and 173b of the penal code that punished unlawful emissions into the soil, air or surface waters if the perpetrator would have reasons to suspect that this could lead to danger for public health or danger of death for another human being (Ubachs 2001, pp. 12–14). However, for a variety of reasons those provisions were also criticized both in Germany (Heine and Meinberg 1988) and in the Netherlands (Faure 1997), primarily because they could only be applied if there had been a violation of administrative duties, making protection awarded by the criminal law completely dependent upon administrative law.

2.2.2 Administrative Dependence of the Criminal Law

In the 1970s and 1980s, criminal law was often considered a complement to a primarily administrative legal framework.[5] That criminal provisions were contained in environmental laws of a mainly administrative character was of more than symbolic importance; it also had practical implications for the kind of protection that the former could offer in environmental matters.

One consequence of the administratively based structure of environmental criminal law is that ecological values were not directly protected through the criminal law. Even severe pollution of soil or water, for example, was not punishable unless the act simultaneously violated an administrative obligation. Administrative dependence, therefore, limited the scope in which pollution could be directly criminalized. Moreover, administrative authorities were given the responsibility to determine the punishable nature of certain polluting acts. Indeed, administrative authorities defined the conditions of a permit and in doing so, they also determined the conditions for criminal liability.[6]

[5] Although not completely since, as I just mentioned, this problem of the administrative dependence of the criminal law also emerged in the provisions contained in the penal code.

[6] This was traditionally the case in many legal systems. For a good comparative overview in that respect see Prabhu (1994, pp. 699–728).

In sum, as long as administrative provisions/obligations are honoured, no protection will be granted through criminal law. If, on the other hand, administrative obligations are not determined at all, neither can protection be granted through criminal law.

2.2.3 Criminal Law as Primary Instrument

In this traditional structure of environmental criminal law, the main (and for many countries the only) instrument that could be used to enforce administrative environmental law was criminal law. This was the case in the above examples from Belgium, France and the UK. In those countries, alternatives to criminal law (e.g. administrative fines) did not exist. Thus, during that period those legal systems did not follow the so-called enforcement pyramid developed by Ayres and Braithwaite (1992), according to which the criminal would only be used at the top of the pyramid after all other mechanisms (persuasion, administrative fines, etc.) had been exhausted.

In most legal systems at the time—including those of Belgium, France and the UK—the criminal law was the primary enforcement tool. However, the situation was more nuanced in Germany. Germany had the *Ordnungswidrigkeitenrecht* (administrative penal law), which is a non-criminal sanctioning system that allows for the imposition of administrative fines (Faure and Heine 2000, pp. 142–147). In addition, other legal systems inspired by the German model, such as Austria, had a similar system of administrative penal law, allowing the imposition of fines (Faure and Heine 2000, pp. 9–13).

2.3 Two Doctrinal Moves

Although this characterization of the environmental criminal law may constitute too rough a generalization, two features were typical for the period (irrespective of the specific form of environmental crime in the legislation): (1) the dependence of environmental criminal law upon administrative law and (2) a tendency towards criminalization of any violation of environmental law, hence the absence of administrative fines.

From different angles, responses have been formulated in legal doctrine against those two approaches. The first originates from German legal doctrine and acts against the absolute dependence of environmental criminal law upon administrative law (Sect. 3.1). The second stems from administrative law as well as from law and economics that argue in favour of administrative fines and for a more limited role of the criminal law (Sect. 3.2).

2.3.1 Environmental Protection through Criminal Law?

A project that was launched by the Max Planck Institute for Foreign and International Criminal Law in Freiburg im Breisgau played an important role in the analysis of environmental criminal law in Europe (and in other continents). Begun in 1985, it was a broad project entitled *Umweltschutz durch Strafrecht?* in which criminal law in numerous countries was analysed with respect to environmental protection, with special attention to the relationship between environmental criminal law, administrative and civil law. The project was coordinated by Günter Heine, who himself has published widely on environmental criminal law in Germany but also internationally (Heine 1986, 1989, 1991). The general tenet of the project was to examine the limits of criminal law in protecting the environment as to see how its effectiveness could be improved, especially in relation to administrative law. Heine and the other scholars who were inspired by his work developed a model of environmental criminal law with a reduced dependence upon administrative law, at least with a more nuanced approach to administrative law.

This model centres on the idea that the narrow relationship between administrative and criminal law should be abandoned. However, this does not necessarily mean that one should immediately forsake any link between environmental criminal law and administrative law. Indeed, such a link may even have certain advantages. First, administrative dependence has the advantage that it respects the *lex certa* principle, which follows from the principle of legality in criminal law. This holds that the legislator should describe the criminalized behaviour as precisely as possible. In case the legislator punishes violation of administrative norms (e.g. conditions in a permit), the criminalized behaviour will usually be relatively clear before the event (De Nauw 1994, p. 85). However, one should also realize that referring to a permit might not always be the ideal way of criminalizing pollution since permit conditions can be vague and ambiguous.

One can also argue that a link with administrative law is in some cases indispensable since 'pollution' would otherwise be a broad and vague category to criminalize. If such a broad terminology were to be applied, it would no longer be clear *ex ante* which behaviour is criminalized and which is not. That would be the case if the legislator were, for example, to criminalize the person who has contributed to climate change. The impossibility of proving a causal link between certain behaviour and the criminalized result would render such a provision inapplicable in practice (Robert 1994, pp. 954–955).

Moreover, the formulation of obligation in administrative law may also contribute to making more precise the concept of unlawfulness in environmental criminal law. Indeed, one can hope that it is probably the administrative authority that is best situated to determine whether a specific form of pollution is lawful or not. Indeed, administrative authorities may be far better qualified (given their expertise and thus their information advantage) than the judge in a criminal court to determine which type of pollution should be considered unlawful or not. This information advantage of administrative authorities is a strong argument in favour of some link between administrative and environmental criminal law.

A consequence of the previous ideas is that probably some link between environmental criminal law and administrative law should be retained. The primary decision on the admissibility of certain polluting acts should remain with administrative authorities, of course, within the limits set by law and respecting general principles of administrative law.

As a result, different types of criminal provisions are necessary to protect the environment, all with a different goal and all with a different relationship to administrative law (Heine 1994, pp. 731–759). An effective environmental criminal law, according to Heine and MPI scholarship, needs to be able to penalize violations of administrative obligations, and unlawful emissions, and should equally contain an independent pollution crime in case serious consequences occur.

2.3.2 Do We Have the Right Regime?

The heading of this section paraphrases the title of a 2002 article by Anthony Ogus and Carolyn Abbot (2002) where they questioned whether the UK which (at that time) had a regime that relied almost exclusively on criminal law to enforce environmental law, had 'the right regime'.

It was, however, especially Ayres and Braithwaite's (1992) ideas concerning the enforcement pyramid that triggered further thinking into the need for applying the criminal law to violations of environmental law. That toolbox approach of Ayres and Braithwaite paralleled the research of law and economics scholars who argued that criminal law was too costly a system to be generally applied to regulatory violations in cases where administrative penalties could also suffice. Ogus (2004) had, therefore, first argued in favour of a restrictive application of the criminal law for reasons of cost effectiveness and later applied these insights (in joint publications with Carolyn Abbot) to the domain of environmental law (Ogus and Abbot 2002). They argued that given the high threshold of proof and the severe sanctions that accompanied criminal law, the criminal legal system would be inherently costly depending on how prosecutors used their discretion in bringing some of the most high-profile crimes to court (Ogus and Abbot 2002, p. 293). Consequently, prosecutors will not use the criminal law for many cases but will instead dismiss them. If the alternative to impose financial penalties is not available in these cases, the large dismissal rates in environmental crime could lead to underdeterrence. Richard Macrory (2006) carried out a wide-ranging review of regulatory enforcement regimes for the UK Cabinet Office. He concluded that enforcement systems should involve less reliance on criminal law and a greater use of administrative penalties.

To summarize, different streams of literature (criminological, law and economics and administrative law) argued for a more limited role for criminal law and hence a larger role for alternatives, such as administrative fining systems. A crucial reason for doing so is that, as the next section demonstrates, criminal sanctions are rarely imposed in practice.

2.4 Data

Relatively little is known about the enforcement of environmental law in practice. That was the case in the 1980s, as it is today. Even in countries like the Netherlands, Belgium, the UK and Germany, data on enforcement activities are rare. Moreover, the way in which data in the member states are collected (if at all) is not at all harmonized. However, a striking fact surfaced in legal systems in which some data are available: even when enforcement authorities formally established that a violation had taken place, very often the cases were not prosecuted and simply ended with a dismissal (Faure and Svatikova 2012). For example, in the Flemish Region in Belgium, the Environmental Inspectorate collected data on the number of cases that were dismissed on the total number of notices of violations. In doing so, it was observed that an average of 64 per cent of notices of violation were dismissed between 1998 and 2004, whereas approximately 7 per cent were prosecuted during the same period (Faure and Svatikova 2012).[7] This low number of prosecutions casts doubt on the effectiveness of the criminal enforcement system.[8]

Similar data can be found in the UK. Bell and McGillivray (2005) report that between 2000 and 2007, around 25,000 pollution incidents were reported, but the prosecution rate was only 5 per cent. Likewise, the German criminologists group that participated in the Max Planck project on the protection of the environment using criminal law reported to the German Law Association, regarding data on the enforcement of environmental law for the period 1975–1986. According to Heine and Meinberg (1988), in 1985 more than 40 per cent of all criminal environmental cases were not prosecuted.[9] In a later study, Lutterer and Hoch (1997) analysed decisions of the public prosecutor concerning prosecuting environmental crime and noticed that in 60 per cent of the cases a dismissal took place, whereas prosecution only followed in 7.9 per cent of the cases.

[7] A few others resulted in transactions imposed by the prosecutor.

[8] For a further discussion of these data on the Flemish Region, see Faure and Svatikova (2010).

[9] The numbers follow from a more detailed study executed by the criminologist Meinberg (1988).

This admittedly small sample of studies indicates that environmental cases are not often prosecuted by the public prosecutor before the criminal court, leading to high dismissal rates. This confirms the assumption made in the law and economics literature that prosecutors will, given the high cost of criminal procedures, focus their efforts on a few select cases, while dismissing many others. Additionally, two other interesting features follow from this literature. On the one hand, the high degree of dismissals resulted in the low probability of being detected and prosecuted. With respect to the Flemish Region and the data provided by the Environmental Inspectorate, there was a probability of 0.2 that on average a company would be inspected on a yearly basis (Faure and Svatikova 2010). The (conditional) probability of being prosecuted based on the number of prosecutions out of the number of notices of violations dealt with by the public prosecutor was even lower, 0.07 (7%). On average, the probability of an inspection taking place, the violation being detected, and the firm being prosecuted was on average less than 1%, meaning that only one in one hundred firms that are in violation would be detected and prosecuted (Faure and Svatikova 2012, p. 265). This obviously raises serious questions on the deterrent effect of the criminal law.[10] These indications obviously provide strong support for the previously mentioned concurrence in the literature that pleaded for a radical change in environmental criminal law towards a more restrictive role of criminal law and in favour of the development of alternative remedies, such as an administrative fining system.

2.5 Policy Changes

The traditional approach towards environmental criminal law (summarized in Sect. 2.2) has been subjected to serious criticism (Sect. 2.3). Moreover, this criticism was largely supported by data indicating the relatively limited capacity of the criminal legal system to deal with

[10] Combined with the fact that when a case was prosecuted and a conviction by the criminal court took place the fines imposed were quite low as well (Faure and Svatikova (2010)).

environmental crime (Sect 2.4). In this section, I discuss the various policy changes that have occurred in this regard.

I first analyse the importance of the Council of Europe Convention of 1998, a relatively early policy document (Sect. 5.1). Next, I look at the importance of the EU Directive on Environmental Crime of 2008 (Sect. 5.2) and question to what extent it is a departure from the traditional enforcement approach and in line with the doctrinal suggestions. Finally, I look at the evolution of legislation in several member states in order to provide examples of where they have departed from the traditional enforcement approach in line with the doctrinal suggestions (Sect. 5.3).

2.5.1 Council of Europe Convention

The influence of the Max Planck project on criminal law is most visibly detected in the 1998 Council of Europe Convention on the Protection of the Environment through Criminal Law. (See Faure and Heine [2000] for the text of the Convention.)[11] In this Convention, the various signatory states agreed to adopt specific provisions to protect the environment in their criminal law. It thus contains minimum provisions on environmental criminal law. Interestingly, many of the ideas presented above can be found in this convention, particularly the three types of provisions mentioned above.

Article 2 of the Convention describes a crime related to unlawful emissions. This article contains a long list of behaviours that the signatory states will criminalize based on their national law. Article 2(1b) refers to:

> The unlawful discharge, emission or introduction of a quantity of substances or ionising radiation into air, soil or water, which causes or is likely to cause their lasting deterioration or death or serious injury to any person or substantial damage to protected monuments, other protected objects,

---

[11] It is also available at <https://rm.coe.int/CoERMPublicCommonSearchServices/DisplayDCTMContent?documentId=090000168007f3f4>.

property, animals or plants. (Article 2(1b) of the 1998 Council of Europe Convention on the Protection of the Environment through Criminal Law)

This provision clearly criminalizes the concrete endangerment of the environment. It is the unlawful emission that is penalized, which goes much further than merely penalizing the transgression of administrative obligations.

However, the Convention also goes a step further; Article 2.1(a) describes an independent crime of serious pollution:

The discharge, emission or introduction of a quantity of substances or ionizing radiation into air, soil or water, which:

causes death or serious injury to any person, or creates a significant risk of causing death or serious injury to any person. (Article 2.1(a) of the 1998 Council of Europe Convention on the Protection of the Environment through Criminal Law)

Note that in this particular case, when the emission has such serious consequences of causing or risking death or injury, there is no longer a requirement that the emission should be unlawful. This is then a truly independent crime in the sense that the provision applies irrespective of the violation of administrative obligations. This provision can also be applied when an operator would follow the conditions of an administrative permit as unlawfulness is no longer a requirement for criminal liability. The rationale is that emissions causing death or serious injury or creating a significant risk can never be justified under administrative law.

Finally, the Council of Europe Convention also has the criminalization of the violation of administrative obligations. However, this, logically, occupies a less important place in the Convention. More particularly Article 4(d) refers to 'the unlawful operation of a plant'. Note, however, that in this particular case, it holds:

Each party shall adopt such appropriate measures as may be necessary to establish as criminal offences or administrative offences, liable to sanctions or other measures under its domestic law.

The drafters of the Convention clearly recognized that in this case ecological values were not endangered in the same way as with unlawful emissions. In this case, member states can rely on administrative offences.

Although this Convention has not yet entered into force, it is an instrument that demonstrates a new attitude towards environmental criminal law. If environmental criminal law is supposed to play an important role in supporting sustainable development, it should not limit itself to sanctioning administrative obligations but should grant more direct protection to ecological values. This has been realized in the Council of Europe Convention, which also refers to unlawful emissions and even recognizes truly independent crimes in the case of pollution that has serious consequences. This Convention is hence an interesting example of the approach whereby various criminal provisions aim at the protection of criminal law, as this had been proposed in (German) legal doctrine. The Convention also explicitly refers to administrative offences, providing a scope for an approach whereby criminal law would only be used as a last resort.

2.5.2 EU Environmental Crime Directive

Harmonization of criminal law at the EU level has a long (and debated) history. It suffices to say that in 2000, a first step was taken by Denmark within the framework of the (then) Third Pillar, with an initiative aiming at fighting serious environmental crime (OJ 39/4). Subsequently, the Council accepted a framework decision on 27 January 2003 on the protection of the environment through criminal law (OJ L29/55 of 5 February 2003). Interestingly, this Council framework decision was, among other things, based on the previously mentioned 1998 Council of Europe Convention on the Protection of the Environment through Criminal Law. In the Decision of the Court of Justice of the EU of 13 September 2005 in case C-176/03, the Court held that 'as a general rule neither criminal law nor the roles of criminal procedure fall within the community competence'. However:

> the last-mentioned finding does not prevent the community legislature, when the application of effective, proportionate and dissuasive criminal penalties by the competent national authorities is an essential measure for combatting serious environmental offences, from taking measures which relate to the criminal law of the Member States which it considers necessary in order to ensure that the roles which it lays down on environmental protection are fully effective.

The result of this court decision was that from that point on, a directive could be used to force member states to introduce criminal sanctions to be imposed on the violation of domestic legislation implementing environmental directives.

Based on this competence awarded because of this decision, a Directive (2008/99) was adopted with respect to environmental crime and another one (2009/123) with respect to ship-source pollution. For reasons of space, the latter will not be discussed. It is, however, interesting to compare how this EU Directive relates to the doctrinal suggestions discussed in Sect. 2.3. In this respect, I focus on two main questions: To what extent is the graduated punishment approach which follows from the legal doctrine reflected in the Directive? To what extent does the Directive incorporate an approach which equally would provide room for alternatives to the criminal law, such as administrative fines? Starting with the latter question, it is striking that the positive comments concerning administrative law which are present in the Council of Europe Convention are totally absent in the EU Directive on Criminal Law. The only instance in which administrative law is mentioned is rather negative; Recital 3 of Directive 2008/99 holds explicitly that criminal penalties 'demonstrate a social disapproval of a qualitatively different nature compared to administrative penalties or a compensation mechanism under civil law'. Moreover, Article 5 of the Directive holds that specific violations need to be regarded as *criminal offences* in the national legislation implementing the Directive.

The lesson, therefore, is relatively straightforward: the Directive focuses exclusively on criminal penalties and does not mention administrative penalties at all. In that sense, the suggestions in the literature to rely not only on the criminal law to punish environmental pollution have not been taken into account, at least not explicitly.[12] What about the incorporation of the graduated punishment approach? Article 3 of Directive 2008/99 distinguishes nine offences. As mentioned above, the graduated punishment approach following from German legal doctrine holds that an optimal environmental criminal law consists of a combination of three types of different criminal provisions.[13] In terms of the specific offences mentioned in the Directive, the formulation of the crimes in the Directive follows the suggestions made in the literature to some extent, since they do not criminalize only administrative disobedience. Note that unlawfulness, as defined in Article 2(a) of Directive 2008/99, requires an act that violates:

(i) the legislation adopted pursuant to the EC treaty and listed in annex A; or
(ii) with regard to activities covered by the Euratom Treaty, the legislation adopted pursuant to the Euratom treaty and listed in annex B; or
(iii) a law, and administrative regulation of a Member State or a decision taken by a competent authority of a Member State that gives effect to the Community legislation referred to in (i) or (ii).

A simple conclusion from this definition of unlawfulness is, therefore, that none of the offences in the Directive follow the independent or autonomous crime model, whereby the administrative link would be completely eliminated and the 'permit shield' does not apply.

[12] Obviously, that does not exclude the possibility for member states to still have administrative penalties or administrative fines. However, for a correct implementation of the Directive, member states do have to provide criminal penalties for the specific infringements which are explicitly mentioned in Directive 2008/99.

[13] These are, as we mentioned in Sect. 3.1 a provision penalizing violations of administrative obligations, a provision penalizing unlawful emissions and the independent crime of pollution in case of serious consequences.

2.5.3 Domestic Level

In terms of what improvements have been made in recent years in member states' legislation, it is worth mentioning that there are obvious differences between each member state, and it is impractical to discuss all changes in detail. Rather, I provide select examples of whether the place of environmental criminal law has changed (Sect. 5.3.1), whether there have been changes in the administrative dependence (Sect. 5.3.2) and whether there is an increasing place for administrative fines within environmental enforcement (Sect. 5.3.3).

The Place of Environmental Criminal Law

One can easily find examples of policy changes involving either the incorporation of environmental crime into the penal code or a codification of environmental law generally, whereby environmental crime also received a specific place in an environmental code. An example of the former has already been mentioned—Germany and the Netherlands were to some extent first movers, since Germany incorporated various criminal provisions in its penal code in 1980 (Heine 1994, p. 733) and the Netherlands in 1989 (Waling *et al.* 1994, pp. 1080–1082). Additional member states followed suite, particularly southern European countries. Portugal adopted similar provisions in Articles 278–281 of its Criminal Code. This new Portuguese Criminal Code, which came into force on 1 October 1995, includes crimes that cause damage to nature (Art. 278), pollution crimes (Art. 279), pollution causing public danger (Art. 280) and danger to fauna and flora (Art. 281; De Figueirdo 1993; Faure and Heine 2000, p. 283; Hünerfeld 1997; Rodrigues 1994).

Spain adopted a new Spanish Criminal Code in 1995 that contains a spectrum of ecological offences in Articles 325–331. These deal with illegal emissions but also crimes related to damaging cultural heritage, flora and fauna and others (Faure and Heine 2000, p. 293; Polaino Navarrete 1997).

Concerning the second development, examples can also be provided of the incorporation of criminal provisions into a code or special environmental law. In the 1990s, many countries developed environmental codes aiming at an integration of environmental law. Integration implies the bringing of different environmental statutes into one document (like an environmental code). Examples of this can be found in the Scandinavian countries, for example, the Environmental Protection Act of 1991 in Denmark (Faure and Heine 2000, pp. 86–88; Jepsen 1994). In Sweden, the major provisions concerning environmental crime can be found in the Environmental Code 1998 (Faure and Heine 2000, pp. 311–319). Recently, these criminal law provisions in this environmental code have been updated.

Likewise, Ireland and the UK already had relatively early general statutes aimed at protecting the environment that also included criminal offences. Ireland had those provisions in the 1992 Environmental Protection Agency Act (Faure and Heine 2000, pp. 192–195); the UK had offences in the 1995 Environment Act (Faure and Heine 2000, 359–360). However, both in Ireland and the UK, these Environment Acts did not completely harmonize or integrate all environmental statutes. Criminal provisions could still be found in other sectorial legislation. Interesting examples of integration of environmental criminal law can be found in the Flemish and Walloon Regions in Belgium.[14] In the Flemish Region, a Decree of 5 April 1995 already contained general provisions on environmental policy. In 2007, a Title XVI 'Supervision, Enforcement and Safety Measures' was added to this Decree, which entered into force on the first of May 2009. This is referred to as the 'Environmental Enforcement Decree'. This Decree contains criminal sanctions that apply to all sectoral legislation (a long list of legislative provisions) which all fall under the scope of application of this Decree. That integration hence implies that the criminal provisions are harmonized into one document and no longer scattered over different decrees and statutes.

[14] Environmental policy is a competence of the regions in Belgium as a result of which the legislative instruments (referred to as decrees) have been drafted at the level of the regions.

A similar process of integration took place in the Walloon Region with a Decree of 5 June 2008, which equally brought together all criminal provisions and sanctions into one single decree.[15]

Administrative Dependence

One can also easily point out many examples in current environmental legislation where the criminal provisions do not merely punish administrative disobedience but criminalize either endangering or damaging the environment as well. Again, one must be circumspect of generalizations since similar provisions were occasionally adopted as far back as the 1990s, in select cases with a better incorporation of the environment as protected interest already existed (such as for example in Germany). These types of provisions, however, increased after the reforms of the 1990s and into the 2000s. When one, for example, envisages the new Article 278 and following in the Portuguese Criminal Code, it is striking that these provisions target endangerment of the environment and serious pollution. There is still some administrative dependence—a condition for criminal liability is still unlawfulness (Faure and Heine 2000, p. 283). The same can be found in the new provisions of the Spanish Criminal Code, which do not only punish administrative disobedience but also illegal emissions; Article 325 criminalizes the engagement in environmentally dangerous activities in infringement of administrative laws. When these activities cause serious endangerment of human health there is, moreover, an aggravated circumstance and hence a higher sanction. These provisions in the new Spanish Criminal Code hence punish the endangerment of ecological values. However, the requirement of unlawfulness still keeps some degree of administrative dependence (Faure and Heine 2000, pp. 293–294).

Similar developments can be found in other more recent instances. In Sweden, for example, Article 29(1) of the Environmental Code 1998 criminalizes the pollution of land, water or air when it occurs in a way

[15] For an analysis of this Walloon Decree, see the contributions in Bosly *et al.* (2010).

that poses considerable risks for human health or detriment to flora and fauna or other significant harm to the environment. Since a legislative change of 2004, also 'changing the surface and groundwater in a manner that harms or may harm human health, animals or plants' is now criminalized (Philipsen and Faure 2015, pp. 14–15). Likewise in France, the formulation of environmental crime has changed in the sense that ecological values are safeguarded with greater independence from administrative protocols (Guihal 2000, p. 541).[16]

When one looks at those different examples one could argue that there is, in most legal systems, still some relationship between environmental crime and administrative law. However, compared to the absolute administrative dependence in the old environmental laws of the 1980s, important changes have taken place. Criminal behaviour is now no longer only described in terms of administrative penalty (e.g. the duty to have a permit), but rather in ecological terms (e.g. causing serious pollution). Moreover, although some relationship with administrative law is retained, the formulation has changed. More recently, the criminal liability no longer requires, for example, violation of administrative obligations, but unlawfulness. The latter notion is undoubtedly broader than a mere violation of administrative interest. In that sense, the lessons coming from the legal doctrine discussed above advocating changing from an absolute to a relative administrative dependence have been followed.

Administrative Penal Law

It was already mentioned that in the 1980s that some legal systems, such as Austria and Germany, had administrative penal laws whereby the legislator had *ex-ante* decided that particular violations would no longer be handled by the criminal law but exclusively through administrative penal law. Also in other member states, such as Portugal, the enforcement of environmental administrative statutes took place through

[16] Article 421-2 of the French Penal Code now has a specific crime of 'ecologic terrorism' (see Prieur 2001).

administrative punishment of those regulatory offences (Faure and Heine 2000, p. 283).

It was especially in the UK where administrative fines were introduced. In England and Wales, the introduction of the Regulatory Enforcement and Sanctions Act (2008) gave some regulatory bodies, including the Environment Agency, the power to impose a greater repertoire of civil (administrative) sanctions. They were introduced by various administrative orders and regulations such as the Environment Civil Sanctions Order (2010). Consequently, in England and Wales, the Environment Agency can impose either a fixed monetary penalty or a variable monetary penalty. The reason for applying those fines is to fill the gap in enforcement where prosecution does not seem to be in the public interest (Faure and Svatikova 2012, pp. 266–268).

Similar changes equally took place in parts of Belgium because of the introduction of the Environmental Enforcement Decree (2008) in the Flemish Region and a similar decree, also in 2008, in the Walloon Region. In case of the former, some environmental crimes have been declassified as administrative offences no longer subject to the criminal law. In that case, the exclusive administrative sanction is the only sanction available. For crimes still forwarded to the public prosecutor, there is a possibility for the Regional Agency to impose an alternative administrative fine, but only in cases in which the prosecutor opts not to prosecute (Faure and Svatikova 2012, pp. 260–261). Recall that for the Flemish Region under the old system (of only criminal enforcement), 65 per cent of the notices of violations were dismissed, which effectively meant that no remedy was imposed at all. Data on the enforcement policy after the introduction of the administrative fining system in 2008 show that the dismissals, that is, the cases where no enforcement reaction whatsoever took place, have been considerably reduced. When the prosecutor now dismisses cases, they are sent to the administrative authority to impose an administrative fine, which results in a substantial reduction of the number of cases where no reaction takes place.[17]

---

[17] See in that respect the Environmental Enforcement Reports of the Flemish High Council for Environmental Enforcement to be found (in English) on <www.VHRM.be>. See also Faure (2011).

It is important to remember, however, that there are still important differences between the member states. For example, in the Netherlands, a variety of different administrative remedies exist but administrative fines have so far not been used in environmental law.[18] In Spain, the introduction of administrative fines has been opposed (Fajardo *et al.* 2015, p. 67). This shows that although some member states employ an alternative approach that focuses on a more reduced role of the criminal law, this is certainly not the case for all EU member states and, as shown above, nor for the EU Environmental Crime Directive.

2.6 Concluding Remarks

In this chapter, I elucidated how environmental crime has been treated by policymakers and legislators and how this has changed over time. At the inception of environmental law in the 1970s, there was little attention for the notion of environmental crime—the focus was on the administrative management of the environment. The goal of criminal law was mainly to support the administrative system as far as it related to the regulation of environmental pollution. Soon it became clear that this way of treating environmental crime was problematic. On the one hand, too much was criminalized (i.e. behaviours that could be treated via other remedies) and, on the other hand, criminal law itself was made much too dependent upon the violation of administrative obligations, thus seriously limiting the capacity of the criminal law to protect the environment. Various currents in legal literature between the 1980s and the 2000s advocated different ways of dealing with criminal law. A graduated punishment approach was advocated, arguing that an effective environmental criminal law system needed a combination of different types of provisions. Proponents of another approach argued that criminal law should be reserved for the most serious infringements, whereas

[18] See Jansen (2015) for a plaidoyer in favour of the introduction of administrative fines in environmental enforcement.

lesser infringements could be dealt with via other means such as civil or administrative penalties.

It seems that these voices have been heard, at least implicitly, by some policymakers. Several legal systems seem to be moving towards a more independent criminalization of environmental harm (not only by reference to a violation of administrative duties) and have also introduced an alternative approach, allowing criminal law to be reserved for the most severe violations.

As I indicated in the introduction and throughout the chapter, the scope of this analysis is, in some ways, limited. One obvious issue is that it is based on generalizations that may be indicative of most but not all cases. Indeed, already in the 1980s, some policymakers had a graduated punishment approach and moved towards administrative fines, but this was certainly not the case for most European member states. It is of course not argued here that where policy changes took place this was always the result of the paradigm shifts discussed in Sect. 2.3. In some instances, this may have been the case (especially where one could point at a direct or indirect influence of specific authors on the policymaker). In other cases, there is a correlation between doctrinal advice and policy change. However, policy changes in line with the suggestions in legal doctrine may have occurred in many member states, but certainly not in all. Moreover, even on an EU-wide level, when looking at the Environmental Crime Directive, there is room for improvement, for example, by mentioning the importance of administrative fining systems.

One positive aspect of the fact that in many EU member states policy changes have taken place is that some comparison of policies and hence some mutual learning may take place with respect to the relative effectiveness of different policies. That, however, supposes that sufficient data is available, for example, on the relative effectiveness of enforcement efforts before and after a policy change.[19] Nevertheless, data on enforcement efforts are still difficult to obtain. The most important policy advice at this moment is therefore undoubtedly that a reliable system

[19] How to measure this effectiveness is already a highly debated issue.

of data collection on enforcement efforts, preferably harmonized among EU member states, should be developed. Only when such data are available is a mutual learning on the effectiveness of various enforcement systems between member states possible, and only then can one expect to increase the effectiveness of the enforcement of environmental law.

The most important priority now should be to focus on a harmonized system of data collection concerning environmental crime. Only when reliable data are available will it also be possible to develop a smart, risk- and evidence-based enforcement approach in the fight against environmental crime.

References

Ayres, I., & Braithwaite, J. (2005). *Responsive regulation: Transcending the deregulation debate*. New York: Oxford University Press.

Bell, S., & McGillivray, D. (2005). *Environmental law,* 6th edn. Oxford: Oxford University Press.

Bosly, H.-D., Carolus, P., De Suray, P., De Temmerman, P., Di Cristofaro, L., Donnay Wouters, J.P., Faure, M., Gobert, P., Jeurissen, I., Masset, A., Pirotte, C., & Staudt, E. (2010). *La Lutte Contre les infractions environnementales: Journée d'Études du 30 Avril 2009*. Brugge: Vanden Broele.

De Figueirdo, D. (1993). Das Portugiesische Strafgesetzbuch von 1982 in der Bewährung. *Zeitschrift für die gesamte Strafrechtwissenschaft, 105*(1), 77–107.

De Nauw, A. (1994). *Les Métamorphoses Administratives du Droit Pénal de l'Entreprise*. Ghent: Mys & Breesch.

Fajardo, T., Fuentes, J., Ramos, I., & Verdú, J. (2015). *Fighting environmental crime in Spain: A country report. Study in the framework of the EFFACE research project*. Granada: University of Granada.

Faure, M. (1992). *Umweltrecht in Belgien. Strafrecht im Spannungsfeld von Zivil- und Verwaltungsrecht*. Freiburg im Breisgau: Max Planck Institute for Foreign and International Criminal Law.

Faure, M. (1997). Het Nederlandse Milieustrafrecht: Dringend aan Herziening toe!. *RM Themis, 1997*(1), 3–12.

Faure, M. (2011). Handhaving van het Milieurecht in het Vlaamse Gewest: Enkele Cijfers. In D. D'Hooge, K. Deketelaere, A.M. Draye (Eds.), *Liber Amicorum Marc Boes*. Brugge: die Keure.

Faure, M., & Heine, G. (2000). *Environmental criminal law in the European Union. Documentation of the main provisions with introductions*. Freiburg im Breisgau: Max Planck Institute for Foreign and International Criminal Law.

Faure, M., & Svatikova, K. (2010). Enforcement of environmental law in the Flemish region. *European Energy and Environmental Law Review, 19*(2), 60–79.

Faure, M., & Svatikova, K. (2012). Criminal or administrative law to protect the environment?. *Journal of Environmental Law, 24*(2), 253–286.

Guihal, D. (2000). *Droit Répressif de l'Environnement,* 2nd edn. Paris: Economica.

Heemskerk, H., & Ubachs, S. (2001). Totstandkoming Artikel 173a en 173b Sr in 1969. In M.G. Faure, Th. A. de Roos, M.J.C. Visser (Eds.), *Herziening van het Commune Milieustrafrecht*, 9–11. Arnhem: Gouda Quint.

Heine, G. (1986). Aspekten des Umweltstrafrechts im Internationalen Vergleich. *Goltdammer's Archiv für Strafrecht*, 67–88.

Heine, G. (1989). Zur Rolle des Strafrechtlichen Umweltschutzes. *Zeitschrift für die Gesamte Strafrechtswissenschaft, 101*(3), 722–755.

Heine, G. (1991). Die Verwaltungsakzessorietät im deutschen Umweltstrafrecht unter Berücksichtigung des österreichischen Rechts. Aktuelle Probleme und Reformüberregungen. *Österreichische Juristen Zeitung*, 370–378.

Heine, G. (1994). Allemagne. Crimes Against the Environment. *Revue Internationale de Droit Pénal, 65*, 731–759.

Heine, G., & Meinberg, V. (1988). *Empfehlen sich Änderungen im Strafrechtlichen Umweltschutz, Insbesondere in Verbindung mit dem Verwaltungsrecht? Gutachten D für den 57. Deutschen Juristentag*. München: Beck.

Hünerfeld, P. (1997). Portugal. In G. Heine (Ed.), *Umweltstrafrecht im Mittel- und Südeuropäischen Ländern*, 359–371. Freiburg im Breisgau: Max Planck Institute for Foreign and International Criminal Law.

Jansen, O. (2015). Op naar een Algemene Boetebevoegdheid in de Omgevingswet. *Tijdschrift voor Omgevingsrecht, 2015*(4), 165–173.

Jepsen, J. (1994). Dänemark. In K. Cornils, & G. Heine (Eds.), *Umweltstrafrecht in den Nordischen Ländern*, 1–235. Freiburg im Breisgau: Max Planck Institute for Foreign and International Criminal Law.

Lutterer, W., & Hoch, H. J. (1997). *Rechtliche Steuerung im Umweltbereich.* Freiburg im Breisgau: Max Planck Institute for Foreign and International Criminal Law.

Macrory, R.B. (2006). *Regulatory justice: Making sanctions effective.* London: Better Regulation Executive.

Mandiberg, S.F., & Faure, M.G. (2009). A graduated punishment approach to environmental crimes: Beyond vindication of administrative authority in the united states and Europe. *Columbia Journal of Environmental Law, 34*(2), 447–511.

Meinberg, V. (1988). Empirische Erkenntnisse zum Vollzug des Umweltstrafrechts. *Zeitschrift für die Gesamte Strafrechtswissenschaft, 100*(1), 112–157.

Ogus, A. (2004). Enforcing regulation: Do we need the criminal law?. In H. Sjögren, & G. Skogh (Eds.), *New perspectives on economic crime*, 42–56. Cheltenham: Edward Elgar.

Ogus, A., & Abbot, C. (2002). Sanctions for pollution: Do we have the right regime?. *Journal of Environmental Law, 13*, 283–298.

Philipsen, N.J., & Faure, M.G. (2015), *Country report on Sweden. Study in the framework of the EFFACE research project.* Maastricht: Maastricht University.

Polaino Navarrete, N. (1997). Spanien. In G. Heine (Ed.), *Umweltstrafrecht im Mittel- und Südeuropäischen Ländern*, 497–545. Freiburg im Breisgau: Max Planck Institute for Foreign and International Criminal Law.

Prabhu, M. (1994). General report. English version. *International Review of Penal Law, 65*(3–4), 699–728.

Prieur, M. (2001). *Le Droit de l'Environnement,* 4th edn. Paris: Editions Dalloz-Sirey

Robert, J.H. (1994). Le Problème de la Responsabilité et des Sanctions Pénales en Matière d'Environnement. *Revue Internationale de Droit Pénal, 65*, 947–958.

Rodrigues, A. (1994). Les Crimes Contre l'Environnement. Quelques Points du Droit Portugais. *International Review of Penal Law, 65*, 1125–1148.

Tiedemann, K. (1980). *Die Neuordnung des Umweltstrafrechts: Gutachtliche Stellungnahme zu dem Entwurf eines Sechzehnten Strafrechtsänderungsgesetzes* (Gesetz zur Bekämpfung der Umweltkriminalität). Berlin: de Gruyter.

Ubachs, S. (2001). De Beweegredenen van de Wetgever bij de Totstandkoming van de Artikelen 173a en 173b Sr. In M.G. Faure, Th. A. de Roos, M.J.C. Visser (Eds.), *Herziening van het Commune Milieustrafrecht*, 12–17. Arnhem: Gouda Quint.

Waling, C., Koopmans, I., Rutgers, M., Sjöcrona, J., van Strien, N., & Tak, P. (1994). Crimes against the environment. *International Review of Penal Law, 65*, 1065–1099.

Winkelbauer, W. (1985). *Zur Verwaltungsakzessorietät des Umweltstrafrechts.* Berlin: Duncker & Humblot.

Legislative Documents

Directive 2008/99/EC on the protection of the environment through criminal law, OJ L328 of 6 December 2008, p. 28.
Directive 2008/123 on ship-source pollution and on the introduction of penalties for infringements, OJ L280 27 October 2009, p. 52.
Framework Decision 2002/80/JHA of 27 January 2003 on the protection of the environment through criminal law, OJ L29/55 of 3 February 2003.
Proposal by the Kingdom of Denmark for a framework decision on environmental crime, OJ 39/4 of 11 February 2000.

Prof. Dr. Michael G. Faure (LL.M.) became academic director of the Maastricht European institute for transnational legal research (METRO) and professor of Comparative and International Environmental Law at the law faculty of Maastricht University in September 1991. He still holds both positions today. In addition, he is academic director of the Ius Commune Research School and member of the board of directors of Ectil. Since the first of February 2008, he is half time professor of comparative private law and economics at the Rotterdam Institute of Law and Economics (RILE) of the Erasmus University in Rotterdam and academic director of the European Doctorate in Law and Economics (EDLE) programme. Since 1982 he is equally attorney at the Antwerp Bar. He publishes in the areas of environmental (criminal) law, tort and insurance and economic analysis of (accident) law.

3

Victims in the 'Land of Fires': Illegal Waste Disposal in the Campania Region, Italy

Anna Rita Germani, Giacomo D'Alisa, Pasquale Marcello Falcone, and Piergiuseppe Morone

A.R. Germani (✉)
Sapienza University of Rome, Rome, Italy
e-mail: annarita.germani@uniroma1.it

G. D'Alisa
Institute of Environmental Science and Technology, Autonomous University of Barcelona, Barcelona, Spain
e-mail: giacomo.dalisa@uab.cat

P.M. Falcone,
Department of Economic and Social Sciences, Polytechnic University of Marche, Ancona, Italy
e-mail: falcone.pm@gmail.com

P. Morone
Unitelma Sapienza University of Rome, Department of Law and Economics, Rome, Italy
e-mail: piergiuseppe.morone@unitelma.it

R. Sollund et al. (eds.), *Fighting Environmental Crime in Europe and Beyond*, Palgrave Studies in Green Criminology,
DOI 10.1057/978-1-349-95085-0_3

3.1 Introduction

The so-called Land of Fires (LoF) indicates an area in the Campania region (southern Italy) where systematically, since the end of the 1980s, toxic waste has been illegally burned and buried. Legambiente, a prominent environmental Italian NGO, first used the term 'LoF' in 2003 to refer to three municipalities in the province of Naples—Giuliano in Campania, Qualiano, and Villaricca—where thousands of tons of toxic waste have been illegally disposed of (Legambiente 2003). Since then, grassroots movements have shown that the affected area is larger and encompasses more than the three stated municipalities. Even if the term is traditionally associated with a specific geographical area, regardless of its extent, we maintain that the LoF should be understood as an economic phenomenon implemented to cut waste disposal costs for legal and illegal businesses, irrespective of where the economic activity is managed.

Organized mafia-like crime plays a significant role in the illegal management of waste in this area; however, organized mafia-like criminals are not the only players. Furthermore, as a certain informer's recent declaration confirms, the illegal waste business already existed well before the mafia joined it.[1] In the public domain, a simplistic view has often prevailed, according to which waste dumping is committed only by mafia clans; however, a more substantial explanation of the phenomenon comprises the interplay of organized mafia-like crime, businessmen, firms, and bureaucrats. The 2014 Legambiente Report argued that the economic returns from the illegal trafficking of hazardous waste in 2010 were approximately €3.1 billion. According to the Italian Financial Police, economic motivation is one of the most important factors that induces firms to illegally dispose of waste: a European company pays about €60,000 to legally dispose of a container full of 15,000 tons of

[1] Nunzio Perrella, a member of the Camorra, the Neapolitan Mafia, recently declared during an interview with a journalist that the illegal waste business was already thriving before the Camorra started to participate in it. See Perella (2016). Perrella is renowned among magistrates, journalists, and Italian citizens for the phrase he said in 1997 during a volunteer declaration to a prosecutor: 'Garbage is gold.'

hazardous waste, while the same amount of waste can be illegally disposed of for only €5000 in Eastern Europe or in Asia.

The lack of economic resources devoted to crime prevention and control, and the strong interaction and collusion between political parties and industrial lobbies are some of the causes that have affected criminal environmental legislation and its effective enforcement negatively. These circumstances, in addition to a diffuse lack of law enforcement at both national and regional levels, have contributed over the years to the worsening of this widespread illegal situation and have thus created the prevalence of a system that has allowed high private gains to be generated at unsustainable social environmental costs (Germani *et al.* 2015). The illegal trafficking of waste is an emblematic example of such a system, which is in turn encouraged by a weak degree of social perception, given that ecocrimes are usually defined as 'crimes without victims', since the victims are not immediately identifiable.

This chapter aims to shed some light on this phenomenon, mainly through the lens of the victims of this environmental crime and challenges the idea that illegal waste trafficking is an environmental crime without victims. Indeed, as we show in this chapter, the victims are the main actors who fought against illegal waste dumping. During the 20 years of environmental conflicts in Campania, the victims have reinforced their networks, thus unveiling the environmental burden of illegal waste trafficking and denouncing the tragic health consequences of such activity. This study is based on a preliminary review of the literature and cases on both the dominant and counternarrative of the phenomenon. An empirical analysis conducted through 34 interviews with 'opinion leaders' of the movement to address the problem of waste in Campania follows; an affiliation network analysis is then employed to study how the victims interacted over time with different grassroots movements and associations, and how their network strategy can explain the strength of the movements' claims. The findings allow us to draw some preliminary conclusions that in recent years victims have played an important role in influencing: 1) the recognition of waste-related crime as a penal felony by Italian legislation, 2) the promotion of epidemiological studies to investigate the relation between health and illegal and legal waste-dumping practices, and 3) the launching of judicial actions against those participants who benefited financially from their illegal waste businesses. Indeed, the Italian victims seem to be the most determined advocates in this situation; together they are networking and combating the illegal waste practices that have considerably affected life in the LoF area and elsewhere.

3.2 Framing the Issue

3.2.1 What Is the Crime in Question?

In the Italian legal system, there is no legal definition of 'Environmental Crime' (EC). In legal terms, EC refers to environmental offences punished by criminal sanctions. According to Italian legal order, most environmental offences are misdemeanours (*contravvenzioni*), which fall outside of the criminal code and do not constitute a coherent system of rules. In fact, the several related laws issued by the Italian legislature result from disconnected interventions in different environment-related fields.[2] Some distinctions for felonies do, however, exist: Article 260 Environmental Code (Legislative Decree 152/2006) provides for the felony of 'organised activities for the illegal trafficking of waste'. However, several massive protests by Campanian citizens against the illegal trafficking and disposal of waste forced the Italian government to introduce a new law against waste-related activities (Law 6 February 2014, No. 6, Article 256-bis Environmental Code), which punishes the illicit combustion of waste and provides harsh penalties for the burning of waste, previously punishable only as a misdemeanour.

Only recently, Law 68/2015 introduced a new chapter (VI bis) to the Italian penal code regarding and defining crimes against the environment: environmental disaster, intentional crimes against the environment, fatal injuries as a result of the crime of environmental pollution, and the traffic of and abandonment of highly radioactive material (and related consequential side effects). In terms of the severity of the applicable penalty, the most significant crimes are: 1) 'environmental pollution' (Article 452a), punished by imprisonment for 2–6 years and a fine

[2] Vagliasindi *et al.* (2015).

from €10,000 to €100,000 (if it causes death or bodily harm, sentences are harsher [Article 452b]); and 2) 'environmental disaster' (Article 452c), punished by imprisonment for 5–15 years.

3.2.2 Who Is Responsible for the Crimes in Question?

Campania region has been plagued by the illegal management of waste for 20 years; not only illegal burning and burying of waste but also certified landfills are compounding the hazard (D'Alisa *et al.* 2014). As explained in the previous section, until recently, Italian environmental legislation, along with legislation governing waste management, did not include criminal charges. This legislative vacuum offered a great opportunity for those industrialists looking for cheap waste disposal solutions to gain huge returns (Pasotti 2010).

In the 1990s, the illegal waste business in Italy thrived;[3] the Freemasons, some components of the state bureaucracy, and the Camorra (the mafia-type crime syndicate that originated in the region of Campania and in its capital, Naples) orchestrated a powerful network capable of disposing of millions of tons of waste per year (Iacuelli 2008). Fifteen years ago, this business was worth more than €7.5 billion per year and caused a loss for the national treasury of €1 billion every year (Commissione d'Inchiesta 2000); presently, it is worth almost €17 billion per year (Legambiente 2013). The turnover in 15 years has more than doubled.

Since then, several strategies have been used to dispose of garbage illegally, such as i) dumping hazardous waste directly in the countryside, ii) dumping hazardous waste in illegal quarries and on the construction sites of infrastructural public works, iii) burning special waste in the countryside and along low-traffic roads, and iv) mixing toxic with domestic waste for disposal in legal landfills and incinerators (Barbieri and Piglionica 2007; Commissione d'Inchiesta 2000; Fontana *et al.* 2008;

[3] According to the Parliamentary Commission of Inquiry on Waste Cycle and Connected Illicit Activities, every year almost 30 per cent of national special waste is illegally disposed of (Commissione d'Inchiesta 2000, p. 7). Campanian businesses produce only a small amount of the national special waste; most of the waste illegally disposed of in Italy is produced by enterprises located in other regions of Italy.

Iacuelli 2008). Campania has become the main target zone of such strategies and the largest final dumping ground in Italy.[4] The impact of such business has been politically, economically, and ecologically disastrous for the entire region. Indeed, even when prosecutors tried to stop the flourish of waste trafficking by shutting down some landfills because of their precarious sanitary conditions, the main consequence of those actions proved no harm to illegal disposal but rather interrupted the urban waste collection. The diminishing capacity of landfills and the absence of a regional waste management plan served as justification in 1994 for the central government to declare a state of emergency for the Campania region and delegate the waste management to an ad hoc commissioner (Armiero and D'Alisa 2012). However, the national government focused its authoritarian intervention on urban waste and completely dismissed the mounting and more problematic issue of the illegal dumping of hazardous waste. The state of emergency caused an increase in civil conflicts and facilitated the proliferation of the Camorra's businesses, which also infiltrated the urban waste management. The result was a crisis of democracy in Campania (D'Alisa *et al.* 2010).

In light of these considerations, it should be clear that organized mafia-like crime cannot bear the sole responsibility for this waste-related environmental disaster; the Camorra is not the only contributor. Although, according to public opinion, mafia clans are the most influential agents involved in the illegal trafficking of waste, recent empirical research (Germani *et al.* 2015) has shown that business firms often strive directly to eliminate illegally the waste they generate, or alternatively they employ the service of mafia-like organizations. Thus, a more substantial explanation of the phenomenon must be articulated concerning the interplay of

[4] The Campania region generates a small amount of special waste as compared to the rest of Italy, not only in absolute terms but also relative to its contribution to the national GDP. For example, in 2009, the production of special waste in Italy was about 134 million tons, of which more than 10 million tons were hazardous (7.5 per cent of the total production). Campania produced slightly more than 6.4 million tons, of which 0.35 million were hazardous (5.8 per cent of the regional production; ISPRA 2012). This means that Campania contributes only 4.7 per cent of the total special waste in Italy and only 3.5 per cent of the national production of hazardous waste, even if the contribution to the national GDP is 6.25 per cent (http://sitis.istat.it/sitis/html). In fact, D'Alisa *et al.* (2012) recommended complementing the conventional waste indicators with two different indicators in order to investigate these critical waste management patterns.

mafia-like groups, businesses, firms, and administrative officers. Such a link between environmental crime and corporate crime should be adequately considered when developing a more effective deterrence strategy.

3.2.3 Who Are the Victims?

In developing the present study, victims were identified as those who perceive to be directly or indirectly, materially or psychologically, affected by an environmental offence. As our interviewees highlight, to be victim of an environmental crime means: i) to be subjected to psychological harm from living in contaminated places, even in the absence of damage to physical health (I#12); ii) to feel like your life is determined by events that are altering the (natural) equilibrium and that cause organic and biological injuries, as well as internal, spiritual wounds (I#23); iii) to suffer physically, emotionally, personally, and through the experience of other people because of the devastating effects generated by the (economic development) model (I#29).

However, the perception of being the victim of an environmental crime did not create a victim complex; an example of Campanian citizens' extensive participation in denouncing this environmental disaster and demanding stricter enforcement is the website *The Land of Fires*, created in 2007 by an activist from Villaricca, a small town in Campania. Since its creation, new videos have been uploaded every day on this very popular online platform that shows columns of toxic smoke as a result of the daily practices of the illegal burning that affects the LoF; currently more than 800 toxic smoke sightings have been mapped.[5] The growing activism over the last 5 years has produced several grassroots committees that have popped up all around the region, many of them forming a social coalition called Stop Biocide,[6] which denounces the disastrous health consequences (i.e. increase of cancer mortality and morbidity) of the illegal trafficking and disposing of industrial waste, and the mounting contamination of air, aquifers, soil, and subsoil.

---

[5] The map is available at http://www.laterradeifuochi.it/, date accessed 21 December 2015.

[6] https://it-it.facebook.com/stopbiocidio.

In the case study in Sect. 3.5, we present the results of our research on victims, which was obtained by collecting and analysing primary data from 34 interviews conducted with opinion leaders living in those municipalities that fall in the perimeter of the LoF as defined by the national government (see Fig. 3.2). Within the questionnaire, the self-perception of being a victim was assessed by asking participants if they had been a victim of some type of environmental harm over the years. The results show how some local associations and grassroots organizations have become a reference point for the victims of waste-related environmental crimes. Furthermore, we established that illegal dumping has not only damaged the environment and affected people but also contributed to eroding trust in institutions and government.

3.2.4 How Has the Illegal Burning and Burying of Toxic Waste Been Enforced or Prevented?

Since the 1980s, the weak enforcement of environmental laws in Campania offered organized crime groups the opportunity to gain huge profits and firms the possibility of substantially lowering their costs. Public institutions tried to develop new legal frameworks for monitoring waste management, but these attempts failed to lead to any real improvement of the situation (Greyl *et al.* 2013). The first regional waste management plan was approved in 1993 in order to reduce the use of landfills in Campania by 50 per cent through the new management of networks of municipalities. However, this measure was not effective, and when landfills had been saturated in 1994, a state of emergency was declared.[7] An ad hoc commissioner with special powers to implement Campania's waste plan was nominated by the national government, replacing the usual authorities (regional, provincial, and municipal) of waste management.

---

[7] D'Alisa and Armiero (2011) and Armiero and D'Alisa (2012) demonstrated the high level of unreliability surrounding the data on urban waste management in Campania. The state of emergency was declared officially because the landfills were full, but there are no consistent data on the available landfills' capacities, nor for 1997 when there were 82 landfills in the region nor for 2007 when there were 9.

The Italian government initially conceived the commissioner as a temporary institution; nonetheless, from 1994 to 2009, it nominated 11 commissioners.

In 1997, 3 years after the state of emergency began, the most important piece of Italian waste legislation was issued, incorporating the main principles and prescriptions of European waste management regulations into Italian law and allocating the related responsibilities among different institutional levels. Legislative Decree 22/1997 (also called the Ronchi Decree) introduced several types of offences, such as the illegal abandonment of waste (Article 50), unauthorized waste management activities (Article 51), the lack of land remediation of contaminated sites (Article 51bis introduced by Legislative Decree 389/1998), the violation of notification requirement, record keeping and required forms (Article 52), and illicit waste trafficking.[8] However, all of these offences were (and are) deemed misdemeanours.

Only in 2001, with the introduction of Law 93/2001, did the national government recognize the first waste-related environmental crime and consequently punish the organized activity of illegal waste trafficking. Such convictions underlined the fact that until 2001 there had been no possibility of opposing organized mafia-like criminal activities, because in Italy a charge of association with the mafia cannot be made if the offences of the accused are simple misdemeanours.

In 2006, Legislative Decree 152/2006, known as the Environmental Code, was approved; it attempted to systematize other Italian environmental norms, such as the Environmental Impact Assessment, the Strategic Environmental Assessment, soil and water protection,

[8] The decree issued in 1997, known as the Ronchi Decree, is named after the minister of environment at the time. It introduced the principle of 'self-sufficiency', which implies that each region should be responsible for the management, and thus disposal, of the urban waste generated in its own territory. The Ronchi Decree implemented not only waste production prevention policies but also waste collection, recycling, and incineration procedures. Moreover, the decree made provisions for limitations on waste disposal to prevent health and environmental contamination risks and made illegal waste disposal a criminal offence. In particular, Title VI/bis divided crimes against the environment into four categories: environmental pollution, alteration of the natural patrimony, damage to cultural patrimony, and illegal trafficking of waste and environmental fraud.

atmospheric pollution, and waste management. In 2008, with waste treatment capacity again beyond saturation, worldwide attention was drawn to the mismanagement in Campania (Naughton 2008; Rosenthal 2008). In order to deal with the crisis, the national government implemented Decree 90, the most powerful ruling approved in Campania for waste management, and also the least respectful of environmental and human rights. The decree planned for the construction of ten new landfills in the region and four incinerators: two in the province of Naples, one in the province of Salerno, and one in the province of Caserta. However, no real measures were taken under this decree to stop corruption and crime in waste management. Meanwhile, several popular protests in Campania demanded precisely that: stop the corruption and the ecocriminals. Finally, a massive demonstration at the end of 2013 prompted the national government to issue Law Decree 136/2013—converted a few months later to Law 6/2014—which introduced a new crime into the Italian penal code: the illicit combustion of waste (Article 256bis Legislative Decree 152/2006). With this law, the national government was forced to recognize the extreme seriousness of the environmental, health, and economic conditions of many municipalities in Campania and declared the illegal burning of toxic waste a crime. Finally, the Land of Fires area was institutionalized.

As mentioned above, inadequate enforcement has been one of the key factors in Campania's deteriorating environmental situation. In addition to this problem, the lack of economic resources devoted to crime prevention and control, the strong interaction and collusion between political parties and industrial lobbies, and the lack of a culture of legality have created in Italy in general, and in Campania in particular, the prevalence of a system that has allowed the creation of high margins for private profit, which hampers both the market and economic policy in their actions to correct allocation or reallocation of resources. All of these factors have generated a complex waste mismanagement phenomenon that has been inadequately addressed by competent regional and national authorities and institutions. The result is widespread illegality and noncompliance with normative requirements.

3.3 The Campania Waste Disaster in Context

Campania and its capital city, Naples, are infamous worldwide as the largest waste management failure in Europe (D'Alisa and Armiero 2011). National government established the state of emergency in 1994, supposedly to tackle the urban waste crisis,[9] but once the emergency was declared over in 2009, the real socioenvironmental disaster emerged. The illegal disposal of industrial waste, which began earlier in the 1980s (Commissione d'Inchiesta 2000), never stopped during the waste emergency regime and persisted 6 years after the national government deemed the emergency resolved. Strictly connected to the illegal disposal of industrial waste in Campania, in fact, has been the decade-long mismanagement of the region's urban waste. Both illegal industrial waste disposal and the failure of its urban waste planning have transformed Campania into the world's icon of waste mismanagement in Europe (D'Alisa and Armiero 2011).

Literature on the waste crisis in Campania has increased enormously in recent years, developing in different fields and involving the perspectives of NGOs, government institutions, historians, and social and medical scientists (D'Alisa *et al.* 2010). The complex picture of this Italian political disaster emerges only if different studies and dimensions of analysis are taken into account: Fontana *et al.* (2008) and Iacuelli (2008) analyse the importance of the toxic waste trade, across Italy and Europe, between the Camorra and corporations; Lucarelli (2007a, b, c), Ianniello (2007), and Raimondi (2007) conduct a legal analysis of the Campanian case, which examines the government's abuse of legal power;

[9] In Italy, the Council of Ministers declared a state emergency in accordance with Article 2 of Law 225/1992, which specifies that civil protection intervention is necessary when natural disasters and catastrophes occur, or any other events that, due to their intensity and extent, require extraordinary means and powers. There are cases when full powers are not delegated to the Head of the Civil Protection Department but to a special commissioner. Such was the case in 1994 when, for the first time, the Committee for the Waste Emergency in Campania was nominated. The declaration of the state of emergency guaranteed the commissioner power to bypass laws and procedures due to the urgent need to deal with the lack of a waste management plan and the diminishing availability of landfill capacity in the region.

Senior and Mazza (2004),[10] Martuzzi *et al.* (2005 2008), Comella (2007), Fazzo *et al.* (2008), and Capocaccia *et al.* (2012) provide health-risk analyses and epidemiological assessments; de Medici (2007) and Ortolani (2008) focus on the impacts of legal and illegal landfill sites on the environment and human beings; Rabitti (2008) examines the institutional responsibilities of the waste mismanagement problem; Armiero (2008) studies the links between society and nature in environmental conflicts; Pasotti (2010) denounces the lack of management expertise in Campania's political establishment; Musella (2008), Di Costanzo and Ferraro (2014), and Capone (2014) highlight the role and the claims of activists in their fight against illegal waste dumping; Armiero and D'Alisa (2012) show the importance of framing Campania's waste crisis as a case of environmental injustice; D'Alisa and Armiero (2011, 2013) underline the inconsistency of database information related to waste flows in Campania; D'Alisa *et al.* (2012) and D'Alisa and Di Nola (2013) investigate the specificity of waste metabolism in the Campania region; Commissione d'Inchiesta (2000) and Barbieri and Piglionica (2007) expose the sociopolitical analyses offered by the Parliamentary Commission of Inquiry on illegal waste trafficking; De Biase (2015) discusses the critics of the current development model, promoted by activists who oppose the reopening of a landfill in Naples; and Cantoni (2016) looks at the epidemiological controversy in Campania (the causal relation between the population's health and the presence of dumps) from a historical perspective.

3.3.1 The Epidemiological Controversy in Campania

In order to verify the impact that the waste cycle in the hot spots of Campania has on health, in 2004 the Civil Protection Department commissioned the World Health Organization with an epidemiological study that was published in 2005.

[10] Senior and Mazza (2004) were among the first to investigate the link between the high level of cancer mortality in an area in the province of Naples and the level of pollution caused by illegal waste disposal—an area that the two scientists came to call the 'triangle of death'.

The results showed 1) high rates of mortality for all the causes of death and for specific cancers in 24 municipalities in the provinces of Caserta (11) and Naples (13), but the main determinants of such high rates were poor lifestyle (i.e. diet, smoking, and infections) and occupational exposure rather than vicinity to waste facilities (legal and illegal); 2) high rates of neonatal malformations in the same area, but no causal relation was found between those rates and the practice of waste dumping, due to the presence of other intensive industrial and agriculture activities existing in the area (Martuzzi *et al.* 2005). Other studies (Fazzo *et al.* 2008) followed and detected anomalies in health conditions in the municipalities in Campania where illegal disposal of waste was more frequent, and they also confirmed the lack of a causal relation between mortality and morbidity rates and the presence of waste malpractices.

There is an evident contradiction between Campanian citizens' daily perceptions of their unhealthy condition, the poor health of their relatives and friends who live in the vicinity of waste sites, and the main conclusions of the studies commissioned by public authorities. The controversy continues to fuel the perceptions of those affected of not being protected by public institutions. It also confirms that there is often a tendency towards weak legal protection by national regulations for victims of environmental crimes (Lynch and Stretsky 2003). In contrast, scholars have argued in favour of the potential benefits of victims' participation in the criminal justice system in a variety of forms, including the decision-making process, consultation, and providing information (Cardwell *et al.* 2011) (Figs. 3.1 and 3.2).

3.4 Research Design and Methodology

In order to examine the role of victims of waste-related environmental crimes committed in the LoF, a social network analysis (SNA) approach was employed, focusing on the role of various organizations upon activists' self-perception as victims. To this end, we derived the Pollution Fighters Affiliation Network (PFAN), taking into account two sets of agents: one consisting of the victims of illegal waste disposal in the LoF and the other

Fig. 3.1 Geographical location of the Campania region. (*Source*: http://www.minambiente.it)

consisting of the organizations through which victims interact over time. The importance of studying affiliation networks rests on the theoretical relevance of people's memberships in society. Simmel (1950, 1955), one of the first social theorists who examined the theoretical implications of

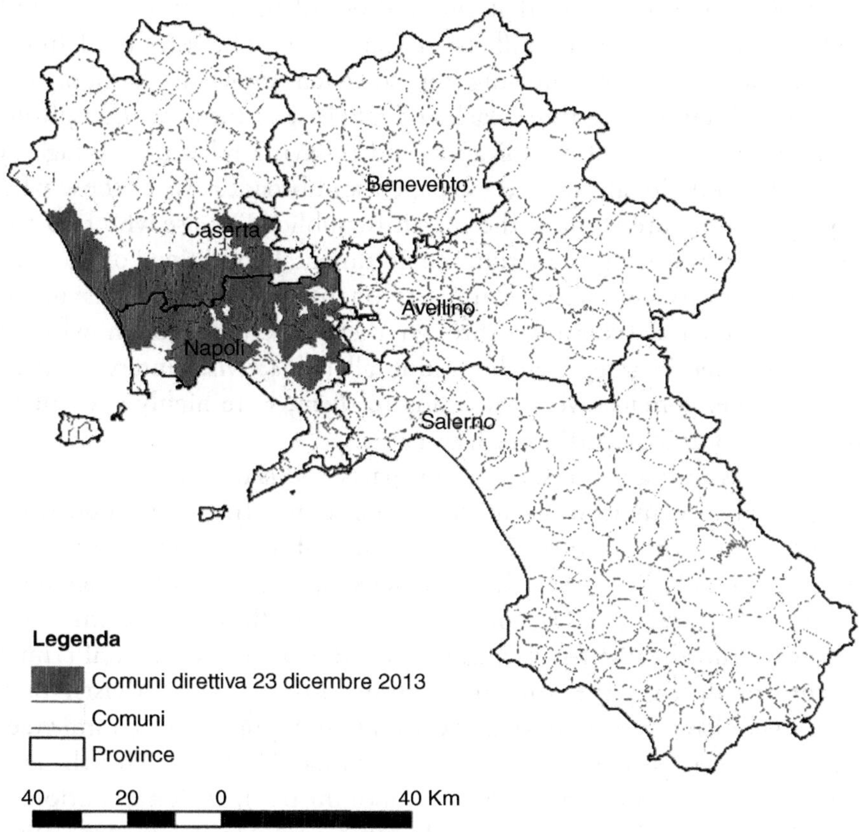

Fig. 3.2 Land of fires (*Source*: elaborated by Burgalassi D. (personal concession)

individuals' affiliations with collectivities, argued that individuals' affiliations (e.g. with family, political parties, trade unions) were crucial in outlining their beliefs and perceptions.

From August to December 2014, 34 face-to-face, semi-structured interviews were conducted with opinion leaders[11] who were part of the

[11] Not all individuals exert an equal amount of influence over others. In this sense, opinion leaders are influential in spreading either positive or negative information about a particular issue. Rogers (1962) emphasized the role of opinion leaders in influencing late adopters during the evaluation stage of the innovation decision process.

archipelago of associations that emerged out of the 20 most recent and enduring environmental conflicts in Campania. The sample of interviewees was built by following the so-called snowball method. We started by interviewing three classes of activists: 1) those acting upfront as the face of the local mobilization and receiving relevant coverage in regional and national media (newspapers and broadcasts); 2) those who appealed to the president of the Italian Republic; 3) those who resorted to courts, denouncing the serious environmental conditions of the LoF and the consequent negative impacts on human health. This initial roster of activists (identified through their expertise and knowledge) was subsequently integrated by asking all the activists interviewed to suggest other contacts who, according to them, were highly relevant in the waste conflict occurring in Campania.

The questionnaire consists of four parts and is designed to provide: 1) general information about the respondents (i.e. age, education, employment, and so on); 2) information about the environmental behaviours and attitudes of the interviewees, their level of engagement in grassroots activities for combating waste trafficking and mismanagement, and their self-perception as victims of environmental crime; 3) information on the kind of relationships that, as activists, they have established with local associations and grassroots committees (e.g. 29th August Committee, Campania Network Health and Environment, Coordination of Fires Committee), regional, national, and international NGOs (e.g. Legambiente, Italia nostra, Rete Lilliput, WWF, Greenpeace, ISDE), research and health centres (e. g. CNR, ENEA, WHO), and public authorities (e.g. Commissioner of the Waste Emergency in Campania, the Department of Civil Protection, Prefects).[12] We investigated the existing ties during what we consider the turning point in the battle over waste in Campania; and finally 4) we developed open questions on how the interviewed activists defined the environment, what kind of actions they considered an environmental crime, and what it meant personally to be victims of such offences.

[12] The interviewees were free to suggest different organizations from those listed.

We set 2008 as the *turning point*[13] for investigating the ties existing among the various entities involved. The reasons for this choice are two: firstly, between 2007 and 2008 tons of waste were piled in the streets, and the images of those mountains of garbage on the roads and submerging Naples and its surrounding municipalities circulated throughout the world by means of various media; secondly, in 2008 the national government issued Decree 90/2008 (converted into Law 123/2008), which imposed 10 landfills and 4 incinerators in Campania and established that any demonstrations in the vicinity of a waste facility would be judged as a penal felony. Such authoritarianism weakened the grassroots movements against the waste crisis in the region for some years, but they emerged again around 2011 and until 2014 gained much popular support.

In this chapter, we present mainly the outcomes of the third section of the questionnaire, which allowed us to investigate how the victims interacted over time with different organizations in order to 1) reinforce their sociopolitical and judicial actions and 2) stop the illegal practices that had considerably affected their lives. In order to study the evolution of the interactions over time and reveal the different properties that networks had before and after our turning point (2008), we asked the respondents to specify the kind of interactions experienced with different organizations from 2004 to 2008 and during the period from 2008 to 2014. More specifically, following Morone *et al.* (2014), we distinguished three types of possible ties between the activists and the organizations: the activist could be a member of such organizations, they could exchange information with them, and/or they could exchange knowledge with them. As a consequence, three different kinds of networks emerged: 'membership networks', 'information exchange networks',[14]

[13] A decisive point at which a significant change or historical event occurs.

[14] In the information exchange network, activists can participate in the initiatives of some organizations even if they are not members of it or even if their activist organization co-organizes demonstrations, seminars, conferences, and so on, with another organization. During these activities, activists belonging to different organizations exchange information about environmental and waste issues. These settings of mutual interactions are very relevant for the circulation of information among activists.

and 'knowledge exchange networks'.[15] However, for the purpose of this chapter, we focus only on the membership network; being a member (and/or a cofounder) of an organization means to be actively involved in most of its initiatives (e.g. meetings, demonstrations, seminars, public assemblies, writing letters to newspapers and authorities, writing and organizing press releases, drafting reports and dossiers, informing on environmental crimes to judicial authorities).

Nodes and edges compose a social network (SN); each node, also called a vertex, identifies an actor (e.g. a person or association); each edge, also known as a tie, denotes a particular relationship (e.g. friendship, sexual relation, membership, paper coauthorship) existing between the two nodes connected by the tie. Finally, the term 'mode' is used to refer to a distinct set of nodes characterized by a certain kind of tie. The most common type of network is a one-mode network. A network data set containing two different sets of nodes is known as a two-mode network. A special type of two-mode network that arises in SN studies is the affiliation network. Although affiliation networks are two mode, they have only one set of actors; the second mode in an affiliation network is, in fact, the set of *events* (such as organizations) to which actors belong.[16]

Our study examines the interactions between activists (the actors) fighting against environmental crime in the LoF and the organizations (the events) of which they are members and/or which they used to gain

[15] The knowledge networks denote a loose interaction between activists and organizations. Such interaction does not mean that knowledge relevant to mobilization cannot emerge out of these organizations that are also central to the information network and membership network. Activists may acquire studies, research results, epidemiological studies, dossiers, and documents even from organizations that they do not trust on a political level or with which they do not interact directly. For example, activists can use the waste management plan drafted by the regional government even if they do not trust the regional authorities (politicians, technicians, and so on) who govern the region or they can read epidemiological reports by the World Health Organization, even though they have no opportunity to meet and debate with the researchers who conducted the study.

[16] Indeed, 'in affiliation network data, the two modes are the actors and the events. In such data, the events are defined not on pairs of actors but on subsets of actors' (Wasserman & Faust 1994, p. 30). Specifically, the first mode is the set of agents N, the second mode is the set of events M; an agent can be related to one or more events.

knowledge about waste management, illegal waste trafficking, and the health consequences of waste-related contamination. We call our affiliation network the PFAN. According to the collected data, the PFAN is composed of 67 actors, 34 of which are citizens (actors) and 33 organizations (events). Organizations are further subdivided into 15 local associations, three national associations, four international organizations, three research centres, two healthcare institutions, and six public institutions.[17]

3.5 The Role of Victims in the Land of Fires: Preliminary Results from the Affiliation Network Analysis

The 34 actors interviewed (59 per cent men and 41 per cent women) have an average age of 43, the youngest being 23 and the eldest 62. More than 50 per cent hold a bachelor degree, 64 per cent of them live in a flat owned by family (the number of family members on average is three), and more than 30 per cent declared a family income of less than €15,000. All claimed to partake in environmentally friendly activities, such as participating in environmental NGOs or grassroots movements (94 per cent), separating their waste collection (100 per cent), endeavouring not to waste energy, water, and food (97 per cent), or using public transportation or bicycle instead of a car. However, almost all respondents declared that the environmentally friendly activities in which they engaged most involved conveying information about waste-related issues (59 per cent) and monitoring (19 per cent). About 80 per cent had no trust in political organizations at different levels (from municipalities up to the European Union), almost 88 per cent stated that they lived close to waste facilities, and 99 per cent identifies as victims of an environmental crime. Those who associated the feeling of being victims with their own bad health or with that of a relative had become activists only recently (after 2011). For the

[17] We report here the results of only 21 of the 32 interviews conducted.

vast majority of the respondents, being a victim meant living under conditions of psychological pressure and always worrying about the state of the environment in which they lived.

One can observe in depiction of the membership network below (Fig. 3.3) that after 2008 the density of the network increased, the architectural features of the system changed drastically, and the overall structure became completely connected. During the period 2004–2008, the membership network was represented by four completely disconnected subnetworks and consisted of a few actors. However, in the period 2008–2014, an increasing number of organizations, generally local, and their members entered the network by actively interacting with each other and forming a unique membership affiliation network. Over this second period, we can observe how the Coordination of Fires Committee occupied a central position in the network; this is a grassroots movement, established with the main objective of coordinating with precision the myriad of local committees that want to fight against the toxic smoke and the illegal burying of hazardous waste. As seen in Fig. 3.3, this movement succeeded in gaining a pivotal position in the evolving social network, coordinating and catalysing the movement around the emerging idea of environmental victims.

The year 2008 saw a turning point in the dynamic evolution of the PFAN under scrutiny. As emerged from our in-depth interviews, before 2008, the struggle among activists and regional and national governments focused predominately on urban waste plans and the unwanted incinerator in Acerra, even though there were activists who had been trying to turn the spotlight on hazardous waste since 2005. This change is reflected in the architecture of the affiliation network, where local associations and grassroots committees (e.g. 29th August Committee, Campania Network Health and Environment, Coordination of Fires Committee) play central roles in aggregating potential victims and in imparting to the local community a stronger awareness of the problem and its associated risks.

After 2008, the movements and existing committees were destabilized by a decisive intervention by the national government to impose 10 new substantially larger landfills, program 3 more incinerators, and declare all acts of dissent in the vicinity of a waste facility a penal felony (D'Alisa *et al.* 2010). Moreover, in 2011–2012, the focus of contention turned

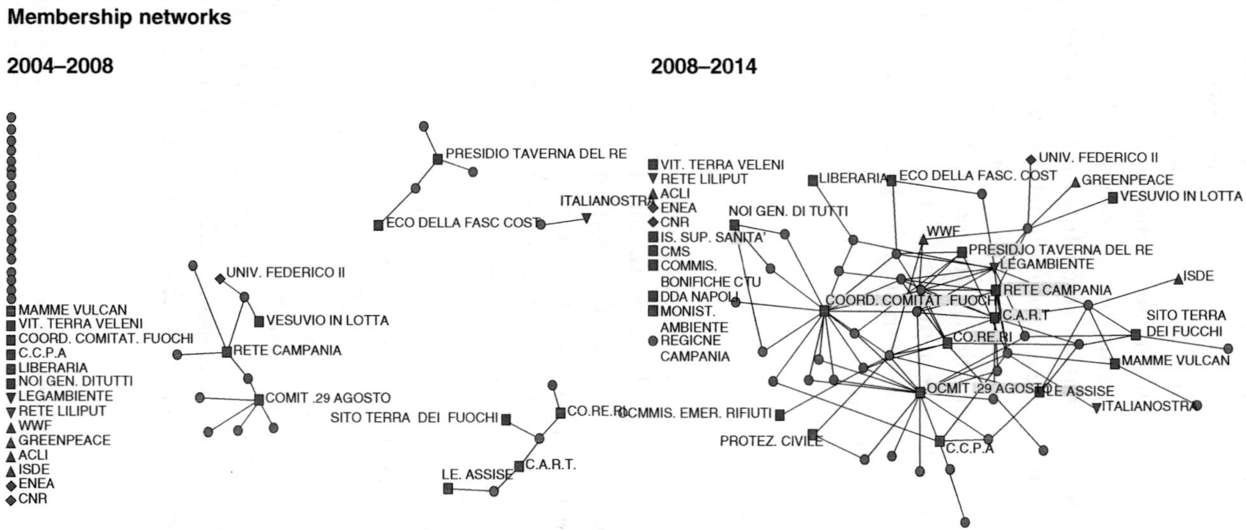

Legend mode networks: Red = Agents; Blue = Events (Circle = Persons; Box = Local associations; Inverted triangle = National organizations; Upright triangle = International organizations; Diamond = Research centers; Square = Healthcare institutions; Circle in box = Public bodies).

Fig. 3.3 The pollution fighters' affiliation networks (multi-relational networks)

towards the correlation between the presence of illegal waste facilities and the increasing rate of diseases such as cancer and asthma.[18] All of these occurrences, on the one hand, increased the level of conflict and, on the other hand, contributed to the emergence of a clearer and more broadly shared feeling of being victims of environmental crimes.

Another interesting feature that emerged from the evolution of the affiliation network over time is the role of national/international institutions. In the depiction of the network, the turning point clearly does not generate any changes to the interactions between local communities and these institutions, thus indicating a mutual distrust. On the contrary, local communities display a growing trust and reliance on local associations and grassroots organizations.

3.6 Conclusions

The picture emerging from the investigation conducted in this chapter builds primarily on the idea that the responsibility for what happened in the LoF lies at various levels and involves multiple actors. Organized mafia-like crime does in fact play a significant role in Campania's waste management sector, and the provincial and local governments' weak power of enforcement has favoured the infiltration of the Camorra into waste trafficking and disposal. However, this illegal business was already thriving well before the Camorra began to participate in it. In order to understand why it happened, a multiplicity of factors must be considered, from inefficient bureaucracy to political patronage, from criminal malfeasance to the corporate nature of the waste-related crimes. Moreover, since Italian waste legislation did not include any criminal charges applicable to environmental dumping until 2001, this void allowed firms to lower their waste disposal and management costs enormously and allowed organized crime to flourish and gain huge profits.

[18] To put it simply, there are activists who associate the increasing rate of mortality and morbidity through cancer and other diseases with the presence of illegal waste sites, and there are government officers who correlate the increasing rate of disease to the poor lifestyle of Campania's citizens.

The collection of primary data by means of semi-structured interviews with opinion leaders of the movement against the waste crisis demonstrates that the increasing level of victims' organizational activities in the LoF, from 2008 until the present, is creating public awareness of the impact of illegally disposing and burning of waste; this research thus sheds light on the capacity of a civil society to influence policy changes and decision-makers at the national level. This trend was corroborated by the SNA performed in this chapter; a dense and well-articulated web of relations emerged in the PFAN. This was particularly true after 2008, a well-identified turning point in our study; after 2008 the number of links connecting (mostly) local institutions and the increasing number of activists started growing very quickly, a fact that resulted in the emergence of a stronger collective feeling of being victims of environmental crimes.

The documented central role of activists, local associations, and victims of environmental crimes has been particularly important in pressuring Italian legislation to issue more stringent laws. It is important to remember that the first legislation on waste-related environmental crime was only introduced years after environmental NGOs had already been reporting on the role of organized crime in environmental business, and that the burning of waste has been deemed an environmental crime only after years of denunciation by activists and massive demonstrations in the city of Naples.

With the enactment of the recent Law n. 68/2015, Italy has finally systematically codified its legislation on environmental crimes in line with the European Union (EU) Environmental Crime Directive (2008/99/EC), which maintains that member states must ensure that environmental crimes are punishable by 'effective, proportional and dissuasive' penalties'. Although the text is not without criticism, Law n. 68/2015 takes a first step towards stricter sanctions against environmental crime by inserting four new types of environmental crimes in the penal code: environmental contamination, environmental disaster, traffic and abandonment of highly radioactive materials, and obstacle to controls. Other important features of the new law are the provisions for aggravating factors for both organized crime groups and mafia-like crime groups and the extension of the prescription period, since the current short statute of limitations is considered a major impediment to convicting many environmental crimes.

However, there is still room in Italy for major changes in terms of preventing future environmental injustices. Notwithstanding the recent normative accomplishments, legislators and institutions still need to make stronger efforts to increase public participation in environmental decision making (e.g. public hearings for environmental impact assessments) and to empower citizens by giving them greater access to pollution data and information. If victims of environmental crimes are to be recognized and protected as such, they will be more likely to combat crime and to contribute to investigations; if they are not, then the criminal justice system will lose important evidence, and their enforcement of the relative laws against criminals will become less effective.

References

Armiero, M. (2008). Seeing like a protester: Nature, power, and environmental struggles. *Left History, 13*(1), 59–76.

Armiero, M., & D'Alisa, G. (2012). Rights of resistance: The garbage struggles for environmental justice in Campania, Italy. *Capitalism Nature Socialism, 23*(4), 52–68.

Barbieri, R., & Piglionica, D. (2007). Commissione parlamentare d'inchiesta sul ciclo dei rifiuti e sulle attività illecite ad esso connesse. *Parliamentary report*, doc. XXIII n. 2, http://www.parlamento.it/documenti/repository/commissioni/bicamerali/ciclo_rifiuti/Documenti/Relazione%20finale%20doc.%20XXIII%20n.%208.pdf.

Cantoni, R. (2016). The waste crisis in Campania, South Italy: A historical perspective on an epidemiological controversy. *Endeavour*, Elsevier, https://hal.archives-ouvertes.fr/hal-01285492.

Capocaccia, R., Comba, P., Conti, S., De Angelis, R., Della Porta, P., Falleni, F., Fazzo, L., Federici, A., Ferrante, G., Francisci, S., La Sala, L., Manno, V., Masocco, M., Minardi, V., Minelli, G., Musmeci, L., Pizzuti, R., Rossi, S., Ruocco, G., Salmaso, S., & Ziemacki G. (2012). *Situazione epidemiologica della regione Campania ed in particolare delle province di Caserta e Napoli (città esclusa), con riferimento all'incidenza della mortalità per malattie oncologiche*, Relazione finale del Gruppo di Lavoro ex D.M. 24. 07. 2012, www.salute.gov.it/imgs/c_17_pubblicazioni_1883_allegato.pdf.

Capone, N. (2014). The assemblies of the city of Naples: A long battle to defend the landscape and environment. *Capitalism Nature Socialism*, *24*(4), 46–54.

Cardwell, P.J., French, D., & Hall, M. (2011). Tackling the environmental crime in the European Union: The case of the missing victim?. *Environmental Liability*, *19*(2), 35–44.

Comella, G. (2007). Emergenza rifiuti e mortalità per tumori in Campania. *Bollettino delle Assise*, *12*, 27–39, http://www.napoliassise.it/bollettino.htm.

Commissione d'Inchiesta (2000). *Commissione Parlamentare d'Inchiesta sul ciclo dei rifiuti e sulle attvità ad esso connesse*, Documento sui traffici illeciti e le ecomafie, www.xitizap.com/scalia.pdf.

D'Alisa, G., & Armiero, M. (2011). La ciudad de los residuos: Justicia ambiental y incertidumbre

D'Alisa, G., & Armiero, M. (2013). What happened to the trash? Political miracles and real statistics in an emergency regime. *Capitalism Nature Socialism*, *24*(4), 29–45.

D'Alisa, G., Armiero, M., & De Rosa, P.S. (2014). Rethink Campania's Toxic-waste scandal. *Nature*, *509*, 427.

D'Alisa, G., Burgalassi, D., Healy, H., & Walter, M. (2010). Conflict in Campania: Waste emergency or crisis of democracy. *Ecological Economics*, *70*, 239–249.

D'Alisa, G., & Di Nola, M.F. (2013). Separate collection target: Why 65% in 2012? Campania case study. In A. D'Amato, M. Mazzanti, A. Montini (Eds.), *Waste management in spatial environments* (pp. 79–95). Abingdon: Routledge.

D'Alisa, G., Di Nola, M.F., Giampietro, M. (2012). A multi-Scale analysis of urban waste metabolism: Density of waste disposed in Campania. *Journal of Cleaner Production*, *35*, 59–70, doi:10.1016/j.jclepro.2012.05.017.

De Biase, M. (2015). Fires of Pianura: The Antidump struggle in the western outskirt of Naples. *Capitalism Nature Socialism*, *26*(1), 39–58.

de Medici, G. (2007). L'emergenza rifiuti in Campania la questione dei siti. *Bollettino delle Assise*, *12*, 6–7, http://www.napoliassise.it/bollettino.htm.

Di Costanzo, G., & Ferraro, S. (2014). The landfill in the countryside: Waste management and government of the population in Campania. *Capitalism Nature Socialism*, *24*(4), 17–28.

Fazzo, L., Belli, S., Mitis, F., Santero, M., Martina, L., Pizzuti, R., Comba, P., & Martuzzi, M. (2008). *Analisi dei clusters di mortalità in un'area con una diffusa presenza di siti di smaltimento dei rifiuti urbani e pericolosi in Campania*, Istituto Superiore di Sanità, www.iss.it/binary/epam/cont/FAZZO_Rifiuti.1159881860.pdf.

Fontana, E., Pergolizzi, A., Ruggiero, P., Dodaro, F., Groccia, C., Ciafani, S., & Del Giudice, R. (2008). *Rifiuti Spa*. Legambiente, http://www.legambiente.it/contenuti/articoli/rifiuti-spa.

Germani, A.R., Pergolizzi, A., & Reganati, F. (2015). Illegal trafficking and unsustainable waste management in Italy: Evidence at the regional level. *Journal of Security and Sustainability Issues*, *4*(4), 369–389, http://dx.doi.org/10.9770/jssi.2015.4(5).

Greyl, L., Vegni, S., Natalicchio, M., Cure, S., & Ferretti, J. (2013). The Waste Crisis in Campania. In H. Healy, J. Martinez-Alier, L. Temper, M. Walter, J.F. Gerber (Eds.), *Ecological economics from the ground Up* (pp. 273–308). London and New York: Routledge.

Iacuelli, A. (2008). *Le vie infinite dei rifiuti: Il sistema campano*. Rome: Edizioni Rinascita.

Ianiello, C. (2007). L'emergenza rifiuti in Campania: I paradossi delle gestioni commissariali. *Rassegna di diritto pubblico europeo*, *6*(2), 137–178.

ISPRA (2012). *Rapporto Rifiuti Speciali: Edizione 2012*. Rome: Istituto Superiore per la Protezione e la Ricerca Ambientale. http://www.isprambiente.gov.it/it/pubblicazioni/rapporti/rapporto-rifiuti-speciali-edizione-2012.

Law 68/2015, http://www.gazzettaufficiale.it/eli/id/2015/05/28/15G00082/sg

Law 6 February 2014, http://www.gazzettaufficiale.it/eli/id/2014/02/08/14G00013/sg.

Law 123/2008, http://www.gazzettaufficiale.it/eli/id/2008/04/30/008G0104/sg.

Law 93/2001, http://www.gazzettaufficiale.it/eli/id/2001/04/26/001G0200/sg.

Law Decree 136/2013, http://www.gazzettaufficiale.it/eli/id/2013/12/10/13G00180/sg.

Law Decree 90/2008, http://www.camera.it/parlam/leggi/decreti/08090d.htm.

Legambiente (2013). *Rapporto Ecomafia 2013*. Milan: Edizioni Ambiente.

Legambiente (2014). *Rapporto Ecomafia 2014*. Milan: Edizioni Ambiente.

Legambiente (2003). *Rifiuti S.p.A.*, http://www.legambiente.it/sites/%26/RifiutiSpa_2003_0000000328.pdf.

Legislative Decree 152/2006, http://www.gazzettaufficiale.it/atto/serie_generale/caricaDettaglioAtto/originario?atto.dataPubblicazioneGazzetta=2006-04-14%26atto.codiceRedazionale=006G0171.

Legislative Decree 22/1997, http://www.gazzettaufficiale.it/eli/id/1997/02/15/097G0043/sg.

Legislative Decree 389/1998, http://www.gazzettaufficiale.it/eli/id/2016/01/18/16G00009/sg.

Lucarelli, A. (2007a). Riflessioni sul piano rifiuti della Campania. *Bollettino delle Assise,* Anno I, Speciale Ottobre-Novembre, No 12-13-14-15, pp. 8–17, http://www.napoliassise.it/bollettino.htm.

Lucarelli, A. (2007b). Governare e gestire la raccolta differenziata. *Bollettino delle Assise* Anno I, Speciale Luglio-Agosto, No 6-7-8-9, pp. 21–30, http://www.napoliassise.it/bollettino.htm.

Lucarelli, A. (2007c). Profili di illeggittimità ed inopportunità del piano regionale dei rifiuti della Campania. *Bollettino delle Assise* Anno I, Speciale Luglio-Agosto, No 6-7-8-9, pp. 5–20, http://www.napoliassise.it/bollettino.htm.

Lynch, M.J., & Stretsky, P.B. (2003). The meaning of green: Contrasting criminological perspective. *Theoretical Criminology, 7*(2), 217–238.

Martuzzi, M., Bianchi, F., Comba, P., Fazzo, L., Minichilli, F., & Mitis, F. (eds.) (2005). *Trattamento dei rifiuti in Campania: Impatto sulla salute umana: Studio pilota,* Report ordered by the Italian Department of Civil Protection, http://www.protezionecivile.gov.it/jcms/it/view_dossier.wp?contentId=DOS14955.

Martuzzi, M., Bianchi, F., Comba, P., Fazzo, L., Minichilli, F., & Mitis, F. (2008). *Trattamento dei rifiuti in Campania: Studio di correlazione tra rischio ambientale da rifiuti, mortalità e malformazioni congenite,* Report ordered by the Italian Department of Civil Protection, http://www.protezionecivile.gov.it/resources/cms/documents/Studio_di_correlazione.pdf.

Morone, P., Tartiu, V.E., & Falcone, P.M. (2014). Assessing the potential of biowaste for bioplastics production through social network analysis. *Journal of Cleaner Production, 90,* 43–54, doi:10.1016/j.jclepro.2014.11.069.

Musella, A. (2008). *Mi rifiuto! Le lotte in difesa della salute e dell'ambiente in Campania.* Dogliani, Italy: Sensibili alle foglie.

Naughton, P. (2008). Army Bulldozers move in on Naples Rubbish Mountain. *The Times* online, 7 January, http://www.thetimes.co.uk/tto/news/world/europe/article2596483.ece, date accessed 28 April 2016.

Ortolani, F. (2008). Emergenza rifiuti in Campania: Due discariche a rischio frana, la terza inquina: Ferrandelle non era idonea' http://www.napoliassise.it/due_discariche_a_rischio_frana_la_terza_inquina.pdf; date accessed 05 Month 2016.

Pasotti, E. (2010). Sorting through the trash: The waste management crisis in Campania and Sicily. *South European Society and Politics, 15*(2), 289–307.

Perrella, N. (2016). Traffico di rifiuti, il pentito: "Abbiamo scaricato anche a Malagrotta a Roma," interview by N. Trocchia, *Il Fatto Quotidiano,*

7 February, http://www.ilfattoquotidiano.it/2016/02/07/traffico-di-rifiuti-il-pentito-abbiamo-scaricato-anche-a-malagrotta-a-roma/2376862/, date accessed 28 April 2016.
Rabitti, P. (2008). *Ecoballe: Tutte le verità su discariche, inceneritori, smaltimento abusivo dei rifiuti*. Rome: Aliberti.
Raimondi, R. (2007). Rapporto sul disastro ambientale dei rifiuti in Campania: Il diritto al risarcimento dei danni. *Bollettino delle Assise*, *12*, 29–33, http://www.napoliassise.it/bollettino.htm.
Rogers, E.M. (1962). *Diffusion of innovations*. Glencoe, IL: Free Press.
Rosenthal, E. (2008). A Whiff of Naples arrives in Hamburg. *New York Times*, 9 June, http://www.nytimes.com/2008/06/09/world/europe/09trash.html?_r=0, date accessed 28 April 2016.
Senior, K., & Mazza, A. (2004). Italian "Triangle of Death" linked to waste crisis. *The Lancet Oncology*, *5*, 525–527.
Simmel, G. (1950). *The sociology of George Simmel* (ed. and transl. K. Wolff). Glencoe, IL: Free Press.
Simmel, G. (1955). *Conflict and the web of group affiliations*. New York: Free Press.
Vagliasindi, G.M., Lucifora, A., Bianco, F. (2015). *Fighting environmental crime in Italy: A country report*, Study in the framework of the EFFACE research project, Catania: University of Catania, http://efface.eu/sites/default/files/EFFACE_Fighting%20Environmental%20Crime%20in%20Italy.pdf.
Wasserman, S., & Faust, K. (1994). *Social network analysis: Methods and applications*. Cambridge: Cambridge University Press.

Anna Rita Germani (PhD, MSc) is Aggregate Professor in Economics in the Department of Law, Philosophy and Economic Studies (Faculty of Law) at the University of Rome 'La Sapienza' where she teaches International Economics and Economics of Public Procurement. Her main research interests focus on environmental law and economics issues, such as public enforcement of environmental laws and judicial and prosecutorial discretion in prosecuting environmental crimes. She has published referred empirical articles on environmental justice and illegal trafficking of waste and, most recently, she is working on environmental crime and victims issues.

Giacomo D'Alisa is a Juan de la Sierva Research Fellow at Institute of Environmental Science and Technology at Autonomous University of Barcelona, Spain. He is an ecological economist and political ecologist. His main line of research deals with waste metabolism and related environmental conflict, political ecology of environmental disaster, commons.

Pasquale Marcello Falcone is a research fellow at Department of Economics and Social Sciences of Polytechnic University of Marche (Italy). He obtained a PhD in Economics at University of Foggia (Italy) and an MSc in Economics at University of Leicester (UK). His research interests span from Environmental Economics and Sustainable Development to sustainability transition theory. Recently he is exploring the role of financial institutions in the transition towards a bio-based economy.

Piergiuseppe Morone is an economist with an interest in evolutionary theory applied especially to sustainable innovation studies. As a postgraduate student he was trained at SPRU-Sussex University where he received in 2003 his PhD in Science and Technology Policy with a thesis on innovation economics, investigating the relation between social network architectures and speed of diffusion of knowledge and innovations. He is now a Professor of Economic Policy at Unitelma Sapienza—University of Rome—with a strong interest in green innovation and sustainability transitions pushing his research at the interface between innovation, food, and agricultural economics and green chemistry, an area of enquiry that has attracted growing attention among social scientists over the last decade. His work regularly appears in prestigious and highly impacted innovation and environmental economics journals. He is vice-chair and Management Committee member of the Cost Action TD1203 on Food waste valorization and he is also an Editor of Open Agriculture, open access journal by De Gruyter Open.

4

Tackling Illegal Fisheries: The Role of Rights–Based Management

Stephanie Newman and Andrew Farmer

4.1 Introduction

Illegal, unreported, and unregulated (IUU) fishing refers to fishing activities that do not comply with national, regional, or international fisheries conservation or management legislation or measures (Agnew and Barnes 2004). IUU fishing activities may have serious detrimental impacts on marine ecosystems, ecosystem services, and the societies that derive benefit from such services. This chapter focuses on the causes, motives, and incentives for committing illegal fishing. In particular, it considers the role of rights-based fisheries management systems as a tool to reduce the incentives of illegal behaviour.

S. Newman (✉) · A. Farmer
Institute for European Environmental Policy,
London, UK
e-mail: afarmer@ieep.eu

R. Sollund et al. (eds.), *Fighting Environmental Crime in Europe and Beyond*, Palgrave Studies in Green Criminology,
DOI 10.1057/978-1-349-95085-0_4

4.2 The Definition of the Environmental Crime

Illegal fishing activities are defined by the international community and the European Union (EU)[1] as activities conducted by fishing vessels in violation of national laws or international obligations, or activities conducted in maritime waters without the permission of that state. In addition to the activities of fishing operators, illegal fishing is often associated with upstream and downstream criminal activities such as money laundering, corruption, document fraud, or handling of stolen goods, although these are not explicitly included in the official definitions (UNODC 2011).

Unreported fishing refers to activities that have not been reported, or have been misreported, to the relevant national authority or regional fisheries management organization, in contravention of their reporting procedures. *Unregulated fishing* refers to activities conducted in areas or for fish stocks in relation to which there are no applicable conservation or management measures, in a manner that is not consistent with state responsibilities for the conservation of marine living resources under international law. IUU fishing is often described as an environmental crime, although technically unregulated fishing does not actually involve the breaking of any obligations in law, so technically only illegal and unreported fishing are illegal and may be encompassed by the term 'environmental crime'. However, the three types of fishing activity are often discussed together, and it is not always easy to distinguish between them in the literature (e.g. data on IUU fishing are often reported together).

It is important to establish what activities precisely are considered to be non-compliant since, by definition, anything that is an infringement of the law is illegal. Illegal fishing therefore covers a wide range of actions. According to the IUU Regulation (EC) No 1005/2008 (see below for overview of regulation of fisheries in EU waters), EU vessels

[1] See Articles 2, 3, and 4 of Council Regulation (EC) No 1005/2008 establishing a Community system to prevent, deter, and eliminate IUU fishing (European Counci 2008).

shall be presumed to be engaging in IUU fishing if they have, contrary to the conservation and management measures applicable in the fishing area concerned, been shown to be (European Council 2008):

a) Fishing without a valid licence, authorization, or permit issued by the flag State or the relevant coastal State.
b) Not fulfilling obligations to record and report catch or catch-related data, including data to be transmitted by satellite vessel monitoring system.
c) Fishing in a closed area, during a closed season, without or after attainment of a quota or beyond a closed depth.
d) Engaging in directed fishing for a stock that is subject to a moratorium or for which fishing is prohibited.
e) Using prohibited or non-compliant fishing gear.
f) Falsifying or concealing its markings, identity, or registration.
g) Concealing, tampering with or disposing of evidence relating to an investigation.
h) Obstructing the work of officials in the exercise of their duties in inspecting for compliance with the applicable conservation and management measures, or the work of observers in the exercise of their duties of observing compliance with the applicable Community rules.
i) Taking on board, transhipping, or landing undersized fish in contravention of the legislation in force.
j) Transhipping or participating in joint fishing operations with support or re-supply from fishing vessels identified as having engaged in IUU fishing, in particular those included in the Community IUU vessel list or in the IUU vessel list of a regional fisheries management organization.
k) Carrying out fishing activities in the area of a regional fisheries management organization in a manner inconsistent with or in contravention of the conservation and management measures of that organization.
l) Use of a fishing vessel with no nationality (a stateless vessel in accordance with international law).

The fishing industry has also been identified as vulnerable to international organized crime and associated with serious illegal activities including trafficking in persons, drugs and arms, smuggling of migrants, and terrorism (UNODC 2011). There have also been reports of poor or forced labour on board fishing vessels (UNODC 2011). The UNODC (2011) found several reported instances where there were links between human and drug trafficking and marine living resource crime (particularly in relation to high value, low volume species such as abalone, sturgeon, or toothfish).

IUU fishing is a global problem, but the effects vary region by region. Unregulated fishing occurs largely on the high seas (Pew Charitable Trusts 2013). Agnew *et al.* (2009a) conducted one of the most extensive studies into the size of illegal and unreported fishing, analysing 54 Exclusive Economic Zones (EEZs), which can extend up to 200 NM from the coast, and 15 regions of the high seas, and covering 46 per cent of the globally reported marine fish caught. The Eastern Central Atlantic exhibited the highest level of illegal and unreported catches (37 per cent of catches between 2000 and 2003; Agnew *et al.* 2009a). Trends show that in the northeast Atlantic IUU, fishing increased in the early 1990s (up from 10 per cent in the 1980s to 12 per cent), attributed to an increase in fishing pressure resulting from the end of a period of exceptionally high cod recruitment. The situation started to improve slightly in the early 2000s (dropping to 9 per cent; Agnew *et al.* 2009a).

4.3 Impacts of Environmental Crime: The Impacts of IUU Fishing

IUU fishing activities can have serious detrimental impacts on marine ecosystems, ecosystem services, and the societies that derive benefit from such services. IUU fishing exerts additional pressures on fish stocks, which may already be under pressure from unsustainable rates of legal fishing activities and can thereby contribute to the depletion of those stocks. In addition to these direct impacts on target fish species, fishing (including IUU fishing activities) can negatively affect non-target commercial species and nonmarketable fish, as well as protected and vulnerable species and habitats (Dayton *et al.* 1995; Gascoigne and Willstead 2009; Grieve *et al.* 2014; Pauly *et al.* 1998; Suuronen *et al.* 2013).

Fishing may also indirectly affect ecosystems via pollution from the discharge of organic waste while processing catches, non-biodegradable litter such as lost nets that can continue to ghost fish, emissions of carbon dioxide and other greenhouse gases, and the alteration of trophic structure and function through targeting low trophic level fish and discarding (Heath *et al.* 2014; Reeves and Furness 2002; Suuronen *et al.* 2013). Furthermore, IUU fishing obstructs fisheries managers from effectively regulating fish stocks in a sustainable manner because the uncertainty associated with estimates of IUU catches impede stock assessments (Watson and Pauly 2001).

In addition to its detrimental environmental impacts, IUU fishing has significant social and economic effects. By exploiting and depleting fish stocks, it reduces the resources available to legitimate fishing enterprises. This can lead to reduced profits and, potentially, unemployment. Often IUU fishing affects small-scale fishing communities in developing countries, with implications for development and food security (UNODC 2011). In economic terms, the value of fish lost to illegal and unreported fishing is estimated to be between USD 10–23.5 billion annually (roughly €8.9–20.9 billion) (Agnew *et al.* 2009a).

While this section has highlighted the importance of IUU fishing in its effects on the environment, it is important to stress that not all fisheries impacts are from IUU activities. Legal fisheries can have negative impacts. For example, Esteban and Carpenter (2015) have developed a database of the specific scientific advice provided to EU fisheries ministers for different stocks and the actual quotas or (total allowable catches (TACs)) and the actual numbers agreed by those ministers. From 2001 to 2015, the agreed TACs exceeded scientific advice by 20 per cent, although this dropped over time. However, 70 per cent of TACs continued to be set above the scientific advice. Member states with the largest gross tonnage above scientific advice were Denmark, the UK, and Spain. Da Rocha *et al.* (2012) analysed the recovery plans for southern hake and Atlantic cod as well as the enforcement of TACs. They concluded that drastic actions would be needed to ensure compliance and deliver stock recovery, with consequences for the incomes of fishers and social effects on coastal communities. Therefore, there is a major challenge to bring legal activities in line with sustainable stock management, let alone deal with IUU fishing.

4.4 Regulation of Fisheries in EU Waters

In EU waters in the North East Atlantic, fisheries are regulated (as in other EU waters) by the EU Common Fisheries Policy (CFP). The CFP aims to promote sustainable fishing by imposing technical measures (such as gear specifications and area/time closures) and by limiting fishing opportunities available to member states (in the form of total allowable catches divided among member states in the form of quotas or in the form of effort limits expressed as days-at-sea). Although these measures are defined at the EU level, member states are responsible for carrying out their quotas and inspecting or sanctioning in the case of infringements.

With respect to the concept of environmental crime, it is important to note that non-compliance with the EU Regulations implementing the CFP is not included within the specific scope of the Environmental Crime Directive 2008/99/EC.

Recognizing that the success of the CFP requires implementing an effective system of control, the EU established a Community system for ensuring compliance with the rules of the CFP (Council Regulation (EC) No 1224/2009), known hereafter as the Control Regulation (European Counci 2009). The Control Regulation governs the collection of data for managing fishing opportunities and aims to ensure that only the allowed quantities of fish may be caught. It applies to all activities covered by the CFP carried out by EU fishing vessels or nationals in member states or Community waters. The Regulation also aims to ensure that the rules are applied across the EU in the same way, with harmonized sanctions. In addition, the Control Regulation brought the control, inspection, and enforcement system in line with Council Regulation (EC) No 1005/2008 establishing a Community system to prevent, deter, and eliminate IUU fishing, commonly referred to as the IUU (Fishing) Regulation (European Counci 2008). The IUU Regulation aims to make sure that no illegally caught fisheries products end up on the EU market. Achieving this requires flag states to certify the origin and legality of the fish, thereby ensuring the full traceability of fishery products traded to and from the EU. It also creates a black list of IUU vessels and countries that have not regulated IUU fishing sufficiently. A final regulation of importance is Council Regulation (EC) No 768/2005 which established the European Fisheries and Control Agency (EFCA) in 2005 (European Counci 2005) to assist the European Commission in facilitating and enhancing cooperation between member states with respect to their control and inspection activities, in order to try and create a level playing field for the fishing industry. The EFCA uses Joint Deployment Plans (JDPs) as its tool to ensure effective enforcement, by organizing the deployment of national, human, and material means of control and inspection pooled by member states.

It is not possible to quantify legal infringements with any degree of accuracy: they are known to take place in different forms, and some violations are detected while others go unnoticed. Several sources of literature provide data on the number of CFP serious infringements reported by member states to the Commission (see European Commission 2003, 2005, 2006, 2007a, 2008; Agnew *et al.* 2009b). Other more recent sources of data on infringements are the EFCA annual reports, which provide comprehensive data for the JDPs, based on the number of inspections undertaken and the detected infringements (ECFA 2013). Although member states are able to carry out inspections on their own, the joint efforts through JDPs make up a significant proportion of all inspections (Beke *et al.* 2014). Consequently, the coverage of these data is reasonable but varies by region: the NAFO and NEAFC JDP accounts for 100 per cent of inspections, whereas the JDPs in the Baltic and the North Sea account for around 30 per cent of member state inspections (Beke *et al.* 2014).

However, it should be recognized that there are issues with data on the number of inspections and detected infringements. First, these relate to outputs, and they do not actually demonstrate trends in compliance. The number of serious infringements is reported as a percentage of the number of active vessels; however, as a metric for measuring trends in compliance, this is a flawed measure—making real sense of data on infringements can only be achieved in light of information on the fishing effort, the area fished, the time period, and the amount of control/inspection effort. Nevertheless, these data can provide some insight into overall trends, and they do highlight that infringements with the rules of the CFP continue to be a concern.

4.5 Factors Affecting Compliance

Non-compliance with fisheries regulations is a complex issue, with numerous intertwined processes and influences. However, for many years, little research was undertaken to establish the underlying causes for non-compliant behaviour amongst fishers (Nielsen & Mathiesen 2003). Traditionally, a purely economic approach was applied, accounting, in its simplest form, for monetized costs and benefits of non-compliant behaviour only (Becker 1968, in Eggert and Ellegård 2003). According to this approach, fishers will weigh the expected net benefits of non-compliance, including the expected penalty in the case of being caught and convicted, with the expected net benefits from compliance, and choose their behaviour based on the most beneficial outcome (Eggert and Ellegård 2003).

The OECD (2005) reports that the choice and design of management regimes is a key driver of IUU fishing. This appears to be a governance-related rather than an economic driver. However, the rationale behind the argument is economic in nature: management regimes drive IUU fishing the way in which they determine the income that fishers will be able to make, and the higher the legitimate income the less likely they will engage in illegal activities. This is linked to the importance of introducing capacity management. The OECD does not, however, explain which management regimes are more conducive to legitimate behaviour, although the economic argument they use suggests the management regime that produces the highest level of income would be the best.

An alternative approach is to take into consideration other social factors, described by Eggert and Ellegård (2003) as 'co-management' or 'cooperative action theory'. This approach emphasizes the role of legitimacy of regulations, institutions, etc., in making fishers comply with the rules. According to this theory, fishers will be more likely to comply if they perceive the regulations or decision-making process that has produced the regulations as legitimate. Another aspect of this approach is the perceived behaviour of others. According to this theory, despite potential benefits of non-compliance, fishers are more likely to comply with regulations if they perceive others to be complying or if they can expect informal sanctions from their peers in cases of violation.

Several studies have attempted to investigate the importance in practice of these different factors (Eggert and Ellegård 2003; Hatcher and Gordon 2005). Hatcher and Gordon (2005) conducted an empirical investigation into the factors affecting UK fisheries compliance, specifically with regard to quota limits, to compare the significance of various social and moral factors versus more 'conventional' economic incentives. In their model, they included such factors as financial incentives to violate, deterrents to violation, variables related to personal moral judgements about violation, variables related to the perceived behaviour and opinions of others, and variables representing the legitimacy of the regulatory system, including the regulations themselves as well as the institutions and processes. An earlier model that relied upon the same data determined that compliance with quotas was positively associated with a personal perception of fair shares, the perception of compliance by other local fishers, and a sense of personal involvement in the quota management system (Hatcher *et al.* 2000). However, the alternative model employed in Hatcher and Gordon (2005), which the authors argue is richer and more robust, found that levels of quota violations in the fishery appeared to be driven by financial incentives. Indeed, they observed that variables related to involvement or participation all had near-zero coefficients, although there was some support for the importance of local structures given that the index of support for producer organization rules was association with lower violation levels (Hatcher and Gordon 2005).

Eggert and Ellegård (2003) conducted a similar investigation in Sweden. They surveyed fishers from the Swedish industrial and small-scale fleets to gauge fishers' attitudes towards the fishery management regulations, including the means and measures to control it, their perception of the risk of control, and their perceptions of the overall compliance with fisheries regulations. They observed that Swedish fishers were far more compliant than would be expected given purely economic considerations. Views concerning the existing regulatory framework were unfavourable: 24 per cent considered the existing management to work badly, about a third considered controls to be completely ineffective, while a majority perceived themselves to have too small an influence on the development of the management policy (Eggert and Ellegård 2003). Fishers estimated that 90 per cent of the catch in their fishery was reported, and although this implied 30,000 tons of unreported landings, a considerably higher degree of violation would be expected in a situation with low legitimacy of regulations, low risk of controls, and mild penalties if the equation were based on economic incentives alone (Eggert and Ellegård 2003). Nevertheless, this points to a compliance problem in the Swedish fishery, and of course, this estimate of unreported catches (only one aspect of non-compliance) may not be particularly robust and could be an underestimate. Interviewees (including industrial fishers) indicated that industrial fisheries (fisheries for herring and sprat destined for fishmeal) were the primary culprits violating regulations. Bearing this in mind, the authors suggest that the culture of profit maximization within these large-scale fisheries—leading to higher investments, greater capacity, and more advanced technology—has translated to economic considerations being more influential in encouraging compliance than moral obligations and peer pressure (Eggert and Ellegård 2003). By contrast, small-scale gillnet fishers are more likely to respond to the latter, noneconomic incentives. The authors postulate that this may be because they mainly come from small harbours in the south and west of Sweden, fish more traditionally, and are therefore more susceptible to peer pressure and have a greater sense of moral obligation (Eggert and Ellegård 2003).

4.6 Rights-Based Management as an Approach to Reduce Illegal Activity

This chapter focuses on the causes, motives, and incentives for committing illegal fishing. In particular, it considers the role of rights-based fisheries management systems in incentivizing or dis-incentivizing illegal behaviour. Rights-based systems of fisheries management exist in most EU member states in some form, and the European Commission sought to introduce an EU system of transferable fishing concessions (defined as a revocable user entitlement to a specific part of fishing opportunities allocated to a member state, which the holder may transfer) in its proposal for the reform of the CFP (COM[2011]417; Europa, 2011). Although this proposal was not approved by the Council and European Parliament, member states are free to implement their own rights-based management systems. As the debate over the usefulness or benefits of such systems continues, it is important to consider the role they play in influencing fishers' behaviour with respect to compliance. Thus, this section reviews the evidence available to try to determine to what extent this management tool plays a role in compliance behaviour.

Rights-based management programmes convey and manage exclusive entitlements to an entity (person, company, vessel, community) to fish in a particular place at a particular time. The European Commission defines rights-based management as 'a formalised system of allocating individual fishing rights to fishermen, fishing vessels, enterprises, cooperatives and fishing communities' (Europa 2007b). There are several types of rights-based management schemes. For example, fishing rights—also known as catch shares (Bonzon *et al.* 2013)—can be based on quota, fishing effort, or access to fishing territory. They can be held by individuals, groups, communities, or regions. They can be fully transferable, non-transferable, or somewhere in between (with regulation of the market or safeguards to limit transfers in certain situations; Bonzon *et al.* 2013). Most well-documented rights-based management schemes are quota based, and the majority are transferable, meaning that participants can buy, sell, and/or lease shares (Bonzon *et al.* 2013). Transferability increases flexibility, enabling a fishery to adjust to annual fluctuations in the catch limit.

By providing exclusive access, rights-based management systems aim to address the 'tragedy of the commons', articulated by Hardin (1968). Managing resources under a common pool or open access (i.e. the opposite of a rights-based approach) typically results in a drive to short-term overexploitation. By contrast, allocating access rights within a fishery provides a means of internalizing externalities arising from the common property nature of fish stocks.

The EU is responsible for limiting total fleet size and for fixing catch and effort levels of EU member states. It also decides technical measures such as restrictions on gear types and characteristics in order to provide additional protection to fish stocks. The EU distributes the total allowable catches and effort units (days-at-sea) among member states according to the principle of 'relative stability'.[2] National authorities then distribute and manage fishing licences, quotas, and effort allocations at the national or regional level. Thus the decision over whether to employ a rights-based management approach is at member states discretion (European Commission 2007b).

Limiting access to a fishery automatically creates a market for fishing rights, reflected, for example, in higher prices for vessels that come with a license as opposed to those that do not. By introducing transferability formally into the rights allocation system, it is possible to ensure greater transparency, legal certainty, and security. It also enables the authorities to establish formal safeguards and regulation of the market (Europa 2007b). This was one reason that the European Commission proposed rights-based management as a management option within the CFP (see Europa 2007b). However, transferability is also one of the most controversial aspects of rights-based management systems. There are now numerous examples of rights-based management scheme implementation in various specific fisheries and localities, in Europe and beyond.

[2] 'Relative stability' is the principle according to which the EU allocates total allowable catches into national quotas. Under this system, total allowable catches for each fish stock are shared between the member states of the EU according to a fixed allocation key based on their historical catches.

These experiences provide numerous lessons on good practices and the limitations and risks of these tools.

The literature is clear that there are several important advantages to rights-based management systems. Research and experience have shown that rights-based management systems can:

- Alter the economic incentives of fishers who no longer compete for their catches, so that highly competitive fishing no longer takes place (Beddington *et al.* 2007).
- Stabilize fishery landings and catch limits (Essington 2010; Essington *et al.* 2012).
- Enable the industry to settle on a fleet capacity that optimizes individual economic yield to vessels or cooperatives (the more efficient fishers will buy out their less efficient counterparts, and in so doing increase the returns to the fishery overall) (Beddington *et al.* 2007; Coelho *et al.* 2011).
- Allow flexible and extended fishing seasons (Coelho *et al.* 2011).
- Increase the profits and value of fisheries (Grafton *et al.* 2006; Grimm *et al.* 2012; Newell *et al.* 2005).
- Enhance the quality of landings and improve markets (by avoiding landings gluts; Coelho *et al.* 2011).
- Improve the safety of operations (resulting from extended seasons and ending the race-to-fish; Coelho *et al.* 2011; Grimm *et al.* 2012).
- Reduce the likelihood of overfishing (Costello *et al.* 2008; Melnychuk *et al.* 2012) and prevent, and even reverse, the collapse of fish stocks (Costello *et al.* 2008).
- Alter fishers' relationships with management actions that protect and enhance fish populations, because the value of a quota share increases as stocks become more abundant (Beddington *et al.* 2007).
- Promote successful community-based co-management of fisheries (Gutiérrez *et al.* 2011).

Despite the numerous advantages of rights-based management approaches, they are not without potential problems. Given that transferable rights have the effect of reducing fleet capacity to optimize economic yield, this can lead to concentration of property rights

(Coelho *et al.* 2011; Sumaila 2010). In economic terms, this is not considered a problem because the proponents of transferable catch shares expect such concentration to take place (this is how they achieve economic efficiency). This can also mean that the job structure increasingly shifts from part-time to full-time jobs (Sumaila 2010). As the number of quota owners declines over time, this can influence employment levels, engendering income disparities and barriers to new entrants into the sector. Sumaila and Watson (2002) report concerns of monopolization within fisheries and larger fisheries operators becoming larger mainly because they have more effective lobbying machinery, rather than because they are more economically efficient than small-scale operators.

As discussed before, compliance is a complex issue—there are numerous potential factors that play a role in motivating illegal behaviour. Rights-based management systems employ incentives to change the behaviour of fishers and their patterns of exploitation. Therefore, it is likely that they would also influence fishers' decisions over whether or not to comply with regulations. There are different ways in which rights-based management may encourage or discourage compliance.

Given that rights-based systems improve the profitability of fisheries, this should automatically discourage illegal activity. OECD (2005) reports that overcapacity is a very powerful driver of illegal fishing, as well as the economic and social conditions of fishers. Rights-based management has been demonstrated to reduce the capacity of fishing fleets and increase the economic situation for those remaining in the fishery. In addition, rights-based management systems convey exclusive rights to the person, community or vessel in question. This exclusive right, if it is conveyed for a sufficiently long period, provides the quota or rights holder with a sense of ownership over the resource. Coelho *et al.* (2013) argue that the advantage of these private-property-based forms of management is that they are self-enforcing: 'as fishers are given almost private property rights to the resource based, some sort of auto-regulation is guaranteed' (p. 467). The sense of ownership should give the property rights users the perception that the results of their actions will affect the net economic benefits that result from resource extraction (Coelho *et al.* 2011). This self-regulation argument is based on the economic approach to compliance of Becker (1968) described above and is often extended beyond simply obeying the rules to lobbying for lower TACs or at least, not lobbying for higher TACs in contravention of scientific advice. In theory, this so-called ownership engages fishers in compliance with the regulations and diminishes enforcement costs (Coelho *et al.* 2013). Furthermore, inadequate enforcement may reduce the value of the property right (by increasing the supply of fish and potentially reducing the stock biomass in the longer term, thereby making shares of the catch worth less in the future). This has been seen to prompt stakeholders to take collective action and fund their own monitoring programmes with a tax on landings and quota (Branch 2009). In the British Columbia groundfish fishery, for example, fishers actually pay for all the on board observer and dockside coverage, to avoid any misreporting of catches (Turris 2000). This example supports the argument that fishers might be more willing to pay for enforcement, to report violators, and to reach collective agreements on acceptable behaviour in order to protect the value of their quota (Branch 2009). Other arguments in support of rights-based management as a tool for greater compliance are:

- Under the flexible rights-based systems where rights can be traded, there is less need for fishers to take illegal actions if they can lease or buy quotas.
- The ownership of rights can be revoked as a sanction and, therefore, can be part of a control system (Branch 2009).

In practice, many rights-based management systems continue to have problems with illegal behaviour (Coelho *et al.* 2013). Illegal activities commonly reported to be present in the absence of effective control and enforcement are data fouling (i.e. high-grading and under-reporting of catches) and quota busting (Coelho 2011). This suggests that the net gain expected from ownership may not be greater than the net gain from committing an offence. This may partly be because not all fishers will have what they consider sufficient entitlement to fishing rights. To differing degrees, in many fisheries, the actual fishers can be leasing quota from quota holders ('armchair fishers' or 'slipper skippers') and may be less likely to obey regulations for the same reason that rented apartments are often poorly maintained compared to those inhabited by the owners (Branch 2009). In this case, it is possible that the long-term economic interests of the quota holder, or the long-term interests of the fish stocks, do not outweigh the short-term economic gains from exceeding the quota. Who holds the quota and who leases it will depend largely on the initial allocation of rights and the degree to which they have been transferred since then, if transferability is permitted under the system. This point links closely to the driver of illegal fishing referred to by Eggert and Ellegård (2003) as the legitimacy of the management structures. While the economic impacts of tradable rights are positive, concerns are raised about their social impacts in terms of fairness and equity (Davis 1996). By concentrating the quota in the hands of fewer people, they can potentially become quota landlords controlling the market. If this is perceived as unfair, it would help people to legitimize illegal activity (along the lines of stealing a loaf of bread to feed a starving family). Thus, apart from the equity concerns, there may also be an enforcement rational to regulating the markets for quota to avoid over-concentration.

Nevertheless, there is evidence that fisheries that use rights-based systems maintain their quotas better. Aps *et al.* (2010) argue that Individual Transferable Quotas would 'create and enforce the missing negative feedback loop that will be constantly pushing the fishery system towards higher economic efficiency and ecological sustainability' (p. 1). This would provide both a smart approach to fisheries management and also be consistent with development of marine spatial planning. Melnychuck *et al.* (2012) conducted a global meta-analysis of 345 stocks to assess whether fisheries under catch shares were more likely to track management targets set for sustainable harvest than fisheries managed only by fleet-wide quota caps or effort controls. They observed that over-exploitation occurred in only 9 per cent of stocks under catch shares compared to 13 per cent of stocks under fleet-wide quota caps, and 41 per cent of stocks under effort controls. They conclude that the reduced variability of catch-share fisheries around their respective target catch rates was likely due to the incentive that placed the responsibility for not exceeding quota on the individual. Similarly, Grimm *et al.* (2012) studied 15 major catch-share fisheries of the United States and British Columbia for compliance with total allowable catches, among other things. They observed that of the 86 TACs set in the studied catch-share fisheries since implementation, only 5 (6 per cent) were exceeded, and by an average of only 7 per cent.

4.7 Conclusions

It is important to note again that environmental crime does not encompass all activities that fall under IUU fishing. Environmental crime, as a concept, usually involves some form of non-compliance with a legal obligation (whether this is administrative or criminal is another issue of debate). IUU fishing includes two types of non-compliant activity, that which is *illegal* and that which is *unreported*. The latter does not mean that the fishing activity itself is illegal, but non-compliance is due to a reporting failure. In most cases, it is assumed that fishers failing to report do so for a reason and that is likely to be due to some form of non-compliance with the fishing activity itself. However, the third aspect of IUU fishing is *unregulated*, which is not a matter of illegality and, therefore, is not included in most concepts of environmental crime. Thus, overall assessments of the extent of IUU fishing cannot be strictly equated with environmental crime. Having said this, the discussion in this chapter of the role of rights-based management focused on a tool that is used within an overall regulatory framework and, therefore, its effectiveness is likely to concern illegal and unreported fishing, rather than unregulated fishing.

Several sources show that there is an issue with the number of CFP serious infringements reported by member states to the Commission. The challenges in addressing such infringements are:

- To ensure fishers know their obligations;
- To be able to track and identify non-compliance;
- To have the enforcement mechanisms in place to tackle non-compliance and act as an incentive for compliance;
- To adopt systems that encourage compliant behaviour.

Rights-based management is a potential mechanism to deliver better fisheries management. The adoption of rights-based management can lead to better compliance with the requirements of fisheries (such as TACs) due to the interest that rights holders have, their ability to lease extra quotas, and other factors. It has, for example, been shown that catch shares increase compliance in meeting catch limits (Branch 2009; Grimm *et al.* 2012; Melnychuck *et al.* 2012). However, there are few reports on whether individual transferable quota fishers better respect fisheries' regulations like area closures, seasonal closures, and minimum landing sizes (Branch 2009). In addition, the benefits of rights-based management depend entirely on the rights being adequately determined. If fishers consider their entitlements insufficient or unfairly distributed, then non-compliant behaviour may occur.

Rights-based management should, therefore, be considered in designing fisheries management. In implementing such a system, it is important to design the catch-share systems properly to ensure the incentives work for compliance as well, that is, to address or limit social equity concerns (see Grimm *et al.* 2012). It is also an important lesson for other situations where there is extraction of natural resources and problems with illegal activity and environmental crime. Equitable distribution of rights in relation to those resources might be an appropriate mechanism for better management of those resources and a possible mechanism to reduce environmental crime.

Finally, even with the design of fisheries allocations that are less likely to result in non-compliant behaviour, effective enforcement and control of fishing activities are still essential to the ultimate success of any management system in place (Europa 2007b). Without adequate enforcement, TACs may be exceeded under any management system. This is important for all areas of environmental crime, where tools may be introduced to lessen the pressure to conduct criminal activity, but which still require the dissuasive pressure of an enforcement system to remain in place.

References

Agnew, D.J., & Barnes, C. T. (2004). The economic and social effects of IUU/FOC fishing: Building a framework. In Gray, K., Legg, F. & Andrews-

Chouicha, E. (Eds.), *OECD Fish Piracy: Combatting Illegal, Unreported and Unregulated Fishing.* Paris: Organisation for Economic Co-operation and Development.

Agnew, D.J., Pearce, J., Pramod, G., Peatman, T., Watson, R., Beddinton, J.R., et al. (2009a). Estimating the worldwide extent of illegal fishing. *PLoS One*, *4*(2), e4570.

Agnew, D.J., White, C., Savage, S. (2009b). *A vision for European fisheries: 2012 reform of the EU common fisheries policy.* Brussels: World Wildlife Fund. A report for WWF by MRAG Ltd.

Aps, R., Fetissov, M., Lassen, H. (2010). Smart management of the Baltic sea fishery system: Myth or reality?. In J. Carroll, A. Andrusaitis *et al.* (Eds.), *Proceedings of 2010 IEEE/OES US/EU Baltic international symposium*, Riga, Latvia (pp. 25–27) August 2010. New York: IEEE Press.

Becker, G. (1968). Crime and punishment: An economic approach. *Journal of Political Economy, 76*, 169–217.

Beddington, J.R., Agnew, D.J., Clark, C.W. (2007). Current problems in the management of marine fisheries. *Science, 316*, 1713–1716.

Beke, M., Roderick Ackermann, R., Blomeyer, R. (2014). The CFP: Infringement procedures and imposed sanctions throughout the EU' IP/B/PECH/IC 201, 3–135. Study requested by the European Parliament's Committee on Fisheries.

Bonzon, K., McIlwain, K., Strauss, C.K., Van Leuvan, T. (2013). *Catch share design manual, volume 1: A guide for managers and fishermen*, 2nd edn. n.p.: Environmental Defense Fund.

Branch, T.A. (2009). How do individual transferable quotas affect marine ecosystems?. *Fish and Fisheries, 10*, 39–57.

Coelho, M.P., Filipe, J.A., Ferreira, M.A. (2011). Rights based management and the reform of the common fisheries policy: The debate. *International Journal Latest Trends Final Ecology Science, 1*(1), 16–22.

Coelho, M.P., Filipe, J.A., Ferreira, M.A. (2013). Modelling enforcement and compliance in fisheries: A survey. *International Journal Latest Trends Final Ecology Science, 3*(2), 464–469.

Costello, C., Gaines, S., Lynham, J. (2008). Can catch shares prevent fisheries collapse?. *Science, 321*, 1678–1681.

Da Rocha, J.M., Cerviño, S., Villasante, S. (2012). The common fisheries policy: An enforcement problem. *Marine Policy, 36*, 1309–1314.

Davis, A. (1996). Barbed wire and Bandwagons: A comment on ITQ fisheries management. *Reviews in Fish Biology and Fisheries, 6*, 97–107.

Dayton, P.K., Thrush, S.F., Agardy, T., Hofman, R.J. (1995). Viewpoint: Environmental effects of marine fishing. *Aquatic Conservation: Marine and Freshwater Ecosystems*, *5*, 205–232.

EFCA (2013). *Annual report 2013*. Bilbao: European Fisheries Control Agency.

Eggert, H., & Ellegård, A. (2003). Fishery control and regulation compliance: A case for comanagement in Swedish commercial fisheries. *Marine Policy*, *27*, 525–533.

Essington, T.E. (2010). Ecological indicators display reduced variation in North American catch share fisheries. *Proceedings of the National Academy of Sciences of the USA, 107*, 754–759.

Essington, T.E., Melnychuk, M.C., Branch, T.A., Heppell, S.S., Jensen, O.P., Link, J.S., Martell, S.J.D., Parma, A.M., Pope, J.G., Smith, A.D.M. (2012). Catch shares, fisheries, and ecological stewardship: A comparative analysis of resource responses to a rights-based policy instrument. *Conservation Letters*, *5*, 186–195.

Esteban, A., & Carpenter, G. (2015). *Landing the blame: Overfishing in EU Waters 2001–2015*. London: New Economics Foundation.

European Commission (2003). Communication from the Commission to the Council and the European Parliament—Reports from Member States on Behaviours Which Seriously Infringed the Rules of the Common Fisheries Policy in 2002. *COM* (2003) 782 final. http://eur-lex.europa.eu/legal-content/en/TXT/?uri=CELEX:52003DC0782.

European Commission (2005). Communication from the Commission to the Council and the European Parliament—Reports from Member States on Behaviours Which Seriously Infringed the Rules of the Common Fisheries Policy in 2003. *COM* (2005) 207 final. http://eur-lex.europa.eu/LexUriServ/LexUriServ.do?uri=COM:2005:0207:FIN:EN:PDF.

European Commission (2006). Communication from the Commission to the Council and the European Parliament—Reports from Member States on Behaviours Which Seriously Infringed the Rules of the Common Fisheries Policy in 2004. *COM* (2006) 387 final. http://eur-lex.europa.eu/legal-content/EN/TXT/?qid=1462804014415&uri=CELEX:52006DC0387.

European Commission (2007a). Communication from the Commission to the Council and the European Parliament—Reports from Member States on Behaviours Which Seriously Infringed the Rules of the Common Fisheries Policy in 2005. *COM* (2007) 448 final. http://eur-lex.europa.eu/legal-content/EN/TXT/?uri=CELEX%3A52007DC0448.

European Commission (2007b). Communication from the Commission on Rights-based Management Tools in Fisheries. *COM* (2007) 73 final. http://eur-lex.europa.eu/legal-content/EN/TXT/?qid=1462804064735&uri=CELEX:52007DC0073.

European Commission (2008). Communication from the Commission to the Council and the European Parliament—Reports from Member States on Behaviours Which Seriously Infringed the Rules of the Common Fisheries Policy in 2006. *COM* (2008) 670 final. http://eur-lex.europa.eu/legal-content/en/TXT/?uri=CELEX:52008DC0670.

European Commission (2011). Communication from the Commission to the European Parliament, the Council, the European Economic and Social Committee and the Committee of the Regions, Reform of the Common Fisheries Policy. *COM* (2011) 417 final. http://eur-lex.europa.eu/legal-content/EN/TXT/?qid=1462804108056&uri=CELEX:52011DC0417.

European Council (2005). Council Regulation (EC) No 768/2005 establishing a Community Fisheries Control Agency and amending Regulation (EEC) No 2847/93 establishing a control system applicable to the common fisheries policy. http://eur-lex.europa.eu/LexUriServ/LexUriServ.do?uri=OJ:L:2005:128:0001:0014:EN:PDF.

European Council (2008). Council Regulation (EC) No 1005/2008 establishing a Community system to prevent, deter, and eliminate IUU fishing. http://eur-lex.europa.eu/LexUriServ/LexUriServ.do?uri=OJ:L:2008:286:0001:0032:EN:PDF.

European Council (2009). Council Regulation (EC) No 1224/2009 establishing a Community control system for ensuring compliance with the rules of the common fisheries policy http://eur-lex.europa.eu/LexUriServ/LexUriServ.do?uri=OJ:L:2009:343:0001:0050:EN:PDF.

Gascoigne, J., & Willstead, E. (2009). *Moving towards low impact fisheries in Europe: Policy hurdles and actions.* Brussels: Seas at Risk.

Grafton, R.Q., Arnason, R., Bjorndal, T. (2006). Incentive-based approaches to sustainable fisheries. *Canadian Journal of Fisheries and Aquatic Science, 63* (3), 699–710.

Grieve, C., Brady, D.C., Polet, H. (2014). Best practices for managing, measuring and mitigating the benthic impacts of fishing—Part 1. *Marine Stewardship Council Science Series, 2,* 18–88.

Grimm, D., Barkhorn, I., Festa, D., Bonzon, K., Boomhower, J., Hovland, V., Blau, J. (2012). Assessing catch shares' effects: Evidence from Federal

United States and associated British Columbian fisheries. *Marine Policy, 36* (3), 644–657, doi: 10.1016/j.marpol.2011.10.014.

Gutiérrez, N.L., Hilborn, R., Defeo, O. (2011). Leadership, social capital and incentives promote successful fisheries. *Nature, 470*, 386–389.

Hardin, G. (1968). The tragedy of the commons. *Science, 162*(3859), 1243–1248.

Hatcher, A., & Gordon, D. (2005). Further investigations into the factors affecting Compliance with U.K. fishing quotas. *Land Economics, 81*(1, February), 71–86.

Hatcher, A., Jaffry, S., Thébaud, O., Bennett, E. (2000). Normative and social influences affecting compliance with fishery regulations. *Land Economics, 76* (3, August), 448–461.

Heath, M.R., Cook, R.M., Cameron, A.I., Morris, D.J., Speirs, D.C. (2014). Cascading ecological effects of eliminating fishery discards. *Nature Communications* article 3893. http://www.nature.com/ncomms/2014/140513/ncomms4893/full/ncomms4893.html.

Melnychuk, M.C., Essington, T.E., Branch, T.A., Heppell, S.S., Jensen, O.P., Link, J.S., Martell, S.J.D., Parma, A.M., Pope, J.G., Smith, J.G. (2012). Can catch share fisheries better track management targets?. *Fish and Fisheries, 13*(3), 267–290.

Newell, R.G., Sanchirico, J.N., Kerr, S. (2005). Fishing quota markets. *Journal of Environmental Economics and Management, 49*, 437–462.

Nielsen, J.R., & Mathiesen, C. (2003). Important factors influencing rule compliance in fisheries lessons from Denmark. *Marine Policy, 27*, 409–416.

OECD (2005). *Why fish piracy persists: The economics of illegal, unreported and unregulated fishing.* Paris: Organisation for Economic Co-operation and Development.

Pauly, D., Christensen, V., Dalsgaard, J., Froese, R., Torres Jr, F. (1998). Fishing down marine food webs. *Science, 279*, 860–863.

Pew Charitable Trusts (2013). *FAQ: Illegal, unreported, and unregulated fishing.* London: Pew. http://www.pewtrusts.org/en/research-and-analysis/fact-sheets/2013/08/27/faq-illegal-unreported-and-unregulated-fishing.

Reeves, S.A., & Furness, R.W. (2002). *Net loss—Seabirds gain? Implication of fisheries management for seabirds scavenging discards in the Northern North Sea.* Sandy, UK: RSPB.

Sumaila, U.R. (2010). A cautionary note on individual transferable quotas. *Ecology and Society, 15*(3), 36.

Sumaila, U.R., & Watson, R. (2002). The rights to fish—An ecological critique of individual transferable quotas. In T. Ward, D. Tarte, E. Hegerl, K. Short (Eds.),

Ecosystem-based management of marine fisheries: Policy proposals and operational guidance for ecosystem-based management of marine capture fisheries. n.p.: World Wildlife Fund for Nature Australia.

Suuronen, P., Chopin, F., Glass, C., Løkkeborg, S., Matsushita, Y., Queirolo, D., Rihan, D. (2013). Low impact and fuel efficient fishing: Looking beyond the Horizon. *Fisheries Research, 119–20*, 135–146.

Turris, B.R. (2000). A comparison of British Columbia's ITQ fisheries for Groundfish Trawl and Sablefish: Similar results from programmes with differing objectives, designs and processes. In R. Shotton (Ed.), *Use of property rights in fisheries management,* Proceedings of the FishRights 99 Conference, Fremantle, Australia, 11–19 November 1999, FAO Fisheries Technical Paper 404/1 (Rome: FAO).

UNODC (2011). *Issue paper—Transnational organized crime in the fishing industry*. Vienna: United Nations Office on Drugs and Crime.

Watson, R., & Pauly, D. (2001). Systematic distortions in world fisheries catch trends. *Nature*, 414, 534–536.

Stephanie Newman is a specialist in fisheries and marine policy. At the Institute for European Environmental Policy she managed and contributed to numerous research projects which aimed to support the sustainable exploitation of marine biological resources, mainly in the contexts of reform of the Common Fisheries Policy and European Fisheries Fund, and the implementation of the Marine Strategy Framework Directive and Birds and Habitats Directives. She has provided the fisheries policy expertise in numerous projects including a study on 'biodiversity proofing' the Multi-annual Financial Framework. She also contributed to the Impact Assessment for the CFP review, and a project mapping the Biodiversity Strategy targets and actions within the wider EU policy framework. Stephanie has an MSc in Marine Environmental Management from the University of York. Her research studied the deviation of EU fishing quotas from scientific advice, and the implementation of ecosystem-based management in Canadian maritime policy, the latter of which she undertook at the Federal Department of Fisheries and Oceans in Newfoundland.

Dr Andrew Farmer Head of the Industry, Waste and Water Programme, Institute for European Environmental Policy, has a PhD from St Andrews University and began his career as a research scientist in the USA and UK. Subsequently, Dr Farmer worked for a UK government agency for 7 years, where he provided scientific and policy advice across a wide range of areas, in particular focusing on analysis of the impacts of activities on the environment and developing inputs to negotiations at international level. Dr Farmer has undertaken extensive research on the implementation of EU legislation and its implementation in the Member States, with a particular focus on the challenges of compliance assessment and enforcement. Dr Farmer has published the following books: *Managing Environmental Pollution* (Routledge) and *Handbook of Environmental Protection and Enforcement* (Earthscan). He was the Editor of the *Manual of European Environmental Policy* published by Earthscan.

5

Wildlife Trafficking: Harms and Victimization

Jennifer Maher and Ragnhild Sollund

5.1 Introduction

In this chapter, we present and discuss findings from an empirical case study on the illegal wildlife trade (IWT) carried out in Norway, the UK, Colombia, and Brazil. This book focuses on the European

We are grateful for initial funding for the project; this research is based upon from The Norwegian Animal Protection Fund.

J. Maher (✉)
Faculty of Business and Society, Lecturer and Subject Leader in Criminology, South Wales, UK
e-mail: jenny.maher@southwales.ac.uk

R. Sollund
University of Oslo, Oslo, Norway
e-mail: ragnhild.sollund@jus.uio.no

R. Sollund et al. (eds.), *Fighting Environmental Crime in Europe and Beyond*, Palgrave Studies in Green Criminology,
DOI 10.1057/978-1-349-95085-0_5

Union (EU), therefore, special attention is given to the UK and Norway. We utilize data from the European Union Action to Fight Environmental Crime (EFFACE) (2016) project (Maher and Sollund 2016; Sollund and Maher 2015) to demonstrate the harms associated with IWT and explain why endangered animals and animal products are trafficked. We also identify offenders, their role in the trade, and the punishment received. Crucially, our emphasis is on the direct victims of the trade, the animals themselves, whether they are trafficked dead or alive.

5.2 A Brief Overview of the Illegal Wildlife Trade

The trade in endangered animal and plant species is regulated through the Convention on International Trade in Endangered Species of Fauna and Flora (CITES) convention. CITES utilizes three appendices:

> Appendix I—lists species threatened with extinction. Trade in animals pertaining to these species is permitted only in exceptional circumstances.
>
> Appendix II—lists species not necessarily threatened with extinction but of whom trade must be controlled in order to avoid exploitation incompatible with species survival.
>
> Appendix III—lists species that are protected in at least one country that has asked other CITES parties for assistance in controlling the trade (CITES 2013a).

Whether trade of a species is restricted, and thereby criminalized, is dependent upon its degree of vulnerability. While most trade in endangered species is regulated under CITES (alongside other conventions), trade is only banned for critically endangered species, and there are many species that are neither listed, nor protected, within these conventions (Reeve 2002). In early 2015, the EU became the 181st body to adhere voluntarily to CITES. Prior to this, the EU adopted Council Regulation (EC) No. 338/97 (European Commission 2016), a framework based upon CITES, but with stricter trade rules[1], comprising four annexes (A, B, C, and D). The first three largely correspond to the CITES appendices. Annex D is the 'monitoring list' used to track the EU import levels of species that might in the future be listed in Annexes A, B, or C (European Commission [EC] 2010; Sina *et al.* 2016). Currently, though, legislation is not harmonized across parties, and consequently regulation, enforcement, and punishment vary from country to country, leading to the appearance of fissures and loopholes within the EU legal response. Further, the EU response to these breaches is compromised due to variations in prioritization and expertise within the criminal justice system (CJS; e.g. a judge failing to reference previous verdicts; Maher and Sollund, in press; Sollund and Maher 2015; Sollund 2013). With Europe being a key location for IWT as a point of transit, a market for consumers (van Uhm 2016) and, to a lesser degree, a source these are significant failings. Transnational, global, and thereby difficult to control, IWT is increasingly identified as a serious and organized crime with far-reaching consequences for both humans and non-humans (Schneider 2012; Sollund and Maher 2015; Wyatt 2013).

Between 2001 and 2010, the EU Trade in Wildlife Information eXchange (EU-TWIX) database recorded more than 50,000 confiscations across EU states.[2] Animal products make up the majority of these seizures (82 per cent), compared to the seizures of live animals (15 per cent; Van Uhm 2016, p. 90). Reptile products constituted 67.7 per cent of the

[1] Regulations include: 1) Council Regulation (EC) No. 338/97 of 9 December 1996 on the protection of species of wild fauna and flora by regulating trade therein including the Annexes containing a list of species regulated in trade. 2) Implementing regulation: Commission Regulation (EC) No. 865/2006 of 4 May 2006 laying down detailed rules concerning the implementation of Council Regulation (EC) No 338/97 by regulating trade therein. These two regulations constitute the legal framework for all EU governments and regulate international as well as internal trade in wild animals and plants in the EU.

[2] 'The EU-TWIX database has been developed to assist national law enforcement agencies, including CITES Management Authorities and prosecutors, in their task of detecting, analysing, and monitoring illegal activities related to trade in fauna and flora covered by the EU Wildlife Trade Regulations. The main section of the database is designed to become a unique source of centralized data on seizures and offences reported by all 28 EU member states. The purpose of EU-TWIX is to assist with strategic analyses and carrying out field investigations' (EU-TWIX, 2015). According to Sina *et al.* (2016), the EU-TWIX database gives an overview on all seizures of illegal wildlife species traded from 2007–2014.

seizures, while mammal products were largely used in traditional Chinese medicine (TCM; Van Uhm 2014, 2016). Birds made up 59 per cent (N = 877) of live seizures destined for the pet trade, followed by reptiles (30 per cent, N = 2,171). In 2014 alone, UK Border Forces (UK customs agency) made 509 CITES seizures including 23 live animal, 139 animal product, 22 caviar, 14 coral, 39 ivory, and 208 TCM preparation (containing animals and/or plants; Data.gov.uk, 2015). UK enforcement agents suggest that these seizures may account for as little as 10 per cent of actual offences. According to the Norwegian Customs Directorate, in Norway, between 2008 and 2014, there were 1,839 CITES-listed live animal and animal product seizures: parrot (several species), reptile (several species), Siberian tiger, leopard, brown bear, lion, crocodile, alligator, sea horse, hippo, corals, and elephant ivory.[3] Note that a seizure does not denote quantity; for example, the 23 UK live animal seizures (see above) totalled 1,289 individual animals. The wildlife reception and rehabilitation centre in Bogotá, Colombia, receives an average of 4,000 animals annually. In the state of São Paolo, Brazil, according to statistics provided by the Environmental Military Police, between 2009 and 2014, they seized 31,534 *canários-da-terra* (canary-of-the-land).[4] In that same period, 4,772 parrots (*Amazona aestiva*) were apprehended in São Paulo (Nassaro in print).

5.3 Green Criminology Perspective

Criminological IWT literature often adopts conventional criminological approaches to provide theoretical explanations and responses (see Hill, in press; Lemieux 2014; Pires and Clark 2011; Pires and Moreto 2011; Schneider 2012; Wellsmith 2010, 2011). The IWT presents a 'suitable target' in terms of Cohen and Felson's (1979) routine activity theory—significant financial rewards and the absence of strong enforcement and punishment are motivation to offend. This perspective points to the

[3] Statistics provided upon request.

[4] Canaries constitute 90 per cent of seized animals, most destined to be caged as 'pets'. This is a contradiction in terms; a bird who is caged can hardly be 'petted', and the cage constructs both a physical and a social distance.

motivation of the offender and, usefully, to other 'essential' causal factors such as situational characteristics and approaches (e.g. law enforcement).

Here we adopt a green criminology justice perspective because it encompasses eco and species justice, as well as concepts of rights, including environmental and ecosystem rights (as per White 2013). We acknowledge—which conventional criminology often fails to do—that acts may be harmful whether criminalized or not (see also Beirne and South 2007; Hillyard *et al.* 2004; Sollund 2015; White 2013), often resulting in victims being subjected to violence and death. We also prefer and use the term 'abduction', rather than 'poaching', for the act of forcefully removing animals from their habitat (see also Sollund 2011). We accept that these animals have individual interests and that if species justice is to be fulfilled, all animals must be considered victims whether they are traded legally or illegally (see also Sollund 2013).

5.4 Methodology

This chapter is based on empirical research carried out as part of the EFFACE project (see Sollund and Maher 2015) that details the EU context of wildlife trafficking through an overview of current academic and expert literature and data collection from four qualitative case studies in locations representing source (Brazil and Colombia), transit (UK), and demand (UK and Norway) countries. Along with trade comparisons, the research identified the nature of IWT and responses to it. Case study data was collected by means of interviews with and observations of experts including non-governmental organization (NGO) staff, environmental authorities, and law enforcement agents. Offender interviews (Norway only) and analysis of penal cases, verdicts, and confiscation reports further supplemented this data.

5.5 Victims

Assuming as a point of departure that animals are sentient beings, are 'subjects-of-a-life' (Regan 1983), who, like humans, have interests in living their lives unharmed, we can confidently acknowledge them as the principal victims of trade, legal, or otherwise. There are a large range of animal victim species; seizures in the UK and Norway alone include mammals, reptiles, fish and other sea animals, and birds. Many are live animals destined for the pet trade, especially birds, reptiles, fish, and corals fall into this category. However, the largest seizures are of animal parts and derivatives. Animal parts and derivatives are made into food, health (dried seahorse, leopard, rhino horn, musk deer, tiger [Minnaar 2013]), ornamental (ivory, stuffed crocodile and parts of crocodile, bears, wolves, birds, bird eggs), and fashion (reptile skins, feathers) products.

Victimization of individual animals can also cause secondary victimization to whole species and ecosystems. During the last 40 years, the Living Planet Index (LPI), which measures more than 10,000 representative populations of mammals, birds, reptiles, amphibians, and fish, has identified a 52 per cent population decline in these populations (World Wildlife Fund for Nature [WWF] 2014b). Although habitat loss likely accounts for much of this, hunting and abduction are serious threats (WWF 2014b, p. 21). The scale of biodiversity loss could be as high as 100,000 species becoming extinct every year, which is 1,000–10,000 times the rate of natural extinction (WWF 2014a, 2014b). According to Baille *et al.* (cited in Rivalan *et al.* 2007), the IWT threatens a third of the world's species, including critically endangered species such as the iconic rhinoceros, tiger, and African elephant. CITES (2013b) currently lists approximately 5,600 animal species as threatened.

5.5.1 Animal Victimization

The clandestine nature of the IWT ensures the animal victims will suffer, causing harms ranging from violence to death. Interviewees provided many examples of the poor conditions in which trafficked animals arrive in the UK and Norway. Consistent with the academic literature, South American interviewees confirmed that only 5–10 per cent of trafficked parrots and reptiles survive transit. Illegally abducted parrots are often forced to wear falsified leg rings taken from captive-bred birds but may suffer a broken leg during this procedure. NGO interviewees expressed particular concern about the impact of IWT on the welfare of the exotic pet trade, identifying it as one of the most pressing UK animal welfare issues. To smuggle reptiles, offenders typically launder them as part of the legal trade. A permit number that licences 50 reptiles may instead transport hundreds in cramped, life-threatening conditions. Live animals confiscated in the UK, Norway, and Colombia have been found taped to bodies, stuffed into tubes, bottles, and socks in luggage, or in small post parcels. Often they have been sedated for more than 12 hours, putting them at further risk.

Victimization may continue even after 'rescue' from the IWT. In Norway, euthanasia of seized animals is the rule rather than the exception, despite the Norwegian Environmental Agency's goal to return confiscated CITES animals to their natural homes. This was not a topic control agents in Norway were discussing, with the exception of the interviewee from the Norwegian environment agency. CITES (2016b) recommends that an action plan should 'identify approved facilities and programs located within the country that have agreed to provide adequate care (including veterinary or phytosanitary care) and that are willing to accept confiscated live specimens of particular taxa'. While there are a few such locations in Norway, their purpose is not to *rescue* confiscated CITES animals but to *display* animals to the public (most frequently at Kristiansand Zoo and Oslo Reptile Park). These centres have reached saturation point and now only welcome the rarest of animals. CITES (Conf. 9.9; 2016b) establishes the responsibility of parties in cases of wildlife confiscation: that the seizure and confiscation of such 'specimens' are generally preferable to the definitive refusal of the import of the 'specimens', and to ensure the animals are not re-entered into illegal trade, including monitoring their return to their country of origin and providing for their confiscation. Norway accomplishes this through confiscation and killing, rather than rescuing and/or repatriating the animals. Consequently, animals do not re-enter the IWT, but they are deprived of a life.

The Norwegian Environment Agency is consulted to determine the outcome of confiscated animals. It usually advises death, especially if the animals are 'only' CITES II species. For example, on 12 August 2014, six African grey parrots smuggled into Norway were confiscated and later killed. On 30 March 2014, 44 birds were brought to Norway on a permit for 36; the eight excess birds were killed. Paradoxically, 'surviving' animals who have endured abduction from their habitats and trafficking over land and water are first 'rescued' and then killed by Norwegian authorities—their 'saviours'—enforcing CITES. Document analysis of hundreds of penal cases revealed that seized reptiles, 'confiscated goods' in the reports, are killed through enforcement, challenging, we suggest, the intention behind the convention. The CITES (2016c) website suggests 'its aim is to ensure that international trade in specimens of wild animals and plants does not threaten their survival'. However, protections are limited at best as individual animals appear only to have value when their whole species is threatened. The purpose of CITES is in fact to protect economic trade; one UK enforcement officer clearly defined their role as enabling trade rather than guarding animal welfare.

In contrast to Norway, the UK has a better track record of rehoming animals. The purpose-built Animal Reception Centre (ARC) at Heathrow Airport and the commitment of agency staff to rehome wildlife ensure this. As rehoming is not a legal requirement, success is due to the cooperation of agencies and good relationships between agencies and interest groups (e.g. zoos and sanctuaries). Nonetheless, problems were identified by interviewees in terms of how interest groups are chosen and monitored (i.e. they need not be licensed or inspected regularly), limited resources (there is limited capacity among these groups to rehome large numbers of the same species), and animals are kept for long periods in what is designed to be temporary accommodation. According to UK enforcement officers, when live animals are seized under CITES, enforcers must have the capacity to accommodate and care for them. Without this capacity, animals cannot be seized even if an offence has taken place. In one example provided by an officer, a shipment of live animals was returned to the country of export as they did not have the capacity to hold these animals. In this situation, the UK may not record the crime or prosecute the offenders, and the victims are likely to be subjected to further victimization and to remain in the IWT.

Rehabilitation centres in Columbia and Brazil aim to return animals to their habitat. However, in the rehabilitation centres in São Paolo and Bogotá, mortality rates are high among the many confiscated animals abducted and trafficked. According to interviewees, 10 per cent of turtles seized survive trafficking to arrive at a zoo or centre; most die or require lifetime care due to the stress and violence of their initial abduction and subsequent transit. Authorities do not have the equipment, logistics, or resources to respond to the needs of the animals. Animals incapable of returning to their habitat, due to injury or a lack of information about their natural habitats, must live in zoos or rescue centres, enduring poor conditions stemming from a lack of resources and space.

5.5.2 Human Victimization

Humans are also victims of the IWT. Harm often involves the removal of natural resources from humans, preventing or limiting the legal trade necessary for generating revenue locally or nationally. The IWT and the destruction of ecosystems has global implications for people—health risks, environmental degradation, economic loss, and social disintegration. Increasingly, IWT is viewed as a security concern, as organized crime and terrorist groups utilize the IWT to destabilize countries and fund arms deals (Sina *et al.* 2016; Wyatt 2013).

On a local level, UK NGOs have identified threats of violence to indigenous people and rangers and the destruction of livelihoods and communities in source countries as a consequence of the IWT. The IWT compromises biodiversity and drains ecosystems, which can destroy food and economic sources for local people, including the possibility of organizing peaceful ecotourism (in contrast to trophy hunting), which supports both animal and human victims. Interviewees indicated that both local rangers and NGO agents are targeted and killed by poachers, with the protection of high-value animals, such as rhinos, being particularly risky.

5.6 Offenders

While there is no recognized IWT offender profile, the literature identifies impoverished hunters and villagers, legitimate business owners, members of crime groups, general consumers, and corrupt officials as offenders (van Uhm 2016; Wyatt 2013). Coming from source countries (in our case, Brazil and Columbia), animals are likely to pass through many hands: 1) local opportunist hunters, and more recently, 2) organized crime hunting groups, 3) middlemen who visit locales encouraging locals to abduct/kill animals before moving them onto 4) traders who transport these animals either within the country or beyond its borders where 5) traders and business people receive and sell wildlife. Wildlife, as pets or products, are often sold to 6) local or 7) tourist consumers in marketplaces or at roadside stands, or processed for global trade, which can be facilitated through 8) corrupt officials.

At this point, wildlife is transported by 9) international business people, organized criminals, tourists, and 10) consumers (e.g. internet purchases delivered via mail services). Within destination countries, wildlife is traded by 11) legitimate business people and organized and 12) opportunistic criminals and/or purchased by 13) consumers and collectors (see Fig. 5.1).

The UK enforcement officers identified not only seasonal peaks and troughs in the IWT market, but also shifting demands dictated by fashion and health trends. Growth in the use of TCM products in the UK over the past decade, for example, has made exotic animal derivatives amongst the most trafficked and seized products. Likewise, recent developments in the health and beauty market have raised demand for caviar in skin creams and exotic animal derivatives as ingredients in fitness supplements. It is clear that these market fluctuations prompt different offender types; less clear is our understanding of whether the consumer creates the market or vice versa.[5]

5.6.1 Offender Motivation

Consistent with academic and expert literature, interviewees in all four locations identified financial reward as an important offender motivation (depending on where in the chain the offender was). However, when considering the purpose of the trade and types of consumers, explaining

[5] In fact, identifying how trends develop and how to subsequently reduce consumer demand is a crucial area for future research.

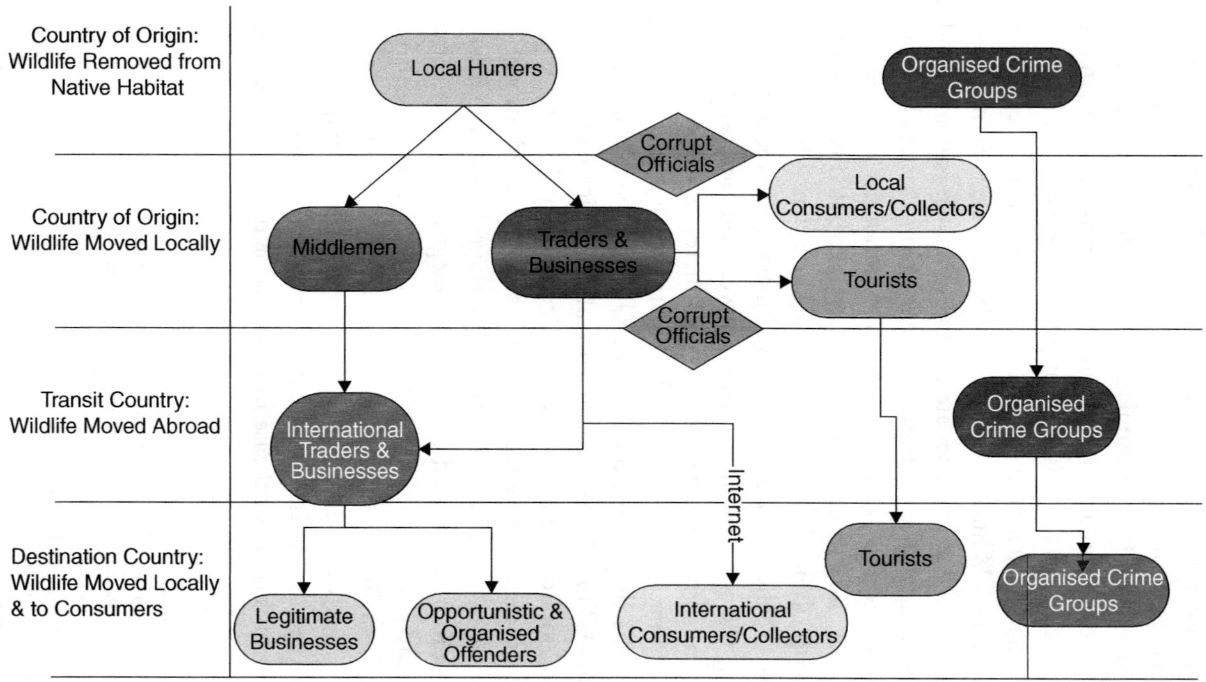

Fig. 5.1 Offenders involved in the IWT from source to destination countries

the causes of IWT and motivations of offenders is more complex than might be assumed (see Fig. 5.1 and Table 5.1). Evidence from UK and Norwegian enforcement agencies suggests that noncompliance (defined as failure to fully comply with regulations and policy requirements, typically a consequence of ignorance or administrative error rather than intentional offending)[6] accounts for a significant portion of their CITES seizures (e.g. tourists bringing back souvenirs/pets) and, as such, offenders are often treated leniently. While ignorance of the law excuses no one, CITES regulations and related policies are complex, change regularly, and include exemptions (tourists, for example, are permitted to bring objects which are 'personal and household effects' or small amounts of otherwise illegal products such as caviar [CITES 2016a; Interpol/IFAW 2013]) which may also contribute to noncompliance. The avian influenza outbreak is an example of where a clearly articulated message by the government (e.g. prohibiting the movement of birds), a well laid out process (enhanced detection and punishment), and strict adherence to procedure (in this case, limitations placed on the legal bird trade) marked a sustained decrease in the illegal bird trade to the UK and the EU more generally.

Evidently CITES is open to interpretation, which can cause confusion and create loopholes that attract organized criminals. One UK enforcement officer described what he saw as the gradual move, by some offenders, from 'bending the rules' in their legitimate businesses to engaging in more organized offences and illegitimate trade. These offenders did not perceive their actions as 'really' breaking the law. Such offending is facilitated by a skewed perception of IWT offences that enables criminals to minimize and justify their behaviour.

Interviewees distinguished collectors from other types of offenders, and an in-depth analysis of a penal case indicated addiction-like behaviour by one

[6] This was apparent in the UK when interviewees explained the negative impact of what appeared to be a simple change to the CITES definition of 'worked' and 'unworked' specimens which caused widespread confusion among UK traders and enforcers alike; legitimate traders feared interpreting the new rules incorrectly, thereby losing their products or being convicted for a CITES offence, and enforcement agencies were uncertain what to enforce. Given the uncertainty and levels of non-compliance, offenders could exploit this confusion as it made it more difficult to get a conviction should they be caught.

Table 5.1 Offender motivation identified in the IWT in the case study locations

Norway	UK	Columbia/Brazil	Examples
Profit	Profit	Profit	Live animals, traditional medicine products
Cultural	Cultural	Cultural	Bones, bush meat, derivatives
Companion	Companion	Companion	Songbirds, parrots, reptiles
Consumption	Consumption	Consumption	Bush meat, turtles
Health	Health	Health	Rhino horn, leopard
Entertainment	Entertainment	Entertainment	Birds, primates
Beauty	Beauty	–	Caviar, furs
Luxury	Luxury	–	Caviar, furs, skins, rhino
Collection	Collection	–	Bird eggs, taxidermy
Souvenirs	Souvenirs	–	Turtle shell, ivory
Status	Status	–	Fur, taxidermy birds
–	–	Experimentation	Primates, reptiles
–	–	Biopiracy	Caged birds, reptiles

offender (Sollund 2015). While many 'ordinary' consumers engage in IWT, a large number of the police files in Norway that were analysed, coded as the illegal keeping of exotic species (the regulation under the Animal Welfare Act), indicated that reptiles were attractive to people involved in other serious crimes (e.g. violence and drugs) and that the conditions under which the animals were kept did not meet minimum welfare requirements (Table 5.1).

Trafficking in Colombia, where there is a long tradition of keeping wildlife as pets, was commonly identified as motivated by the desire for pets and food, especially widespread among the lower and rural strata of the population, large numbers of whom have moved into cities in recent decades. This urbanization, commonplace in Latin America, is transitioning ITW practices and creating new markets. White meat from sea mammals, turtles, and capybaras is trafficked in large quantities, principally for Easter, when red meat is forbidden. In London, the heart of the UK illegal bush meat trade, consumers are reportedly motivated by the desire to eat traditional or gourmet foods, which are often legally sourced in their native countries.

Traders and middlemen in source countries profit by bringing animals to city markets. In Bogotá, frequent trafficking hotspots are Plaza de Restrepo, Corabastos (Colombia's central market), and the pet shops of Caracas Street. Locals, often indigenous people, are the usual abductors, taking animals for small but necessary financial gain, not all of them needing encouragement by middlemen when they lack alternatives and a ready income. For Colombian police, receivers of animals at reception store houses make better targets for arrest. The middlemen (see Wyatt 2013) who travel to re-collect animals (by this stage these animals have been handled by up to seven individuals), are of particular interest. It is worth noting that buyers can commission purchases through catalogues, upon which middlemen will place an order, for an ocelot, for example. The abductors will then catch the animal for payment on delivery. This way the involved avoid the risk of losing the animal and being arrested in police raids. Night monkeys, extensively used in malaria research, were reportedly abducted to supply demand (Goyes 2015; Maldonado *et al.* 2009).

5.7 Formal and Informal Reactions to Wildlife Victims and Offenders

Control of IWT involves both formal and informal responses. At a national and global level, formal control is exercised by way of international treaties and domestic legislation that support domestic enforcement, prosecution, and judicial response, all facilitated by a small number of key personnel. The subsequent responses put in place are complex and diverse, necessitating multi-agency cooperation (creating an overlap between formal and informal responses). Variations between case study locations are evident in both the practice and effectiveness of formal responses, with deficiencies specifically linked to limited resources and low prioritization within the CJS. Informally, considerable work is carried out by NGOs, both nationally and internationally, to help control and prevent IWT. However, variation also exists in terms of the nature of NGO involvement and their responses to the harms to victims.

5.7.1 Rules and Regulations

Norway (from 1976), the UK (from 1976), Colombia (from 1981), Brazil (from 1975), and the EU (from 2015) are party to CITES and, as such, are required to monitor and regulate the trade of more than 35,000 wild species through the adoption of domestic legislation that implements CITES at a national level (CITES 2016c). According to Reeve (2002), a 1973 study by Environmental Resources Management found 75 per cent of parties viewed CITES as effective in deterring IWT. However, as there is no empirical assessment of CITES, EU regulations, or EU member states' domestic legislations, it is difficult to evaluate the effectiveness of such regulations. Reeve (2002) also provides a comprehensive analysis of CITES compliance and argues that although CITES is a flagship wildlife agreement, it is compromised by being a self-policed system with no global enforcement agency to oversee compliance. She suggests the key risks to CITES are the dissolution of borders (as this makes the permit system irrelevant, since with porous borders no permits need to be presented) and chronic underfunding, both of which are problematic in the EU. Once illegal wildlife/products enter an EU country it becomes more difficult to identify and apprehend the offenders (see also Van Uhm 2016), due to the porous borders between countries. As there is considerable variation among member states and partnership countries such as Norway in terms of the priority given to regulating and enforcing this offence, the EU response is only as strong as its weakest state in terms of enforcement. The development of organized criminal networks poses new challenges for legal responses to and resources for IWT, the most significant being they have the ability to destroy species at a phenomenal rate and have a growing lucrative market worldwide (e.g. China, Vietnam). Furthermore, as other serious crime offences (e.g. drugs and arms) are more highly prioritized than IWT crackdowns in these illegal markets may displace organized offenders towards the high profit, low-risk IWT.

Arguably, the greatest deficiencies in CITES and related legislation are the provisions for trafficked animals' welfare; confiscated wildlife are routinely killed. The lack of welfare facilities in Norway suggests this is not a priority there. Unfortunately, as parties are not required to record or publish outcomes for seized animals, it is impossible to establish how prevalent this problem is across the EU.

What follows is an overview of the domestic legislation regulating the IWT in each location:

- UK CITES offences may fall under Control of Trade in Endangered Species [Enforcement] Regulations 1997 (COTES) or Customs and Excise Management Act 1979 (CEMA) and can be linked to breaches in international (e.g. Council Regulation [EC] No 1/2005 on Animal Welfare in Transportation) and national (e.g. Animal Welfare Act [AWA] 2006) laws (Her Majesty's Stationery Office 1997, 1979). The legislation and policies in place were largely identified by UK interviewees as plentiful and adequate. For example, by including the International Air Transport Association (IATA) Live Animals Regulations (LAR) standards as part of CITES compliance, it is easier to prosecute offenders for abuse linked to trafficking, as there is no need to prove 'suffering' as per the AWA 2006. However, concerns were raised with regard to the timeliness of legislation updates, the clarity of legislation for enforcement purposes, and the limited protection it offers animals. UK national wildlife legislation, for example, was regarded as outdated and disjointed; COTES and CEMA require revision, while (EC) No 1/2005 uses IATA LAR standards from 2004 not 2015 (therefore offenders can be convicted of breaches by 2004 not 2015 standards).
- Norwegian legislation contains several laws and regulations that prohibit the importation of live animals to Norway, among them *Viltloven* (Wildlife Law 2009 §47; Lovdata n.d.b),[7] The Law of Biodiversity (Lovdata n.d.c) and the Animal Welfare Act (Lovdata n.d.d).[8] Another law, often applied in CITES cases, is the law

[7] Revised in 2009.

[8] Regulations that apply are: FOR-1976-11-20-3 Regulation of 20 November 1976 about the prohibition against the importation, commercialization, or keeping in captivity of alien (exotic) animals. (§1). Other regulations which apply are FOR-2004-02-20-464 about the animal welfare conditions for import of live animals. http://lovdata.no/dokument/SF/forskrift/2004-02-20-464.

regulating importation and exportation from 6 June 1997, with a maximum sentence of 6 months in prison. This may be used both for CITES-listed flora and fauna. The Norwegian CITES regulation, November 2002 nr. 1976 is today, in regard to animals, based on the Wildlife Law §56, with a maximum prison sentence of 2 years, but the previously mentioned law is still applied in court. The Norwegian CITES regulation was revised in 2013, based on the Law of Regulation of Importation and Exportation from 6 June 1997, the Wildlife Law, Law of Environmental Protection on Svalbard, the Svalbard Environmental Act, and the Law of Biodiversity.[9] A suggestion for yet another revision of the regulation was sent for public consultation by the Norwegian Environment Agency on 7 May 2015. Changes suggested will impose stricter control of, and demands regarding permits for appendix II species and demands about internal chipping and labelling. With the CITES regulation based in the Law of Biodiversity, breaches of CITES can be registered as crimes rather than misdemeanours. Because several laws and regulations (frequently applied for other offences) now variously are applied for CITES crimes, specific CITES crimes often remain unaccounted for in the system, even when animals belong to CITES species.

- In Colombia, the laws most often applied in relation to trafficking are Decreto 1608 de 1978 (Código Nacional de los Recursos Naturales (on natural resources), Ley 599 de 2000 (Código Penal [Penal Law]) artículos 328 y 329, Ley 84 de 1989 (On animal welfare), and Ley 99 de 1993, artículo 1.
- In Brazil, federal laws that apply are Decreto 24.645 de 1934 [Decree 24.645 of 1934] and Animal Welfare Act Lei 5197 de 1967 [about protection of fauna]. The first part concerns wildlife: Lei 6938 de 1981 (regards national policy on protecting the environment] and Lei

http://lovdata.no/dokument/SF/forskrift/1976-11-20-3. And FOR-1991-07-02-507. Regulation about prohibition of imports of animals and other contagious objects http://lovdata.no/dokument/SF/forskrift/1991-07-02-507.

[9] The CITES regulation in Norway: https://lovdata.no/dokument/SF/forskrift/2002-11-15-1276.

9605 de 1998 [Law 9605 of 1998] (regards penal sanctions and administrative punishment for harmful acts against the environment). Regulation in both Columbia and Brazil are compromised by fragmented and complex legislation, which is seldom adequately enforced.

5.7.2 Enforcement

Whether CITES provides effective protection for animal victims and punishment for offenders has been subject to debate (Kievit 2000; Maher and Sollund 2015; Reeve 2002; Sollund 2011). Arguably, the presence of a legal market, which CITES fosters, motivates IWT as it hides, facilitates, legitimizes, and encourages wildlife trade (Sollund 2011). Warchol *et al.*'s (2003) study demonstrates this link, finding various forms of fraud in the legal bird trade, including forging CITES certificates/permits, under-reporting the actual number of animals being transported, selling wild-caught birds as locally bred, dyeing feathers and smuggling birds in cylinders and sending them as air freight, and bribery of officials. This is supported further by Shepherd *et al.* (2012), UN Office on Drugs and Crime (2012), Wyatt (2009), and Van Uhm (2016) who identified the use of forged CITES import and export certificates, wild-caught animals laundered as captive bred, corruption among those responsible for regulating the trade, failure to reduce demand for illegal ivory through the sale of ivory stockpiles, and links between legal and illegal enterprises.

The development of specialist IWT enforcement agencies in the UK has helped raise the official and public profile of IWT, generating greater understanding of the prevalence and nature of the IWT and enabling more effective enforcement. However, many enforcement officers in the UK and Norway with IWT responsibilities have other generic and specialist roles and find IWT duties are de-prioritized and often carried out outside normal work hours. The specialist Heathrow CITES team and the National Wildlife Crime Unit are central to the success of the UK IWT response. However, there was a notable absence of resources in other enforcement locations, forcing officers to fund their own investigative technology. Resources are also a problem in Norway, where customs officials complained they were refused the computer program Green Parrot developed to help identify CITES species and CITES certificates (Crawford 1997).

Due to the limited resources available for enforcing IWT and the need for maximum impact in key locations (e.g. at Border Inspection Posts [BIPs]), UK agencies increasingly focus on SMART enforcement. The National Wildlife Crime Unit establishes UK-wide enforcement priorities based on data analysis and expert advice, thereby generating evidence-based targets, risk-based targeting, and intelligence-focused enforcement. Key enforcement agencies (see Maher and Sollund 2015 for a detailed breakdown of UK IWT agencies within the CJS) have developed national databases and reporting procedures for wildlife offences to enhance intelligence and identify organized crime in IWT. However, the set priorities are based on data that, according to UK interviewees, are neither complete nor robust enough to be considered intelligence. Intelligence gathering is limited as enforcement systems are not shared; there are problems with data reliability and missed opportunities in not using data provided by other agencies (e.g. NGOs). In Norway, the lack of priority and resources has resulted in low detection, poor recording, and delays in prosecution. Norway, usually reputed for its databases (Statistics Norway has data going back to 1828), does not consistently code CITES cases—they have been registered as misdemeanours rather than crimes (Svae-Grotli 2014)—making it impossible to track offences or to identify the nature or prevalence of these offences.

Personnel from both NGOs and enforcement agencies highlighted the usefulness of strategic meetings and conferences (both national and international) dedicated to a partnership response to the IWT. However, in Norway such meetings, involving customs, police, the Environment Agency and the Food Safety Authority were irregular and rarely prioritized by enforcement agencies. While the Norwegian Environment Agency emphasized customs' deplorable lack of focus on freight companies, customs' response was that they were reliant on the competence of a very few officers (who were unable to distinguish CITES species from non-CITES species and genuine CITES permits from forged

CITES permits). The enforcement response is characterized (and compromised) by conflicting opinions on the prioritization of the IWT and the lack of CITES competence in relevant enforcement sectors (such as police, customs, judiciary).

In the UK, NGOs enhance the formal response, concealing some of the resource deficiency detailed above; making successful partnerships between enforcement agencies, NGOs, and other stakeholders is crucial to the enforcement response. In 2012, for instance, the NGO World Animal Protection stepped in to fund the London Metropolitan Wildlife Crime Unit in response to government funding cuts. This NGO has since established a successful partnership with enforcement agencies, providing forensic toolkits to aid investigation, contributing to targeted operations (e.g. Operation Charm), and sharing data for analysis and publication, to raise awareness and lobby for funding (Interview data).

However, such partnerships, both local and international, are also characterized by a lack of trust due to data confidentiality concerns. For the same reason, communication between international enforcement agencies was also identified as problematic. While EU-TWIX was described by UK officers as an essential enforcement tool for communicating and enabling the swift exchange of information/intelligence between member states, the effectiveness of this exchange was largely dependent on regular inputs from enforcement agencies in all member states. Reportedly, engagement varies considerably from one country to another.

5.7.3 Prosecution and Sanctions

Within the UK and Norway, the prosecution and sentencing of IWT offenders was perceived, by most interviewees, to be the weakest link in the criminal justice response. Prosecution rates were described as very poor, due to inexperienced officials and a lack of expertise and interest within the CJS and judiciary. Many difficulties were detailed between Norwegian enforcement officers and the prosecution services: cases were delayed, not prosecuted or poorly prosecuted, and no feedback was provided to enforcement officers. While UK enforcement officers detailed many examples where they worked closely with the prosecution service to enable a successful prosecution, they argued there were many more occasions where this did not happen and cases were not prosecuted (at all or unsuccessfully). There is little accountability in the UK Crime Prosecution Service (CPS), as only the Scottish CPS records IWT prosecutions or their outcomes. Case files from Norway revealed that cases were passed from prosecutor to prosecutor before finally being brought to trial, and such delays consistently resulted in lenient punishment because the delay was regarded as a burden for the accused.

When prosecutions are successful in the UK and Norway, the resulting sanctions are generally lenient, often delayed, and disproportionate to the harm caused. In order for legislation to have a preventative impact, certainty of punishment is more important than severity (Andenæs 1950); interviewees suggested that in the best-case scenario, some attention was paid to severity and in the worst, both certainty and severity were absent. In Norway, because IWT offences are regarded as misdemeanours rather than serious crimes, most offences are penalized very leniently with a fine, normally between 5,000 and 10,000 kroner.[10] If cases are taken to court they end with brief, suspended prison sentences and a fine. This is irrespective of how the cases are coded, whether animals are dead or alive. Within the UK, there are inconsistencies in how the different regulation and enforcement agencies apply penalties (e.g. fine, cautions). Interviewees believed for regulation to be effective, specialist training was required at all levels of the CJS, in particular for the CPS and judiciary due to the perceived lack of expertise and experience. However, training is reportedly neither provided (UK, Norway) nor desired (UK) due to the lack of priority given to IWT by these countries. In both locations, interviewees communicated a sense that the welfare of animal victims was not of primary concern for those prosecuting or sentencing IWT cases.

In Colombia, trafficking crimes are usually punished with a fine imposed by the environmental authorities; 2 per cent are punished as

[10] One euro is 9,27 NOK.

a criminal offence according to interviews. The punishment depends on the vulnerability of the species involved and on its economic value, which is also taken into account in some cases in Norway and the UK when determining the size of the fine. Likewise in Brazil, fines are widely applied: the São Paolo police imposed fines worth 27 million real in 2012 (about USD 12 million), and 29 million real (USD 13 million) in 2013. This money goes to the Ministry of Environment, as opposed to Norway where these fines are absorbed by the state budget.

5.7.4 Informal Prevention and Control

Norwegian NGOs play a minor role in informing and educating people about IWT, for example, the WWF has limited social media presence. South American NGOs, in contrast, are integral to the conservation and protection of wildlife and also in educating and supporting local people: Traffic (regional in Latin America), Corredor das Oncas (Brazil), and Proaves and Entropika (Colombia), the latter in the case of birds and primates, respectively. Likewise, UK NGOs have a fundamental role in educating the public, raising awareness, and campaigning for political support and funding to prevent IWT. They also collect evidence and, from a national and international perspective, help establish the nature and extent of IWT and support enforcement. A recent example of a successful NGO partnership involved World Animal Protection working with Crimestoppers[11] to provide the public with a free helpline to call and report IWT offences. Key UK enforcement agencies, such as customs, are also active in providing training (using confiscated goods) for enforcement and non-enforcement personnel and developing educational tools for members of the public. These agencies have developed an international reputation for their training and assistance to enforcement officers around the world.

[11] Independent not-for-profit helping law enforcement agencies locate criminals and solve crimes, providing an anonymous 24/7 phone number for the public to call and report a crime.

5.8 Concluding Thoughts/Recommendations

The focus of this chapter is on the harms and victimization of animals within the IWT. In conclusion, we identify the steps necessary to prevent future harm and victimization, suggesting a two-pronged approach. First, focus on preventing the victimization of animals is essential both within the legal wildlife trade and the IWT. Second, the existing formal and informal responses require re-evaluation and coordination in order to successfully respond to the IWT.

Preventing victimization will require reducing demand, limiting supply, and recognizing that animals are victims in the trade. If species justice is to be fulfilled, it must be accepted that these animals have individual interests and are victims, whether they are traded legally or illegally. If these animals are *only* considered to be property, commodities, and products in conventions, regulations, enforcement, and sentencing, their individual rights will be ignored and efforts to reduce demand will be limited. The IWT is widespread and multifarious in the four case study locations, and while a ban on wildlife trade in the near future is unlikely, there are smaller steps that can be taken to reduce, and ultimately ban, the trade, thereby preventing victimization and the aforementioned global impacts. Specifically, a sea change in attitudes towards the necessity of the 'uses' for these animals is required. Relying on our moral compass to bring this change about is inadequate. Rather, through research and science, we can establish change—acknowledging the intelligence, cognitive capacities, needs, and capabilities of these animals—based on data not available when CITES was established (e.g. Pepperberg's [2009] findings on the frequency of trafficking African grey parrots).

Shutting down consumer markets through creating awareness was recognized as the most important measure to be taken in Colombia and Brazil, and this knowledge must be expanded to consumer markets in the EU and beyond (e.g. in relation to the harmful consequences of the pet trade and trade in TCM). Enforcement agencies, politicians, NGOs, corporations, academics, and the media have a role to play; as our findings suggest, many consumers are unwittingly involved in legal and illegal trade due to lack of awareness. There must be a clear message to consumers, traders, and hunters in the legal trade and real consequences for those who engage in the illegal trade.

The development and enforcement of CITES and related legislation is central to the protection of animal victims, the focus of which should be to keep wildlife in their habitat by removing opportunities, motivation, and rewards for offending. The role of the EU as a (predominantly) transit and demand location means it is difficult to affect the trade at the point of origin, where the animals are removed from. However, this would be possible through the harmonization of regulations and enforcement practices in member states, international and national cooperation within enforcement agencies and between agencies, and increasing resources (financial, specialist training). Such coordinated efforts would strengthen the weakest areas in the EU and source countries. Furthermore, augmentation of animal welfare would be possible through revision of Council Regulation (EC) No 1/2005, in line with the enhanced welfare standards set out in the IATA LAR 2014/5.

Our findings suggest that formal responses to IWT are complex, diverse, and vary considerably from one location to another, including their effectiveness. While awareness and interest in IWT is growing in the EU, generally, formal responses suffer from a lack of priority, awareness, and coordination among relevant agencies. Evidence of the difficulties in enforcing and complying with CITES and related regulations were plentiful in our research. Confusion creates loopholes for offenders to take advantage of, reduces compliance, and impacts upon successful enforcement and prosecutions. The risk of detection is low, and punishment is generally absent or too lenient to create awareness or act as a deterrent. Prioritization of CITES cases across the CJS is required, which includes use of the full punishment threshold provided for in legislation.

We recommend that coordination between agencies and countries be enhanced in order to produce more robust data, to evidence the nature and prevalence of the trade, to enable and improve enforcement, and to create accountability (most importantly, in terms of the outcomes for animal victims and the prosecutions taken and sentencing received). Commitment to the use of EU-TWIX (and/or a global equivalent) is a simple option for enhanced cooperation. Another resource, freely available in all four locations, but not utilized, is the ICCWC Wildlife and Forest Crime Analytical Toolkit, which could help enforcement agencies identify the nature of the problem and the resources required, strengthen their enforcement strategy, and identify alternative responses to the trade. To cease being prime destinations for IWT, the EU, UK, and Norway must acknowledge the serious, negative consequences and increasingly organized nature of IWT, strengthen political will, reform their responses, better integrate the role of NGOs in the enforcement process, and better support informal responses (e.g. general awareness campaigns).

Well aware that the following might seem naive, we still argue that one way CITES and prospective regulations can develop would be to help phase out the current exploitative use of wildlife, and instead, generate profit from less harmful alternatives and provide genuine protection for animals. For example, rather than trophy hunted, animals could be 'shot' with a camera, rather than killing and trading animals for profit, revenue could be generated from protecting animals in ways, not only beneficial to the animals, but to local communities (with global effect), whose members could guide tourists to *see* animals in their natural habitats. CITES should better explore its role in reintroducing animals to habitats where they have been run into extinction and enhance its role as protector of entire ecosystems. CITES could *protect* wildlife, rather than regulating trade in it and thereby prolonging suffering and contributing to species extinction.

References

Andenæs, J. (1950). Almenprevensjonen-illusjon Eller Realitet [General deterrence—Illusion or reality], *Nordisk Tidsskrift for Kriminalvidenskab, 33*, 103–133.

Beirne, P., & South, N. (2007). Introduction to green criminology. In P. Beirne & N. South (Eds.), *Issues in green criminology* (pp. xiii–xxii). Devon: Willan

CITES (2013a). *How CITES works.* https://cites.org/eng/disc/how.php. Accessed 27 April 2016.

CITES (2013b). *The CITES species*. http://www.cites.org/eng/disc/species.php. Accessed 27 April 2016.
CITES (2016a). *Control of trade in personal and household effects*. https://cites.org/eng/res/13/13-07R16.php. Accessed 2 March 2016.
CITES (2016b). *Disposal of confiscated live specimens of species included in the appendices*. https://cites.org/sites/default/files/eng/res/all/10/E10-07R15.pdf. Accessed 12 March 2016.
CITES (2016c). *What is CITES?* https://cites.org/eng/disc/what.php. Accessed 2 February 2016.
Cohen, L.E., & Felson, M. (1979). Social change and crime rate trends: A routine activity approach. *American Sociological Review, 44*(04), 588–608.
Crawford, A. (1997). *Making CITES work: Examples of effective implementation and enforcement*. Cambridge: Traffic International.
Data.gov.uk. (2015). *Convention on international trade in endangered species (CITES) seizures and volumes*. http://data.gov.uk/dataset/convention-on-international-trade-in-endangered-species-cites-seizures-and-volumes/resource/334c3200-324f-4e51-b51d-b4f287908177. Accessed 12 March 2016.
EFFACE (2016). *European Union action to fight environmental crime*. http://efface.eu/. Accessed 27 April 2016.
European Commission (2010). *Wildlife trade regulations in the European Union. An introduction to CITES and its implementation in the European Union*. Luxembourg: European Commission.
European Commission (2016). *The European Union and trade in wild Fauna and Flora*, http://ec.europa.eu/environment/cites/legislation_en.htm. Accessed 27 April 2016.
EU-TWIX (2015). EU-TWIX: A tool to facilitate information exchange on illegal wildlife trade in the European Union. http://www.eutwix.org/. Accessed 25 April 2016.
Goyes, D.R. (2015). Denying the harms of animal abductions for biomedical research. In R. Sollund (Ed.), *Green harms and crimes: Critical criminology in a changing world* (pp. 170–208). London: Palgrave.
Her Majesty's Stationery Office (1979). Customs and excise management act 1979. http://www.legislation.gov.uk/ukpga/1979/2/contents. Accessed 24 April 2016.
Her Majesty's Stationery Office (1997). The control of trade in endangered species (Enforcement) regulations 1997. http://www.legislation.gov.uk/uksi/1997/1372/made. Accessed 24 April 2016.

Hill, J. (in press). A systems thinking perspective on the motivations and mechanisms driving wildlife poaching. In R. Sollund (Ed.), *Green harms and crime: Social injustice, protest and oppression*. London: Palgrave.

Hillyard, P., Pantazis, C., Tombs, S., Gordon, D. (2004). *Beyond criminology: Taking harm seriously*. London: Pluto Press.

Interpol and IFAW (International Fund for Animal Welfare) (2013). *Project web: An investigation into the ivory trade over the internet within the European Union*. Lyon: Interpol.

Kievit, H. (2000). Conservation of the Nile Crocodile: Has CITES helped or hindered? In J. Hutton, & B. Dickson (Eds.), *Endangered species—Threatened convention: The past, present and future of CITES*. London: Earthscan.

Lemieux, A. (ed.) (2014). *Situational prevention of poaching*. London: Routledge.

Lovdata (n.d.b.). Lov om jakt og fangst av vilt (viltloven). https://lovdata.no/dokument/NL/lov/1981-05-29-38. Accessed 19 May 2016.

Lovdata (n.d.c.). Lov om forvaltning av naturens mangfold (naturmangfoldloven). https://lovdata.no/dokument/NL/lov/2009-06-19-100?q=biologisk mangfold. Accessed 19 May 2016.

Lovdata (n.d.d). Lov om dyrevelferd. https://lovdata.no/dokument/NL/lov/2009-06-19-97. Accessed 19 May 2016.

Maher, J., & Sollund, R. (2016). Law enforcement of the illegal wildlife trade: A comparative strengths, weaknesses, opportunities and threats [SWOT] Analysis of the UK and Norway. In J. Schneider, A. Di Nicola, T. Wyatt (Eds.), *Journal of trafficking, organized crime and security—Special issue on illicit trafficking in wildlife and forest resources*. Boca Raton Brown Walker Press.

Maldonado, A.M., Nijman, V., Bearder, S.K. (2009). Trade in night monkeys Aotus spp. in the Brazil–Colombia–Peru Tri-border Area: International wildlife trade regulations are ineffectively enforced. *Endangered Species Research*, *9*(2), 143–149.

Minnaar, A. (2013). The poaching of Rhino in South Africa: A conservation, organised and economic crime?. In D. Sorvatzioti, G. Antonopolous, G. Papanicolaou, R. Sollund (Eds.), *Critical views on crime, policy and social control*. Nicosia: University of Nicosia Press.

Nassaro, M.R.F. (In print, 2016). Wildlife trafficking in the state of Sao Paulo, Brazil. In D.R. Goyes, H. Mol, A. Brisman, N. South (Eds.), *Environmental crime in Latin America: The theft of nature and the poisoning of the land*. London: Palgrave Macmillan.

Pepperberg, I.M. (2009). *The Alex studies: Cognitive and communicative abilities of grey parrots*. Cambridge: Harvard University Press.
Pires, S., & Clarke R. (2011). Are parrots CRAVED? An analysis of parrot poaching in Mexico. *Journal of Research in Crime and Delinquency, 49*(1), 122–146.
Pires, S., & Moreto, W. (2011). Preventing wildlife crimes: Solutions that can overcome the 'tragedy of the commons'. *European Journal of Crime Policy, 17*(2), 101–123.
Reeve, R. (2002). *Policing international trade in endangered species. The CITES treaty and compliance*. London: Earthscan.
Regan, T. (1983). *The case for animal rights*. Berkley: University of California Press.
Rivalan, P., Delmas, V., Angulo, E., Bull, L., Hall, R., Courchamp, F., Rosser A.M., Leader-Williams, N. (2007). Can bans stimulate wildlife trade?. *Nature, 447*, 529–530.
Schneider, J. (2012). *Sold into extinction: The global trade in endangered species*. Santa Barbara: Praeger.
Shepherd, C.R., Stengel, C.J., Nijman, V. (2012). *The export and re-export of CITES-listed birds from the Solomon Islands*. Petaling Jaya: Traffic Southeast Asia.
Sina, S., Gerstetter, C., Porsch, L., Roberts, E., O' Smith, L., Klaas, K., Fajardo, T. (2016). *Wildlife crime*. Brussels: European Parliament.
Sollund, R. (2011). Expressions of speciesism: The effects of keeping companion animals on animal abuse, animal trafficking and species decline. *Crime, Law and Social Change, 55*(5), 437–451.
Sollund, R. (2013). Animal trafficking and trade: Abuse and species injustice. In R. Walters, D. Westerhuis, T. Wyatt (Eds.), *Emerging issues in green criminology: Exploring power, justice and harm*. London: Palgrave. 72–93.
Sollund, R. (2015). Wildlife trafficking in a globalized world: An example of motivations and modus operandi from a Norwegian case study. In A. Francesco (Ed.), *Problematic wildlife. A cross-disciplinary approach*. Switzerland: Springer International Publishing. 553–573.
Sollund, R., & Maher, J. (2015). *Illegal wildlife trade: A case study report on the illegal wildlife trade in the United Kingdom, Norway, Colombia and Brazil*. http://efface.eu/illegal-wildlife-trade-case-study-report-illegal-wildlife-trade-united-kingdom-norway-colombia-and#overlay-context=case-studies. Accessed 12 April 2016.
Svae-Grotli, I. (2014). En Forbrytelse å la Alvorlig Miljøkriminalitet Forbli Forseelser. [A crime to allow serious environmental crime remain misdemeanors], *Miljøkrim, 1*, 30–36.

United Nations Office on Drugs and Crime (2012). *Wildlife and forest crime analytic toolkit* (revised ed.). Vienna: United Nations.

Van Uhm, D. (2014). Illegal wildlife trade to the EU and harms to the world. In T. Spapens, R. White, W. Huisman (Eds.), *Environmental crime and the world.* London: Ashgate. 43–67.

Van Uhm, D. (2016). *Uncovering the illegal wildlife trade. In the world of poachers, smugglers and traders.* New York: Springer.

Warchol, G., Zupan, L., Clarke W. (2003). Transnational criminality: An analysis of the illegal wildlife market in Southern Africa. *International Criminal Justice Review, 13*(1), 1–26.

Wellsmith, M. (2010). The applicability of crime prevention to problems of environmental harm: A consideration of illicit trade in endangered species. In R. White (Ed.), *Global environmental harm: Criminological perspectives.* Devon: Willan. 132–150.

Wellsmith, M. (2011). Wildlife crime: The problems of enforcement. *European Journal of Crime Policy, 17*(2), 125–148.

White, R. (2013). *Environmental harm: An eco-justice perspective.* Bristol: Policy Press.

Wyatt, T. (2009). Exploring the organization of Russia far east's illegal wildlife trade: Two case studies of the illegal fur and illegal falcon trades. *Global Crime, 10*(1 & 2), 144–154.

Wyatt, T. (2013a). *Wildlife trafficking: A deconstruction of the crime, the victims, and the offenders.* London: Palgrave Macmillan.

WWF (World Wildlife Fund for Nature) (2014a). *How many species are we losing?* http://wwf.panda.org/about_our_earth/biodiversity/biodiversity/. Accessed 5 December 2014.

WWF (World Wildlife Fund for Nature) (2014b). *Living planet report 2014. Species and spaces, people and places.* http://wwf.panda.org/about_our_earth/all_publications/living_planet_report. Accessed 12 April 2016.

Dr Jennifer Maher is a senior lecturer at the Centre for Criminology, University of South Wales, UK. Her research interests include animal abuse, green criminology, human-animal studies, and youth gangs and violence. She recently concluded research on wildlife trafficking from the UK perspective for the FP7 (European Commission) EFFACE project. She has published internationally in peer reviewed journals and books, in 2011 co-edited with Piers Beirne a special Issue on 'Animal Abuse and Criminology' in the journal Crime,

Law and Social Change and is co-editor in the forthcoming books: The international Handbook on Animal Abuse Studies and Greening Criminology in the 21st Century: Contemporary Debates and Future Directions in the Study of Environmental Harms.

Dr. Ragnhild Sollund is a professor in criminology at the University of Oslo. She has authored, edited, and co-edited 10 books, of which five in the field of green criminology, including *Global Harms: Ecological crime and speciesism*, Nova science publishers (2008); *Eco-global crimes: contemporary problems and future challenges*, (Ashgate 2012); and *Green harms and crimes: Critical criminology in a changing world*, (Palgrave, 2015). Her main research interest is currently legal and illegal wildlife harms; including wildlife trafficking and the illegal killing of protected predators. Before turning her research interest to environmental crimes, she did extensive research within the fields of migration, especially the situation for female migrants, and police racial profiling. She teaches criminology at the University of Oslo at BA/MA level, and is also supervising students at all levels.

6

Illegal Shipments of E-waste from the EU to China

Andrea Illés and Kristof Geeraerts

6.1 Introduction

Over the past two decades, the cross-border transport of e-waste[1] has significantly increased alongside the rise of illegal e-waste shipments from advanced economies to developing economies and newly industrialised economies. This has, without doubt, become a complex and serious environmental crime. Citizens of the European Union (EU) are consuming

[1] E-waste is the informal name for electrical and electronic devices that are at the end of their 'useful' life.

A. Illés (✉)
Institute for European Environmental Policy (IEEP),
London, UK
e-mail: ailles@ieep.eu

K. Geeraerts
Research Affairs and Innovation, University of Antwerp, Antwerp,
Belgium
e-mail: kristof.geeraerts@uantwerpen.be

R. Sollund et al. (eds.), *Fighting Environmental Crime in Europe and Beyond*, Palgrave Studies in Green Criminology,
DOI 10.1057/978-1-349-95085-0_6

electrical and electronic appliances more than ever. As a result, e-waste is one of the fastest growing waste streams within the EU (EEA 2012). At the same time, more stringent e-waste processing and recycling regulations in the EU are increasing the costs of legitimate treatment (OECD 2012), thereby enabling cheaper illegal activities that generate significant savings. For the illegal actors involved, illegal shipments to less advanced economies represent an economic opportunity; nevertheless, those receiving the e-waste, in particular those working in the informal e-waste processing sector,[2] where dismantling and recycling techniques are rudimental compared to the formal sector and do not comply with health and environmental safety standards,[3] are threatened by significant environmental, social, and health risks. The toxicity of this illegal trade has become renowned (see for instance BAN and SVTC 2002; Bridgen *et al.* 2005; ILO 2012) and is best shown by the images of endless piles of discarded computer monitors, television screens, copper wiring, and printed circuit boards in parts of Asia and Africa. These illegal e-waste shipments represent the costs to be paid for a throw-away approach to electrical and electronic equipment that has been a luxury primarily enjoyed by those in advanced and newly industrialised economies. In the world of developing and newly industrialised economies, China represents the largest downstream destination for e-waste exported from Europe. According to the United Nations Office on Drugs and Crime, around 80 per cent of the total global amount of e-waste ends up in Asia, with around 90 per cent being shipped to China (UNODC 2013, p. 105).

At the international level, the Basel Convention on the Control of Transboundary Movements of Hazardous Wastes and Their Disposal aims to control these illegal e-waste shipments, and this has been translated into EU law via the EU's Waste Shipment Regulation (WSR) (EU Parliament

[2] For instance, disassembling computers in small workshops or at home.

[3] When it comes to analysing environmental crime, one should understand the overlap between licit (formal) and illicit (informal) markets, as well as the close connection between legal and illegal actions. According to White (2009) a licit market is state regulated, open to public scrutiny, and based on legal activities, while an illicit market is unregulated, untaxed, and part of the subterranean, also called 'black', market. While there is a clear distinction between the two concepts, legal versus illegal and licit versus illicit, it should be recognised that an illegal activity may take place not only in the illicit (informal) sector but in the licit (formal) sector as well.

and EU Council 2006). Although the WSR forbids the export of e-waste from the EU to non-OECD countries, vast amounts of e-waste are estimated to illegally leave Europe each year. The EU legislative framework to fight illegal e-waste shipments also includes the Waste Electrical and Electronic Equipment (WEEE) Directive (EU Parliament and EU Council 2012), which establishes the definition of e-waste (see Box 6.1).

Box 6.1 Definition of e-waste and waste in EU legislation

According to the WEEE Directive, e-waste 'means electrical or electronic equipment which is waste within the meaning of Article 3(1) of Directive 2008/91/EC, including all components, subassemblies and consumables which are part of the product at the time of discarding'

The Waste Framework Directive (2008/91/EC) defines waste as 'any substance or object which the holder discards or intends or is required to discard'

Source: EU Parliament and EU Council, 2008; EU Parliament and EU Council, 2012

This chapter describes the illegal e-waste shipments from the EU to China (see geographical scope in Fig. 6.1), highlighting the estimated volumes of illegally exported e-waste, the key actors involved in the

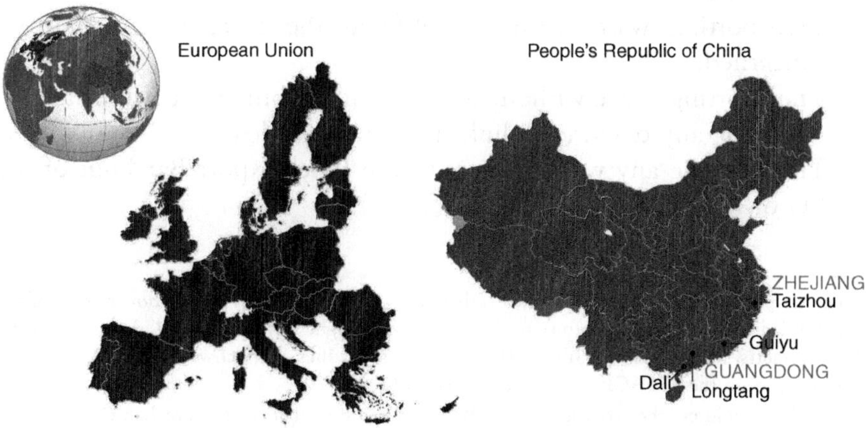

Fig. 6.1 Geographical scope of the case study: The EU and China's key informal dismantling and recycling sites. (*Source*: own representation)

illegal activities, the victims and the harms they suffer, and the legal framework of both the EU and China aiming to tackle this environmental crime.[4] As a conclusion, a set of policy recommendations is outlined that aim to support the fight against these illegal shipments. The research method applied includes an extensive literature review, a document analysis, and the undertaking of a limited number (five) of semi-structured interviews with key stakeholders, including waste experts and inspectors from national authorities, academics, and members of society.

6.2 What Is the Environmental Crime in Question?

6.2.1 The Nature of the Illegal Activity

The focus of this chapter is on illegal shipments of e-waste from the EU to China. One of the reasons for focusing on illegal shipments to China is that this country is considered to be the largest downstream destination for e-waste exported from Europe and North America. Under EU law, according to the WSR, illegal shipments of e-waste can take various forms. These include:

- Transporting waste without notifying the competent authorities concerned;
- Transporting waste without the consent of competent authorities;
- Falsifying any documents linked to the waste loads;
- Transporting any waste subject to the Basel Export Ban[5] out of the EU or the

[4] The chapter is primarily based on two earlier case studies written by the authors as part of the EU-funded research project European Union Action to Fight Environmental Crime (EFFACE). See Geeraerts, Mutafoglu, and Illés (2015) and Geeraerts, Illés, and Schweizer (2015). For more information on the EFFACE project, see Efface.eu (2016).

[5] In order to address the weakness of the Basel Convention that it does not ban the export of hazardous waste from advanced economies to less advanced economies, the Basel Ban Amendment (Basel Convention, 2014) was introduced in 1995, which does not allow the export of hazardous waste from OECD to non-OECD countries.

- Organisation for Economic Co-operation and Development (OECD) countries (e.g. transporting hazardous waste to non-OECD countries or exporting waste for disposal outside the EU);
- Mixing certain types of wastes; or
- Classifying hazardous waste as non-hazardous.

Even though all forms of illegal waste shipment violate the EU WSR, the impact of the different types of activities is not the same. The illegally exported e-waste shipments from the EU to China are not processed in a safe way and therefore pose significant environmental and human health risks. E-waste offences have also been connected to theft, smuggling, and financial offences such as money laundering and tax evasions (Huisman *et al.* 2015, p. 24).

In most cases, there is a very thin line between illegal and legal actions; a close connection between the legal and illegal e-waste markets indeed exists (Huisman *et al.* 2015, p. 24). Several studies suggest that many, if not all, legitimate companies dealing with e-waste are involved in illegal e-waste activities, either intentionally or unintentionally (Baird *et al.* 2014; Europol 2011). The Countering WEEE Illegal Trade (CWIT) project,[6] which studied numerous cases of e-waste offences in detail, concluded that in many cases, registered companies such as sorting and consolidation sites, recyclers, end processors, and logistics operators were involved (Huisman *et al.* 2015, p. 24).

In addition to minor unintentional (or intentional) violations or non-compliance by individuals or registered companies, illegal e-waste shipments may be the work of criminal organizations, that is, organizations following a criminal business model (Huisman *et al.* 2015, p. 24). A wide range of studies carried out by or on behalf of the United Nations (UN), the UN Office on Drugs and Crime (UNODC), Interpol, the EU, and several NGOs, confirm the link between illegal waste shipment and organised crime (Fajardo 2014). According to these studies, the illegal

[6] The CWIT project was a 2-year project ending in late 2015 funded by the 7th EU Framework Programme for Research and Innovation (FP7). It aimed to provide a set of recommendations to counter the illegal trade in e-waste. For more information, see Cwitproject.eu (2016).

export of e-waste involves less structured and centralized groups that are often only formed for a short period to commit the crime but do not stay together after the illegal action (Fajardo 2014). The 2011 EU Organised Crime Threat Assessment (Europol 2011, p. 40) concluded that these small informal groups usually consist of five to ten people, out of which at least one member has an ethnic link to the destination country.

6.2.2 The Extent of the Illegal Activity

Given the fact that the illegal shipment of e-waste is by its nature not explicitly tracked, the availability and quality of overall statistical data are low. Data unreliability also results from the lack of differentiation between new and used electrical and electronic equipment exported from the EU. This is an issue as the EU WSR does not prohibit the export of used (second-hand) electrical and electronic goods to non-OECD countries, creating a substantial loophole frequently used by exporters. Significant amounts of used goods, which in fact are non-functioning and thus should be considered e-waste, are shipped from the EU to the developing and newly industrialised economies as second-hand goods (EEA 2009, pp. 13–14).

Nevertheless, attempts to estimate illegal shipments for the years 2005 and 2012 have been made by Geeraerts, Mutafoglu, and Illés (2015) and are presented in Table 6.1. First, the estimate by Zoeteman *et al.* (2009) of the amounts of EU e-waste imported into China in 2005 was taken. Secondly, the EU e-waste imported to China in 2012 was estimated by applying Zoeteman *et al.*'s methodology to 2012 figures (Geeraerts et al. 2015). More details on the methodology can be found in Box 6.2.

Box 6.2 The methodology applied to estimate the extent of illegal e-waste shipments from the EU to China for 2005 and 2012

According to Zoeteman *et al.* (2009, p. 10), 0.74 million tonnes of e-waste originating from the EU were imported into China in 2005. This estimate was calculated as follows.

First, the generation of e-waste in the EU in 2005 was calculated by multiplying the number of EU inhabitants (475 million in 2005) by the average e-waste generated (15 kg/inhabitant/year) equalling to 7.01

million tonnes in 2005[7] (Geeraerts et al. 2015, p. 20; Zoeteman *et al.* 2009, p. 28).[8] In addition, Zoeteman *et al.* (2009) made separate estimates for four categories of e-waste including large household appliances, small household appliances, office and communication waste (e.g. computers and mobiles), and entertainment electronics (e.g. TVs and radios).

Second, the share of illegally exported e-waste was estimated. Zoeteman *et al.* (2009, p. 29) assumed that 10–20 per cent of the total amount of EU e-waste is illegally exported from the EU, and that 30 per cent of all used computers, TVs, and mobiles (two out of the four e-waste categories) generated in the EU are legally exported to developing and newly industrialised economies for reuse.[9] By adding up these figures, Zoeteman *et al.* (2009) estimated that 1.89 million tonnes of e-waste and used electronic goods left the EU in 2005 (Geeraerts, Mutafoglu, and Illés, 2015, p. 21; Zoeteman *et al.*, 2009, p. 29).[10]

Third, Zoeteman *et al.* (2009) estimated that 60 per cent of EU export ended up in Asia, of which 65 per cent was assumed to go to China and 35 per cent to India (5 per cent presumably going to smaller Asian countries. These estimations were based on, among others, estimations of amounts of e-waste processed regionally.) As a result, the import in China of e-waste from the EU was estimated to be around 0.74 million tonnes in 2005 (Geeraerts et al. 2015, p. 21–22; Zoeteman *et al.* 2009, p. 35).[11]

Based on this methodology, Geeraerts et al. (2015, pp. 20–23) estimated the volumes of e-waste illegally shipped (including used electronic goods shipped for reuse though ending up mostly as e-waste in China) from the EU to China for the year 2012.

First, they took the estimate of the Solving eh E-waste Problem (StEP) project: 9.91 million tonnes of e-waste generated in the EU in 2012 (StEP 2015).[12] Second, the share of illegally exported e-waste for 2012 was

---

[7] 475,000,000 (inhabitants) × 0.015 tonnes (15 kg/inhabitant/year) = 7,005,000 tonnes.

[8] In line with Zoeteman *et al.* (2009), Huisman *et al.* (2008, pp. 39–91) assumed that this amounted to 8.3 to 9.1 million tonnes, whereas UNODC (2013, p. 103) estimated the EU had generated 6.5 million tonnes of e-waste in 2008.

[9] Nevertheless, a considerable amount of these legally exported products become e-waste during the transport (e.g. as a result of insufficient protection during transport) or a short period of time after arriving in the destination country (BIO IS, 2013).

[10] 0.15 × 7,005,000 (e-waste) + 0.3 × (0.2 + 0.2) × 7,005,000 (used electronic goods) = 1,891,350 tonnes.

[11] 0.6 × 0.65 × 1,891,350 tonnes = 737,627 tonnes.

[12] The StEP project aims to tackles the problems of e-waste by bringing together all relevant stakeholders and carrying out research in the field.

estimated by applying the methodology of Zoeteman *et al.* (2009), thereby assuming that 15 per cent of all e-waste generated in the EU is exported illegally (and assuming that this percentage had not changed over the years),[13] and that 15 per cent of used electrical and electronic goods are shipped to developing and newly industrialised economies, mainly for reuse. The latter figure was taken from a 2013 study commissioned by the European Commission (BIO IS, 2013). It was thus estimated that approximately 2.98 million tonnes of e-waste and used electronic goods left the EU in 2012 (Geeraerts et al. 2015, p. 21).[14] Third, the imports from the EU into China were estimated, thereby assuming that in 2012, as in 2005, around 40 per cent (0.65 × 0.6) of EU exports ended up in China; approximately 1.16 million tonnes of e-waste.[15]

Table 6.1 Overview of key e-waste volume figures estimating the extent of the illegal activity in 2005 and 2012

Year	E-waste generated in the EU (mn tonnes)	E-waste exported from the EU (mn tonnes)	E-waste imported into China from the EU (mn tonnes)
2005	7.01[a]	1.89[a]	0.74[a]
2012	9.91[b]	2.98[c]	1.16[c]

Sources: [a]Zoeteman *et al.* (2009); [b]StEP (2015); [c]Geeraerts *et al.* (2015)

Estimates of total figures of e-waste imports in China are also available. According to the UNODC (2103, p. 110) approximately eight million tonnes of e-waste was imported into China in 2012.

It should be noted that given the uncertainties outlined earlier, the volumes indicated are rough estimates, which often are based on assumptions and extrapolations and should therefore be revisited and revised in light of further research. In this respect, the final report of the CWIT project (Huisman *et al.* 2015), which was published more recently, needs to be mentioned as it presents new and detailed assessments of the volumes of e-waste generated in the EU and of the volumes of e-waste exported

[13] Zoeteman *et al.* (2009) estimated that in 2005 10–20 per cent of the total amount of EU e-waste was illegally exported to non-EU countries.

[14] 0.15 × 9,918,000 (e-waste) + 0.15 × 9,918,000 (used electronic goods) = 2,975,400 tonnes.

[15] 0.6 × 0.65 × 2,975,400 tonnes = 1,160,406 tonnes.

from the EU, though volumes of exports to China or other destination countries have not been estimated. The CWIT consortium estimates that in 2012 the 28 member states of the EU, together with Norway and Switzerland, generated 9.45 million tonnes of e-waste (Huisman *et al.* 2015, p. 12), which is a slightly lower estimate than the 9.9 million estimate for the EU28 from the StEP project (StEP 2015) and used by Geeraerts, Mutafoglu, and Illés (2015). More importantly, the CWIT project estimated that 1.5 million tonnes of e-waste were exported out of the EU (200,000 tonnes of which is documented export of equipment), whereas Geeraerts, Mutafoglu, and Illés (2015) came up with an estimate of three million tonnes. How can this difference be explained?

First, both estimates of illegal exports are based on somewhat different estimates of the e-waste volumes generated in the EU, as explained earlier. However, this explains only a small portion of the difference. Most of the difference can be explained by the different methodologies applied to estimate the volumes of the exports.[16] Finally, the CWIT estimate may be considered as more conservative than the estimate by Geeraerts, Mutafoglu, and Illés, (2015). Just to give one example, Huisman *et al.* (2015) state that the estimate of 200,000 tonnes of documented export of used electrical and electronic appliances represents a minimum value, as this figure is based on detailed mass balances for five high-income countries only. Flows for other countries could not be quantified, although it is likely that these flows exist in other rich countries as well.[17]

[16] While Zoeteman *et al.* (2009) and Geeraerts, Mutafoglu, and Illés (2015) merely took an assumption-based percentage from the volumes of e-waste produced in the EU, the CWIT project (Huisman *et al.* 2015) conducted detailed assessments of the e-waste flows in the EU28+2, such as e-waste officially reported as collected and recycled; e-waste recycled under non-compliant conditions in Europe; e-waste scavenged for valuable parts; and discarded e-waste to arrive at the number of 1.5 million tonnes that is exported from the EU.

[17] Huisman *et al.* (2015) also refer to significant amounts of refrigerator compressors (84,000 tonnes which are scavenged) and IT components (180,000 tonnes) which are initially processed within the EU but end up being exported to Asia for further processing. These flows are not taken into account when estimating the flows that are being exported out of the EU. Instead, these numbers are incorporated into the estimate of 1.7 million tonnes that are initially processed within the EU and more in particular into the 750,000 tonnes of scavenged e-waste parts and fractions which do not make it to the official collection points.

Given the uncertainties surrounding the share of illegal exports (and the share of e-waste imported in China), Geeraerts, Mutafoglu, and Illés, (2015) have also generated a more conservative estimate.[18] According to this estimate, two million tonnes of e-waste in 2012 were exported from the EU, which is significantly closer to the CWIT estimate of 1.5 million.

6.2.3 Overview of Key Actors Involved

Research has shown that there is a very wide range of actors who are either directly or indirectly involved in the illegal export of e-waste from the EU to China (Bisschop 2012; Huisman *et al.* 2015). The export chain starts with the electrical and electronic equipment producers, retailers, and consumers, followed by formal and informal collectors, refurbishers, recyclers—a point where organised crime groups also link in—and ends with the informal dismantling and recycling sector in China. Figure 6.2 provides an overview of these actors and the linkages between them.

On-site investigations by the Environmental Investigation Agency (EIA) confirmed that after e-waste is disposed by consumers at collection points, the waste passes through a large number of hands before it reaches its final destination in developing and newly industrialised economies (EIA 2011). In view of this complex chain, civic amenity sites play an important role; on-site investigations in the UK, for instance, found that such sites routinely sell the disposed e-waste to external companies which then illegally export the e-waste from the EU to developing and newly industrialised economies (EIA 2011), but waste brokers, as well as waste tourists,[19] can also play an important role at this point of the export chain (Interpol 2009, pp. 20–23). At the same time,

[18] This was done within the context of the 'minimum export/import scenario', assuming a minimum export out of the EU and a minimum import of EU-waste into China. In this scenario, it was assumed that 10 per cent of EU e-waste is exported illegally out of the EU (instead of 15 per cent in the 'default scenario'), and that 10 per cent of e-waste is exported legally as used electronic goods (instead of 15 per cent).

[19] Waste tourists, who are in many cases involved in illegal activities, are individuals or groups who come from the destination countries and specifically travel to the EU to buy e-waste for export and/or sale (Interpol, 2009).

in contrast to illegal e-waste shipments to Africa, forwarding agents do not take an important part in illegal e-waste shipments to East Asia where shipping companies directly handle these shipments (Sander and Schilling 2010, pp. 61–65).

Even though the import of e-waste has been officially banned in China since 2000, vast amounts of e-waste are still crossing the Chinese border via a number of different routes. It then ends up in the informal dismantling and recycling sector that has been growing since the 1990s when imported e-waste began to enter China and individual recyclers started to use imported e-waste as sources for raw materials (Wang *et al.* 2013, pp. 21–28). The informal recycling sector primarily employs rural migrants

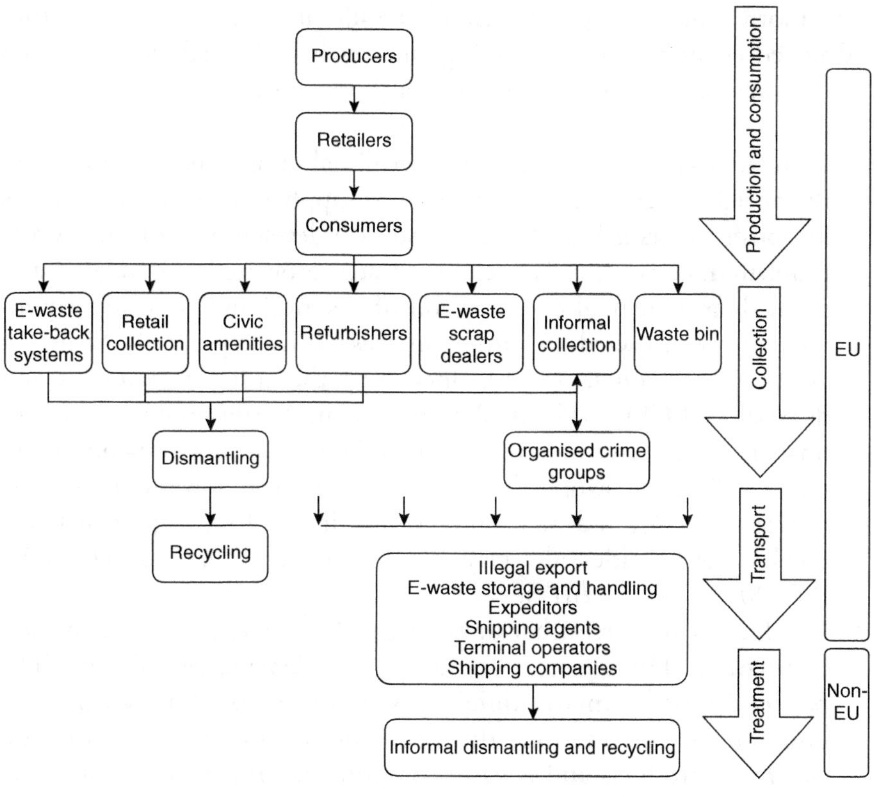

Fig. 6.2 Overview of key actors involved. (*Source*: authors' compilation based on Bisschop (2012) and Huisman *et al.* (2015))

from the agrarian regions of China, who are paid very low wages (on average USD 1.5 per day, Wang *et al.* 2013, pp. 21–28). The informally and illegally processed products are then, in most cases, sold by waste brokers to the manufacturing sector, both formal and informal (UNODC 2013). Nevertheless, compared to the unregulated informal sector, the formal state-regulated recycling sector is still at its early stages and mainly deals with domestically generated e-waste in China.

6.2.4 Motivations and Drivers behind the Illegal E-waste Shipments

The motivations and drivers behind the illegal e-waste shipments from advanced economies to developing and newly industrialised economies are characterised by three components (Bisschop 2012):

- Push factors are those forces that drive illegal shipments of e-waste from their origin. These factors are also called supply-side factors. One of the key push factors is linked to the historical development of the e-waste problem; today e-waste is one of the fastest growing waste streams, and given the exponential consumption of electrical and electronic equipment, it is projected to further increase (Bisschop 2012). Stringent e-waste legislation in the EU increasing the costs of treatment and disposal (OECD 2012) is also important. Furthermore, the recent financial crisis seems to have made recycling and dismantling businesses more willing to avoid the costs of legitimate e-waste processing (Eurojust 2014), and poor enforcement in the EU, in particular the low level of penalties, also plays a major role (BAN and SVTC 2002; ILO 2012; OECD 2012).
- Pull factors are forces that draw illegal shipments of e-waste to their destination. These factors are also called demand-side factors. The profits arising from the differences in the costs of treatment and disposal, as well as from the resale of functioning electrical and electronic products and e-waste components form an important pull factor (Liddick 2011; Odeyingbo 2011). In fact, large groups in China are dependent on the income from such illegal activities

(Li 2012). Furthermore, China's manufacturing sector has been gradually increasing the demand for such activities where the illegal activities feed into the legal e-waste industry (Bisschop 2012).

- Facilitating factors (i.e. factors that are contextual elements that make illegal shipments of e-waste possible) are low transportation costs to Asia, given that cargo ships from southeast Asia to Europe sail back to Asia in many cases with empty containers (Salehabadi 2013); the anonymity of containers (Bisschop 2012); the inadequate protection of e-waste collection points against theft (CWIT 2014), and the fact that e-waste can be easily mixed up or sold as second-hand electrical and electronic goods (Baird *et al.* 2014; Bisschop 2012).

6.3 Who Are the Victims and What Is the Harm They Suffer?

6.3.1 Overview of Key Groups of Victims

The most affected victims of the illegal e-waste shipments from the EU to China are those directly involved in the informal e-waste processing activities in China. The rudimentary methods employed in the informal recycling and dismantling sector put those involved in these practices in direct human health risks and create significant environmental risks. As the informal activities are spatially highly concentrated, exposure is highest in those Chinese towns involved in the informal sector (Breivik *et al.* 2014), including for instance Guiyu, Longtang, and Dali (see map in Fig. 6.1).

As discussed above, the majority of workers in the informal sector are poor, rural migrants, who are already at the margins of Chinese society; many are from ethnic and religious minorities (Hicks *et al.* 2005). Likewise, the presence of children, pregnant women, and young women with babies at the e-waste recycling and dismantling sites shows how these illegal e-waste processing activities impact those members of society who are most vulnerable and at risk (China Labour Bulletin 2005; ILO 2012). The impact of e-waste processing on these vulnerable groups highlights the inherent social inequalities and environmental discrimination reinforced by the illegal import of e-waste.

At the same time, the impact of informal e-waste dismantling and recycling is felt, not only at the e-waste processing sites, but in surrounding communities as well. In Beilin, China, it was shown that the homes of e-waste processing workers had high levels of toxic substances, putting even those who are not directly engaged in the industry at risk (Brigden *et al.* 2005). In addition, informal e-waste processing and recycling in some cases take place at the homes of the workers.

Contamination of food and water sources also poses significant risks to communities in the surrounding regions and eventually to the nation as well (Sepúlveda *et al.* 2010).

6.3.2 Key Environmental and Human Health Impacts

The illegal shipment of e-waste from the EU to China significantly affects the environment, societies, human health, and economies at multiple levels and carries significant risks on the ground (see Fig. 6.3). In not much more than a decade, e-waste has become the central factor in determining everyday realities for those living and working at sites of informal e-waste management (Hicks *et al.* 2005) and has brought substantial financial gains to those involved in the illegal shipments. It can be observed that imbalances in the global market economy, in access to resources, and in e-waste regulation are driving illegal e-waste flows and informal local management practices in China which exacerbate these inequities and, most critically, are degrading the natural environment and ecosystems and generating a number of acute human health risks (BAN and SVTC 2002; ILO 2012).

Environmental Impacts in China

The intensive informal and thus uncontrolled recycling and processing of e-waste in China has resulted in the release of large amounts of contaminants into the local environment, including heavy metals such as cadmium, lead, and mercury; polybrominated diphenyl ethers

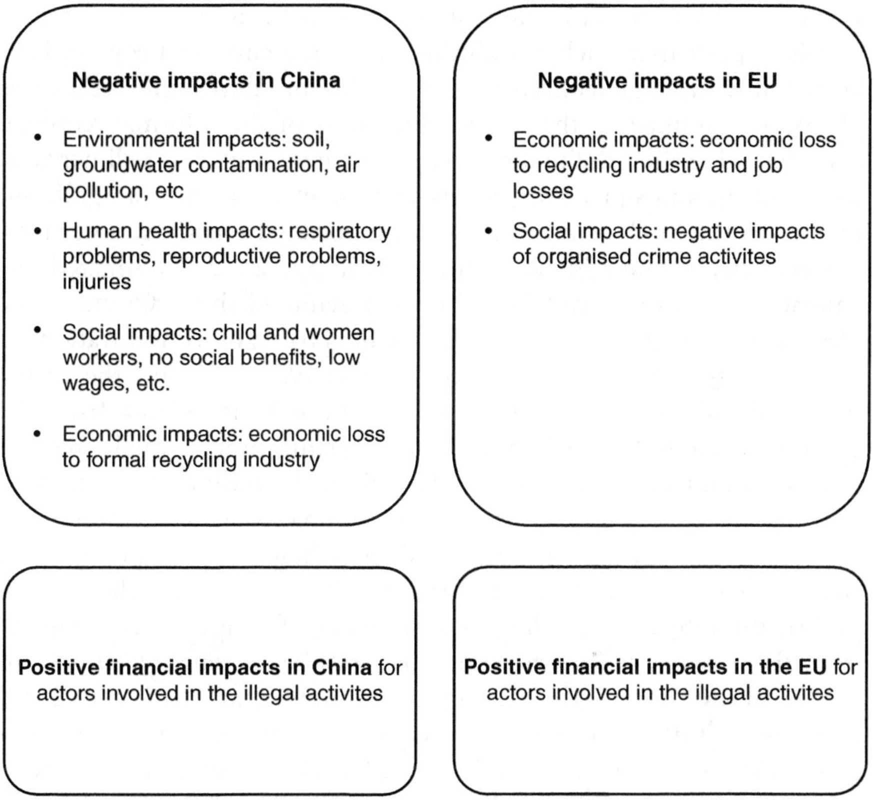

Fig. 6.3 Overview of key impacts of illegal e-waste shipments from the EU to China. (*Source*: authors' own representation)

(PBDEs); polychlorinated dibenzo dioxins/furans (PCDD/Fs); polychlorinated biphenyls (PBCs); chlorofluorocarbons (CFCs); and polycyclic aromatic hydrocarbons (PAHs).

Field and laboratory studies have shown the detrimental impact of toxic compounds released from informal e-waste processing on the environment, including air, soil, and water systems, as well ecosystems, plants, and animals (Walters and Santillo 2008). Many on-site investigations (see for instance Deng *et al.* 2007, Li *et al.* 2007, Wong *et al.* 2007) have found that the concentrations of various toxic compounds exceed the international standards and norms and therefore pose a significant risk to the environment and citizens living in the area. Heavy metals in particular, such as cadmium, lead, mercury, and copper, have been found in high concentrations in the air, dust, soil, sediments, plants, and animals in the surrounding areas of the informal recycling and processing sites. Pollutants can accumulate in soils and sediments, as well as plants and aquatic organisms, and therefore can have a significant impact on the food chain, which in turn poses serious risks to humans.

Geeraerts, Mutafoglu, and Illés (2015, pp. 24–25) estimated the annual emissions of a number of contaminants of the 2005 and 2012 illegal e-waste imports from the EU to China based on concentrations of components of Swiss e-waste (see Morf *et al.* 2007) and the earlier estimated volumes of e-waste illegally imported into China from the EU (see Table 6.2). Even though the recycling process might remove some contaminants, it is assumed that, given the rudimentary nature of this process, large amounts of toxic contaminants are still entering the local environment of the informal recycling and dumping sites. According to the estimates of Geeraerts, Mutafoglu, and Illés (2015, p. 24), the informal recycling and dumping of illegal e-waste imports from the EU has led to the (potential) release of roughly 10 and 16 tonnes of PCBs into the Chinese environment in 2005 and 2012, respectively. Other estimates have suggested that approximately 2,139 and 3,365 tonnes of lead and 7,598 and 11,952 tonnes of nickel were released in China in 2005 and 2012, respectively.

While these figures already indicate the seriousness of China's environmental problem as a result of informal e-waste recycling and processing activities, the magnitude of the actual contaminant emissions is much higher given that illegal e-waste imports are arriving not only from the EU but also from other developed parts of the world, such as the United States, South Korea, and Japan, given that the informal sector also processes a significant amount of domestically produced e-waste.

The pollutants released as a result of the informal e-waste recycling and processing activities not only harm the environment but have a much broader impact on the lives of those living in the surrounding areas. As a result of the contamination of groundwater, the drinking water supplies in Guiyu have been deteriorating to the extent that since

Table 6.2 Potential emissions of environmental pollutants in China from informal e-waste recycling or dumping in 2005 and 2012

Contaminant	Presence in e-waste	Typical e-waste concentration (mg/kg)	Annual emissions in China from e-waste imported from EU (tonnes)	
			In 2005[a]	In 2012[b]
Polychlorinated biphenyls (PCBs)	Condensers, transformers	14	10.3	16.2
Antimony (Sb)	Flame retardants, plastics	1,700	1,254.0	1,972.7
Cadmium (Cd)	Batteries, toner cartridges, plastics	180	132.8	208.9
Chromium (Cr)	Data tapes, floppy discs	9,900	7,302.5	11,488.0
Copper (Cu)	Wiring	41,000	30,242.7	47,576.6
Lead (Pb)	Solder, CRTs, batteries	2,900	2,139.1	3,365.2
Mercury (Hg)	Fluorescent lamps, batteries, switches	1	0.5	0.8
Nickel (Ni)	Batteries	10,300	7,597.6	11,952.2
Tin (Sn)	Solder, LDC screens	2,400	1,770.3	2,785.0
Zinc (Zn)	Batteries, CRTs	5,100	3,761.9	5,918.1

Source: Geeraerts *et al.* (2015); Morf *et al.* (2007); Robinson (2009)
[a]Assuming that, in 2005, 737,627 tonnes of e-waste were imported from the EU to China
[b]Assuming that, in 2012 1,160,406 tonnes of e-waste were imported from the EU to China

the late 1990s, clean drinking water has had to be shipped in from neighbouring towns (BAN and SVTC 2002, p. 16). The human health impacts of these pollutants are presented below.

Human Health Impacts in China

Geeraerts, Mutafoglu, and Illés (2015) demonstrate that illegal e-waste shipments from the EU have been, and probably still are, contributing to significantly increased incidences of chronic disease in China, threatening, not just workers at the informal sites but also residents of e-waste recycling areas and adjacent regions, as well as future generations. Illegal exports from the EU (together with exports from North America and other advanced economies) have resulted, and probably still result, in a high prevalence of skin, gastric, respiratory, hematic, neurological, prenatal, natal, and infant diseases in China. These diseases result from the exposure to e-waste and its hazardous components via informal processing and recycling and the resulting intake of contaminants through diet, inhalation, and soil/dust ingestion.

Select scientific studies (Grant *et al.* 2013) focusing on China show an association between exposure to e-waste and compromised physical health such as decreased lung function (i.e. lower forced vital capacity); decreased physical growth of children (i.e. lower weight, height, and body-mass index); reduced reproductive health (i.e. increases in spontaneous abortions, stillbirths, and premature births, and reduced birth weights and birth lengths); and changes in cellular expression and function (i.e. increased DNA damage).

Geeraerts, Mutafoglu, and Illés (2015) in particular sought to quantify the impact of lead poisoning resulting from e-waste exposure on children's neurological development, expressed in terms of children's IQ scores. It has been suggested that for each 10 µg/dl of blood lead, IQ is reduced by at least one to three points (Morgan 2013 quoted in Science Communication Unit 2013). It is indeed well known that lead, like other heavy metals, persists in the environment and leads to poisoning at low concentrations through bioaccumulation in plants and animals or bioconcentration in the food chain (Song and Li 2014). Furthermore, the oral ingestion of contaminated food is an important pathway for the uptake of lead, and children in particular are susceptible to heavy metal exposure due to high gastrointestinal uptake (Ogunseitan 2013). Lead in human bodies is known to interfere with behaviour and learning abilities (Grant *et al.* 2013; Song and Li 2014).

Based on data from various studies, Geeraerts, Mutafoglu, and Illés (2015) concluded that almost all children living in informal e-waste recycling centres such as Guiyu and Taizhou are, or at least have been, subject to a level of lead exposure that exceeds the dietary intake value per day at which neurodevelopmental toxicity affects children as determined by the European Food Safety Authority (EFSA) Panel on Contaminants in the Food Chain (EFSA 2010).[20] Geeraerts, Mutafoglu, and Illés (2015) also refer to several studies that state that very high average blood lead levels have been found in children in Guiyu and Taizhou, indicating that the daily dietary intake value (as determined by the EFSA Panel) has been exceeded multiple times.[21]

According to Geeraerts, Mutafoglu, and Illés (2015), this implies that potentially the neurological development of all the children living in these informal e-waste recycling areas has been affected. It was estimated that roughly between 16,000 and 26,000 children born in Guiyu in the period 1995–2013 have had blood lead levels exceeding the earlier mentioned daily dietary intake level and, as a result, have experienced a drop in intelligence due to the developmental neurotoxicity impact of informal e-waste recycling and dumping. For China as a whole, it was estimated that the neurological development of between 58,000 and 93,000 children born in the period 1995–2013 has been affected as a result of e-waste exposure. It was subsequently estimated that these children combined lost between 70,000 and 112,000 IQ points as a result of informal e-waste recycling and dumping activities, amounting to an average reduction of intelligence of 1.2 points per child.

---

[20] The benchmark dose approach (BMD) by definition is a dosage which is associated with a specified change in response, the benchmark response (BMR). The benchmark dose level (BMDL) is the BMD's lower confidence bound, and it is usually used as a reference point. For instance, for a BMR of 1 per cent, the BMDL, the benchmark dose lower confidence limit, can be interpreted as $BMDL_{01}$ and indicates a dose where the response is likely to be smaller than 1 per cent. The term 'likely' is defined by the statistical confidence level, usually 95 per cent. The EFSA Panel determined that the reference point for the risk characterisation of lead when assessing the risk of intellectual deficits in children measured by the full-scale IQ score is 12 μg/L (B-Pb) at the 95th percentile lower confidence limit of the benchmark dose (BMD) of 1 per cent extra risk ($BMDL_{01}$). For this BMDL of 12 μg/L (B-Pb), the corresponding dietary lead intake value for developmental neurotoxicity in 6-year-old children calculated by the EFSA Panel is 0.50 μg/kg bw per day (EFSA, 2009)

[21] The blood levels exceeded the $BMDL_{01}$ of 12 μg/L (corresponding to the 0.50 μg/kg bw per day dietary intake value) multiple times, with most blood lead levels significantly higher than 100 μg/L (or 10 μg/dl) (EFSA, 2010)

Geeraerts, Mutafoglu, and Illés (2015), however, noted that these figures provide an initial order of magnitude estimate. More accurate estimates might be generated in future research on the basis of more detailed data.[22] Furthermore, due to a lack of data on the precise contribution of EU-borne e-waste to the overall e-waste exposure and to the overall exposure to pollutants, it was not possible to quantify the health impacts in China from EU-borne e-waste only.

Finally, many more quantifications can be carried out for other pollutants (and for combinations, 'cocktails', of pollutants), for other health impacts (e.g. cardiovascular effects), and for other groups of people (e.g. adults living in regions adjacent to informal e-waste recycling areas). Neither health impacts in the longer term have been quantified. In fact, some longer term risks may yet to develop and will need to be understood (Geeraerts, Mutafoglu, and Illés, 2015, p. 45).

6.4 How Do Law Enforcement Agencies React to These Crimes?

6.4.1 The EU Legal Framework and Its Effectiveness and Enforcement

The current EU legal framework to tackle illegal e-waste shipments to developing and newly industrialised economies, which translates the international Basel Convention on the Control of Transboundary Movements of Hazardous Wastes and their Disposal (see Box 6.3) into EU law, primarily includes the WSR (EU Parliament and EU Council 2006) and the Waste Electrical and Electronic Equipment (WEEE) Directive (EU Parliament and EU Council 2012).

[22] More detailed data on the number of children exposed to e-waste, on blood lead levels in children, and on the contribution of e-waste exposure to these blood lead levels. It remains to be seen whether these data can be generated or will become available in the near future.

Box 6.3 The Basel convention

The transboundary movement of e-waste at the international level is guarded by the Basel Convention on the Control of Transboundary Movements of Hazardous Wastes and Their Disposal, which came into force in 1992 and currently has 183 Parties. The Basel Convention seeks to provide enhanced control of the transboundary shipment of hazardous and non-hazardous waste and to reduce the frequency of such movements. It regulates the import and export of waste streams, poses requirements for notice and consent of the movements of the wastes, and aims to act as an incentive for environmentally sound management of the waste streams.

The Basel Convention, however, does not ban the export of hazardous waste from advanced economies to less advanced economies. In order to address this gap, the Basel Ban Amendment was introduced in 1995, which does not allow the export of hazardous waste intended for final disposal and bans the export of hazardous wastes destined for recycling and recovery from OECD to non-OECD countries. Nevertheless, until now the amendment has not been ratified by three-fourths of the parties and therefore it has not yet entered into force.

Source: UNEP, 1989; Basel Convention, 2014

The EU WSR requires member states to control waste shipments; the authorisation of a specific waste shipment depends on the nature of the transboundary movement (import, export, or transit); the processing method (disposal or recycling); the type of waste (less hazardous or more hazardous)[23]; and the country of destination (OECD or non-OECD countries). Overall, the WSR imposes stricter requirements on shipments that are disposed than on waste shipments that are recovered. It also imposes strict requirements on shipments posing significant environmental and health risks and on shipments destined to non-OECD countries. In contrast to the Basel Convention, the EU WSR bans the export of e-waste to non-OECD countries.

Even though the requirements of the EU WSR establish a robust framework to tackle illegal shipments, weaknesses have been detected. A recent report by the Dutch Court of Audit (Algemene Rekenkamer 2013)

[23] The WSR classifies waste as 'green' (less hazardous) or 'amber' (more hazardous) and lists hazardous waste that is subject to export prohibition (EU Parliament and EU Council 2006).

compiling the results of eight national audits[24] on the enforcement of the WSR revealed that huge differences exist between the analysed member states in terms of the number and nature of inspections, the availability of resources, the number and nature of enforcement organisations involved, and the existence of enforcement strategies. The audits found that the involvement of multiple enforcement organisations, including customs, police services, environmental agencies, and environmental inspectorates created challenges to coordination and cooperation. The information management in the countries audited was found to be inadequate for the purpose of enforcing the WSR. Furthermore, huge differences among EU member states have been revealed in relation to the extent to which environmental crimes are prosecuted and the way infringements are penalised. Findings also showed that most European countries make only limited use of sanctions (Algemene Rekenkamer 2013). The substantial differences in enforcement between member states have led to the phenomenon of 'port hopping' where illegal e-waste exporters choose those ports where control is regarded to be the weakest (EC 2013).

In recognizing such weaknesses, the WSR was revised in mid-2014 with the aim to reinforce a range of measures to ensure a more uniform implementation of the regulation throughout the EU (EU Parliament and EU Council 2014). By 1 January 2017, member states have to establish risk-assessment inspection plans, which must include the objectives and priorities of the inspections, the geographical area covered by the inspection plans, and the tasks assigned to each authority involved. The inspection plans must be regularly reviewed and updated at least every 3 years. The amendment grants inspectors more power to demand documentary evidence from suspected illegal waste exporters and therefore shifts the burden of proof regarding the distinction between waste and product to the suspected illegal exporters. Upstream inspections are also reinforced, and the new regulation includes a minimum number of physical checks in the waste shipment inspections. Member states are

[24] Bulgaria, Greece, Hungary, Ireland, Poland, Norway, the Netherlands, and Slovenia.

also required to strengthen cooperation between the different enforcement authorities and provide training for inspectors.

In 2012, amendments were also introduced to the WEEE Directive, some of which have a direct effect on e-waste shipments. Article 10 on the shipments of e-waste, referring to the WSR and the recast Directive (EU Parliament and EU Council 2012), was added, which introduced tighter requirements on providing documentary evidence of the functionality of used electrical and electronic equipment that may be exported. Furthermore, the recast WEEE Directive has raised the mandatory e-waste collection targets, which indirectly also affects illegal e-waste activities as it has the potential to reduce the risk of leakage of e-waste from the formal collection and treatment into illegal circuits.

These extensive amendments have great potential to address the weak points in the enforcement chain of e-waste shipments, in particular inspections. At the same time, because the WSR amendments need only be implemented by 2017, it is yet to be seen how willing the individual member states will be to provide the necessary resources (such as budget and staff) to implement the new provisions in a meaningful way. Therefore, the amendments per se cannot guarantee a sufficient improvement in enforcement.

6.4.2 Chinese E-waste Legislation and Policies and Their Effectiveness

In 2000, the Chinese government introduced an official ban on importing e-waste into China via the Notification of the Import of the Seventh Category of Solid Waste (No. 19/2000). Since then further regulations targeting e-waste have been implemented in China, establishing the 'polluter pays principle', the 'reduce, reuse, and recycle' approaches to e-waste, as well as aims to reduce the use of hazardous and toxic substances in electrical and electronic equipment (Wang *et al.* 2013, pp. 29–32).

In essence, the Chinese government has to tackle its e-waste problems in two key areas: 1) stopping the illegal import of e-waste into the country and, simultaneously, 2) fighting informal e-waste recycling activities and improving the formal e-waste recycling sector. With regard to the latter, in the last 10–12 years, the Chinese government has made great efforts to introduce advanced e-waste recycling technologies and waste management principles from Western countries. Nevertheless, attempts to formalize the Chinese e-waste recycling sector have proven to be very difficult and challenging (ILO 2012; Li 2012). Formal recycling and treatment facilities are not able to collect sufficient volumes of e-waste and cannot compete with the low costs of the informal processing sector. In becoming aware of such difficulties, the Chinese government has chosen an approach to incentivize informal recyclers to shift to formal processes and to divert e-waste volumes from the informal sector to the formal sector (ILO 2012). The changes to the Chinese economy, including increased employment opportunities and higher salaries, are also expected to reduce the role of the informal recycling sector. At the same time, the consumption of electrical and electronic products and, therefore, the volumes of domestically generated e-waste, are increasing, which has started to gradually transform China into an e-waste exporter to poorer countries, often African ones (Kennedy 2015).

In recent years, the Chinese government has also been stepping up its efforts to halt or reduce illegal e-waste imports. In 2013, China's first major campaign Operation to Green Fence, which was launched to enforce its waste quality legislation, aimed to better control the containerized waste imports. Between February and November 2013,[25] Chinese environmental and custom officials undertook more robust and stringent inspections and physical checks of shipments of various types of wastes, including e-waste, plastic, paper, and textiles, primarily from Europe and North America coming into mainland China. As a result of the operation, hundreds of thousands of tonnes of waste have been rejected, and shipping companies were told to return these shipments to the sender. The import licences of many companies were suspended,

[25] Even though the Chinese government has not confirmed this officially, Michael Lion, current chairman of Sims Metal Management Asia Limited, in a seminar in New York in June 2015 said that Part II of the Operation Green Fence may be coming soon (LeBlanc 2015).

and, according to the International Solid Waste Association (ISWA), in the first three months of the campaign, 55 shipments were stopped and 7,600 tonnes of recyclable materials rejected, resulting in containers piling up in the ports (Earley 2013).

At the same time, a legal loophole that allows the illegal import of e-waste into mainland China to be facilitated via Hong Kong is often used by exporters. Even though Hong Kong is a Special Administrative Region (SAR) of China, there is a legislative difference between the two countries and the ban on e-waste imports adopted in Chinese legislation does not apply in Hong Kong. Subsequently, second-hand electrical and electronic devices and e-waste can be imported into Hong Kong, and once they have been imported they can easily be transported to other countries, including mainland China (Yoshida 2005 quoted in Wang *et al.* 2013). Furthermore, illegal exports of e-waste to China often avoid detection by going through Taipei, Vietnam, or the Philippines from where e-waste is transhipped to smaller ports in China, where customs officers can be bribed by the exporters (ILO 2012; Wang *et al.* 2013).

6.5 Conclusions: Policy Implications and Recommendations

As indicated above, the recently introduced amendments to the EU WSR and the WEEE Directive have the potential to improve inspection and enforcement. Nevertheless, the success of these changes will greatly depend on whether national policymakers will see the fight against transnational e-waste crimes as a priority and whether individual member states will be willing to provide the necessary resources, including sufficient budgets and staff, to implement the new requirements.

There is a very thin line between illegal and legal actions in relation to transnational e-waste shipments and, therefore, it is suggested that the focus of enforcement within the member states should not only be strictly on crimes. National authorities should be encouraged even further to introduce a more integrated approach towards enforcement. The quality of inspections, intelligence, and evidence gathering prior to prosecution should be improved, for example, through intelligence-based risk assessments; better detection techniques; smarter upstream inspections to prevent illegal activities moving downstream in the e-waste chain; and providing specialized training for staff, including police, customs, and environment inspectors. There is also a great need to further improve and harmonize prosecution in the EU as the types of sanctions used within member states and their effectiveness vary greatly. Furthermore, national policymakers should aim to improve national-level cooperation among authorities involved in fighting illegal e-waste shipments and other e-waste crimes, for instance, by setting up a national task force, and should also involve other stakeholders through multi-stakeholder networks. In order to enhance cooperation in the EU at supranational level, EU policymakers could play a facilitating role and support various initiatives, such as the establishment of joint multinational investigation teams specifically focusing on illegal e-waste shipments or the setting up of a list of contact points of national prosecutors where relevant case law best practices could be shared.

Even though improving the enforcement of the WSR, and in particular inspections, is key to tackling illegal e-waste shipments leaving the EU, other more underlying problems of e-waste crimes also need to be addressed. First, the source of the problem, that is, the large volume of e-waste and the toxic substances within it, should be targeted. There is a great need for policies that are even more than now directed towards the prevention and reduction of e-waste; the reduction of the consumption of electronic and electrical products in Europe and the production of more environmentally friendly products, which contain less toxic substances and are easier to dismantle and recycle, are essential. Second, the collection of e-waste should be improved by enhancing security at collection points to avoid thefts, making collection points more accessible and visible for the public, and increasing the number of collection points. This recommendation is also seen as a key priority by Huisman *et al.* (2015), who suggest that actions on collection points need to take place in the short term (in 1–3 years) as this has great potential to improve the entire e-waste chain in a relatively short period. Third, the reuse of used electronic and electrical appliances should be improved by harmonizing the definition of reuse, by developing and harmonizing reuse standards and guidelines, and by providing training and capacity building for the reuse industry, including the refurbishment industry. Fourth, more targeted awareness raising is needed to make sure that consumers of electronic and electrical products are aware of correct e-waste disposal methods, the shipment of illegal e-waste and how their disposal behaviour may contribute to it, and the environmental and public health damage caused by these illegal shipments. Finally, in order to have a better overview of the magnitude of the problems linked to illegal e-waste shipments, reporting and monitoring activities also need to be improved.

References

Algemene Rekenkamer (2013). *Coordinated audit on the enforcement of the European waste shipment regulation: Joint report based on eight national audits.* The Hague: Algemene Rekenkamer/Netherlands Court of Audit. http://www.eca.europa.eu/sites/cc/Lists/CCDocuments/other%20publications/Coordinated_audit_on_the_enforcement_of_the_European_Waste_Shipment_Regulation.pdf.

Baird J., Curry, R., Cruz, P. (2014). An overview of waste crime, its characteristics, and the vulnerability of the EU waste sector. *Waste Management & Research*, *32*, 97–105.

BAN, & SVTC (2002). *Exporting harm: The high-tech trashing of Asia.* US: The Basel Action Network (BAN) and Silicon Valley Toxics Coalition (SVTC). http://www.ban.org/E-waste/technotrashfinalcomp.pdf.

Basel Convention (2014). *Basel convention ban amendment.* http://www.basel.int/Implementation/LegalMatters/BanAmendment/Overview/tabid/1484/Default.aspx. date Accessed 25 November 2014.

Bisschop, L. (2012). Is it all going to waste? Illegal transports of e-waste in a European trade hub. *Crime, Law and Social Change, 58*(2012), 221–249.

Breivik, K., Armitage, J. M., Wania, F., & Jones, K. C. (2014). Tracking the global generation and exports of e-waste. Do existing estimates add up? *Environmental science & technology*, *48*(15), 8735–8743.

Brigden, K., Labunska, I., Santillo, D., Allsopp, M. (2005). *Recycling of electronic wastes in China & India: Workplace & environmental contamination.* Amsterdam: Greenpeace International. http://www.greenpeace.org/international/PageFiles/25134/recycling-of-electronic-waste.pdf.

China Labour Bulletin (2005). *The plight of China's e-waste workers.* http://www.clb.org.hk/en/node/16058/print.

CWIT (2014). *Countering WEEE illegal trade project workshop Lyon 16 & 17 October 2014.* http://www.cwitproject.eu/cwit-workshop/.

Cwitproject.eu (2016). Countering WEEE Illegal Trade. http://www.cwitproject.eu/, date accessed 11 January 2016.

Deng, W., Louie, P., Liu, W., Bi, X., Fu, J., Wong, M. (2007). Distribution of PBDEs in air particles from an electronic waste recycling site compared with Guangzhou and Hong Kong, South China. *Environment International, 33*(8), 1063–1069.

EC (2013). *Commission staff working paper: Impact assessment accompanying document to a legislative proposal and additional non-legislative measures strengthening the inspections and enforcement of regulation (EC) No 1013/2006 of the European parliament and of the council of 14 June 2006 on shipments of waste.* Brussels: EU. SWD(2013) 268.

EEA. (2009). *Waste without borders in the EU? Transboundary shipments of waste.* Copenhagen: European Environment Agency. http://www.eea.europa.eu/publications/waste-without-borders-in-the-eu-transboundary-shipments-of-waste.

Efface.eu (2016). *EFFACE – a research project on environmental crime.* http://www.efface.eu. date Accessed 11 January 2016.

EFSA Assessment and Methodological Support (2009). Guidance of the scientific committee on use of the benchmark dose approach in risk assessment [1]. *EFSA Journal,* 1150, doi: 10.2903/j.efsa.2009.1150.

EFSA Panel on Contaminants in the Food Chain (2010). Scientific opinion on lead in food. *EFSA Journal, 8*(4), 1570, doi: 10.2903/j.efsa.2010.1570.

EIA (2011). *System failure: The UK's harmful trade in electronic waste.* London: Environmental Investigation Agency. http://www.greencustoms.org/docs/EIA_E-waste_report_0511_WEB.pdf.

EU Parliament and EU Council (2003). Directive 2002/96/EC of the European Parliament and of the Council of 27 January 2003 on Waste Electrical and Electronic Equipment (WEEE). OJ L 37. 13.2.2003, 24–38.

EU Parliament and EU Council (2006). Regulation (EC) No 1013/2006 of the European Parliament and of the Council of 14 June 2006 on shipments of waste. OJ L 190, 12.7.2006, 1.

EU Parliament and EU Council (2008). Directive 2008/98/EC of the European Parliament and of the Council of 19 November 2008 on waste and repealing certain Directives. OJ L 312. 22.11.2008, 3–30.

EU Parliament and EU Council (2012). Directive 2012/19/EU of the European Parliament and of the Council of 4 July 2012 on waste electrical and electronic equipment (WEEE). OJ L 197. 24.7.2012, 38–71.

EU Parliament and EU Council (2014). Regulation (EU) No 660/2014 of the European Parliament and of the Council of 15 May 2014 amending Regulation (EC) No 1013/2006 on shipments of waste. OJ L 189, 27.6.2014, 135–142.

Eurojust (2014). *Strategic project on environmental crime.* The Hague: Eurojust. http://www.eurojust.europa.eu/doclibrary/Eurojust-framework/Casework/Strategic%20project%20on%20environmental%20crime%20%28October%202014%29/environmental-crime-report_2014-11-21-EN.pdf.

Europol (2011). *OCTA 2011. EU organised crime threat assessment.* European Police Office. https://www.europol.europa.eu/content/publication/octa-2011-eu-organised-crime-threat-assesment-1465.

Fajardo, T. (2014). *Legal analysis of international instruments on organised crime in the perspective of fighting environmental crime. Study in the framework of the EFFACE research project.* Granada: University of Granada.

Geeraerts, K., Illés, A., Schweizer, J-P. (2015). *Illegal shipment of e-waste from the EU: A case study on illegal e-waste export from the EU to China. A study compiled as part of the EFFACE project.* London: Institute for European Environmental Policy.

Geeraerts, K., Mutafoglu, K. and Illés, A. (2015). *Illegal e-waste shipments from the eu to china. quantitative and monetary analysis of illegal shipments and its environmental, social and economic impacts. A study compiled as part of the EFFACE project.* London: Institute for European Environmental Policy.

Grant, K., Goldizen, F.C., Sly, P.D., Brune, M.N., Neira, M., van den Berg, M., Norman, R.E. (2013). Health consequences of exposure to e-waste: A systematic review. *Lancet Global Health*, *1*, 350–361.

Hicks, C., Dietmar, R., Eugster, M. (2005). The recycling and disposal of electrical and electronic waste in China—legislative and market responses. *Environmental Impact Assessment Review*, *25*, 459–471.

Huisman, J., Botezatu, I., Herreras, L., Liddane, M., Hintsa, J., Luda di Cortemiglia, V., Leroy, P., Vermeersch, E., Mohanty, S., van den Brink, S., Ghenciu, B., Dimitrova, D., Nash, E., Shryane, T., Wieting, M., Kehoe, J., Baldé, C.P., Magalini, F., Zanasi, A., Ruini, F., Männistö, T., Bonzio, A. (2015). *Countering WEEE illegal trade (CWIT) summary report, market assessment, legal analysis, crime analysis and recommendations roadmap*, August 30, 2015, Lyon, France, http://www.cwitproject.eu/wp-content/uploads/2015/09/CWIT-Final-Report.pdf.

Huisman J., Magalini, F., Kuehr, R., Maurer, C., Oglivie, S., Poll, J., Delgado, C., Artim, E., Szlezak, J., Stevels, A. (2008). *2008 review of directive 2002/96 on waste electrical and electronic equipment (WEEE)—Final report*. Bonn: United Nations University.

ILO (2012). *The global impact of e-waste: Addressing the challenge*. Geneva: International Labour Office. http://www.ilo.org/wcmsp5/groups/public/—ed_dialogue/—sector/documents/publication/wcms_196105.pdf.

Interpol (2009). *Electronic waste and organised crime: Assessing the link (Phase II Report for the Interpol Pollution Crime Working Group)*. http://www.interpol.int/Crime-areas/Environmental-crime/Resources.

Kennedy, J. (2015). *China's role in illegal trade of toxic e-waste rising sharply*. https://www.chinafile.com/reporting-opinion/environment/chinas-role-illegal-trade-toxic-e-waste-rising-sharply.

LeBlanc, R. (2015). *Operation green fence: Key questions addressed*. http://recycling.about.com/od/Resources/tp/Operation-Green-Fence-Key-Questions-Answered.htm.

Li, G.-M. (2012). WEEE management in China. In V. Goodship, & A. Stevels (Eds.), *Waste electrical and electronic equipment (WEEE) handbook*, 526–549. Oxford: Philips Woodhead Publishing.

Li, H., Yu, L., Sheng, G., Fu, J., Peng, P. (2007). Severe PCDD/F and PBDD/F Pollution in air around an electronic waste dismantling area in China. *Environmental Science and Technology, 41*(16), 5641–5646.

Liddick, D.R. (2011). *Crimes against nature: Illegal industries and the global environment*. Santa Barbara: Praeger.

Morf, L.S., Tremp, J., Gloor, R., Schuppisser, F., Stengele, M., Taverna, R. (2007). Metals, non-metals and PCB in electrical and electronic waste—actual levels in Switzerland. *Waste Management 2007, 27*, 1306–1316.

Ni, H.-G., & Zeng, E.Y. (2009). Law enforcement and global collaboration are the keys to containing e-waste tsunami in China. *Environmental Science & Technology, 43*(2009), 3991–3994.

Odeyingbo, O.A. (2011). *Assessment of the flow and driving forces of used electrical and electronic equipment into Nigeria and within Nigeria*. Unpublished Master's Thesis. BTU Cottbus: Cottbus.

OECD (2012). *Illegal trade in environmentally sensitive goods. OECD trade policy studies*. OECD Publishing. http://www.oecd-ilibrary.org/trade/illegal-trade-in-environmentally-sensitive-goods_9789264174238-en.

Ogunseitan, O.A. (2013). The Basel convention and e-waste: Translation of scientific uncertainty to protective policy. *Lancet Global Health, 1*, 313–314.

Robinson, B.H. (2009). E-waste: An assessment of global production and environmental impacts. *Science of the Total Environment, 408*, 183–191.
Salehabadi, D. (2013). Transboundary movements of discarded electrical and electronic equipment. *StEP Green Paper Series.* http://www.step-initiative.org/files/step-2014/Publications/Green%20and%20White%20Papers/StEP_GP_TBM_20130325.pdf.
Sander, K., & Schilling, S. (2010). *Transboundary shipment of waste electrical and electronic equipment / Electronic scrap—optimization of material flows and control.* Dessau-Roßlau: Umwelt Bundesamt. http://www.umweltbundesamt.de/sites/default/files/medien/461/publikationen/k3933.pdf.
Science Communication Unit, University of the West of England, Bristol (2013). *Science for environment policy in-depth report: Soil contamination: Impacts on human health.* Report produced for the European Commission DG Environment, September 2013, http://ec.europa.eu/science-environment-policy.
Sepúlveda, A., Schluep, M., Renaud, F.G., Streicher, M., Kuehr, R., Hagelüken, C., Gerecke, A.C. (2010). A review of the environmental fate and effects of hazardous substances released from electrical and electronic equipments during recycling: Examples from China and India. *Environmental Impact Assessment Review, 30*, 28–41.
Song, Q., & Li, J. (2014). Environmental effects of heavy metals derived from the e-waste recycling activities in China: A systematic review. *Waste Management, 34*, 2587–2594.
StEP (2015). *StEP E-waste WorldMap, European Union, overview of e-waste related information.* http://www.step-initiative.org/step-e-waste-world-map.html. Accessed 26 April 2016.
UNEP (1989). *Basel convention on the control of transboundary movements of hazardous wastes and their disposal.* http://www.basel.int/portals/4/basel%20convention/docs/text/baselconventiontext-e.pdf.
UNODC (2009). *Transnational trafficking and the rule of law in West Africa: A threat assessment.* Vienna: United Nations Office on Drugs and Crime. https://www.unodc.org/documents/data-and-analysis/Studies/West_Africa_Report_2009.pdf.
Walters, A., & Santillo, D. (2008). *Evidence of environmental and health impacts of electronics recycling in China: An update.* Amsterdam: Greenpeace International.
Wang, F., Kuehr, R., Ahlquist, D., Li, J. (2013). E-waste in China: A country report. *StEP Green Paper Series.* http://ewasteguide.info/files/Wang_2013_StEP.pdf.

White, R. (2009). Researching transnational environmental harm: Toward an eco-global criminology. *International Journal of Comparative and Applied Criminal Justice, 33*(2), 229–248.

Wong, C., Duzgoren-Aydin, N., Aydin, A., Wong, M. (2007). Evidence of excessive releases of metals from primitive e-waste processing in Guiyu. *Environment Pollution, 148*, 62–72.

Zoeteman, B., Krikke, H.R., Venselaar, J. (2009). Handling electronic waste flows: On the effectiveness of producer responsibility in a globalizing world. *CentER Discussion Paper Series No. 2009–74*. http://dx.doi.org/10.2139/ssrn.1476332.

Andrea Illés is a policy analyst in the Climate and Environmental Governance Programme of the Institute for European Environmental Policy (IEEP) in London. She holds an MSc in environmental policy from Imperial College London and a BSc in Biology from Eötvös Loránd University (Budapest). At the Institute, Andrea works on a wide range of pan-European policy research projects for EU institutions, Member State governments and other clients concerning environmental governance, environmental crime, the use of market-based environmental policy instruments, with a special focus on the potential for environmental tax reform in Europe, and the development of EU climate and energy policy. Before joining the Institute, Andrea has worked on energy efficiency in buildings at the Centre for Climate Change and Sustainable Energy Policy at the Central European University in Hungary.

Kristof Geeraerts is an information and research manager 'EU research funding' at the University of Antwerp. A political and environmental scientist by training, Kristof has been working as a (senior) policy analyst for many years at the Institute for European Environmental Policy (IEEP) in Brussels. At IEEP he undertook research in the wide area of EU environmental governance and with a particular focus on strategic and horizontal policy issues such as sustainable development, the EU Environment Action Programs, environmental crime, environmental liability, and national-level implementation of EU environmental law.

7

The EU Action to Protect the Environment in Kosovo and to Fight Environmental Crime

Teresa Fajardo del Castillo

7.1 Introduction

Kosovo is one of the poorest and most polluted countries in the world. Environmental harm and environmental crime in Kosovo are a consequence not only of the tragedy of war but also of endemic poverty and a weak state institutional system prone to corruption and organized crime. In this scenario, is it possible for the European Union (EU) to export its legal model of environmental protection to Kosovo, including the possibility of protecting the environment through criminal law? To answer this question, in this chapter I examine not just EU's efforts to introduce environmental protection in the negotiations that led to the Stabilisation and Association Agreement of 2015 with Kosovo but also the new Kosovo

T.F. del Castillo (✉)
Public International Law and International Relations, University of Granada, Granada, Spain
e-mail: fajardo@ugr.es

R. Sollund et al. (eds.), *Fighting Environmental Crime in Europe and Beyond*, Palgrave Studies in Green Criminology,
DOI 10.1057/978-1-349-95085-0_7

legal order with its political, economic, and human contexts that pose innumerable problems to the protection of the environment. Shaping Kosovo into a democratic country that abides by the rule of law and adheres to the basic principles of law and justice is a long-term project despite the efforts of the last decades: the peace-building intervention and the international administration of the United Nations in which the EU played a crucial role (Blockmans and Wessel 2009). The transformative effect of the international intervention and the instrumental role played by the laws adopted by the Provisional Institutions of Self-Government resulted in a new entity distinct from Serbia (Hay 2014). The Constitutional Framework for Provisional Self-Government adopted in 2001 by the United Nations Mission under the mandate of Security Council Resolution 1244/99 (UNMIK) established that

> the Provisional Institutions of Self-Government shall be responsible for aligning their legislation and practices in all areas of responsibility with relevant European and international standards and norms, with a particular view to facilitating closer economic, social and other ties between the people of Kosovo and other Europeans, and in awareness that respect for such standards and norms will be central for the development of relations with the Euro-Atlantic community. (Morina *et al.* 2011, p. 283)

Since the adoption of this resolution, the EU has exercised a tutelage over Kosovo to produce not just an exemplary legal system on paper but also to build capacity where success depends on enforcement and compliance of new laws but also on the legitimacy of the EU's intervention in the region. However, Kosovo is still in the making.

Kosovo as a new entity faces many challenges in its efforts to protect the environment. There has been no effective environmental protection in the past, but now as an autonomous government under the watch of the EU one of its many goals is to establish the necessary degree of governance to enforce an environmental legal framework, which has its origin in legislation adopted by the UNMIK. Kosovo must now incorporate the EU environmental law *acquis,* the entire body of laws adopted by the EU to protect the environment in order to comply with its commitments. Before the 2008 declaration of independence, the

Kosovo Provisional Institutions of Self-Government adopted environmental legislation taking into account EU environmental law standards. Thus, the Law on Nature Conservation had as one of its aims to bring 'environmental standards in Kosovo into harmony with those of the European Union'.[1]

After the declaration of independence, this legislation has been complemented and in some cases repealed by new environmental laws that continue to envisage incorporating the EU environmental *acquis*, given that accession to the EU is a long-term goal. In 2012, Kosovo adopted a new criminal code that foresees in its Chapter XXVIII criminal offences against the environment, animals, plants, and cultural objects. However, this primary law needs to be fully developed through secondary legislation. From a legal point of view, an environmental crime is any serious infringement of administrative and criminal laws protecting the environment. However, in order to establish the existence of these environmental crimes, law enforcement agencies need standards of protection to be adopted through secondary legislation whose infringement would trigger prosecution. Despite the fact that most environmental statutes are already adopted and in force, most indicators of compliance such as limits of admissible spills, standards of emissions, standards of quality or the designation of zones of protection still have to be incorporated in the laws of Kosovo before new laws protecting the environment can be put in place that include punishment for the most serious damage to the environment. Kosovo's fledgling legal system, in which environmental harm derived from human activities has been criminalized but for which prosecution is not yet in place, makes it necessary to consider non-legal definitions of environmental crime.

On paper, Kosovo has a basic legal framework to protect the environment and to fight against environmental crime but no institutional capacity to enforce it. Most of the difficulties in implementing and enforcing this legal environmental regime are related to the general

[1] See Law No. 02/L-18 on Nature Conservation available at http://www.assembly-kosova.org/common/docs/ligjet/2005_02-L18_en.pdf.

problems of weak administrative infrastructure and judiciary, corruption, and organized crime (Fajardo 2015; Perrielo and Wierda 2006). These problems are aggravated by the lack of public and private sectors capable of assuming responsibility for services still carried out by the state, UNMIK, or the EULEX, the EU Mission for the Rule of Law in Kosovo. The informal sector is providing most of the environmental-related services, such as domestic waste treatment and basic energy supply, but this has resulted in environmental harm. In some cases, the recently adopted legislation is still being contravened, for example, the illegal harvesting of trees for heating fuel is one of the most serious environmental issues facing Kosovo. The lack of waste management throughout the country is also a challenge. Who is liable for environmental pollution must also be resolved before private companies, including the energy sector, can resume mining and industrial activities. Privatization of coalmines in the country has been considered one of the most important drivers of Kosovo's new economy. However, environmental protection has not been a part of mining history in Kosovo, and at the present, environmental legislation is not being enforced as evinced by the Trepca Mine, opened in the thirteenth century, which is one of the country's primary sources of air, soil, and water pollution. The Trepca Mine is also the source of lead poisoning that is affecting internally displaced members of Roma, Askhali, and Egyptian ethnic minorities who were resettled near the abandoned facilities of the mine by the United Nations authorities during the international administration (Bejtullahu and Dobrushi 2005).

The building of a new society and a new economic order that leave behind the war and its damage has not yet been attained. The war has left Kosovo segregated into ethnic areas where the central government nor EULEX do not intervene (Weber and West 2014), much less protect the environment. For example, there are considerable environmental problems in the Serbian municipalities of Kosovo that require a solution but are beyond the control of the Kosovo authorities (Kemp *et al.* 2013). There are no comprehensive official data on those areas in domestic or European reports (MESP and KEPA 2014).

7.2 The EU and the Protection of the Environment in Kosovo

The EU is committed to paving the way for Kosovo to become a country that abides by European values and principles and establishes relations with Serbia. The EU has invested in Kosovo by creating new laws in accordance with EU laws and institutions that are fashioned after EU member states' institutions. However, the payback is uncertain. Kosovo has a less than clear attitude towards this EU commitment because of its unstable political environment, which has led to its suspension of the implementation of the 2013 EU-brokered agreement between Serbia and Kosovo (EEAS 2013).

On 27 October 2015, after long and difficult negotiations that began in 2013, the EU signed the Stabilisation and Association Agreement, a legal instrument designed to guide relations between Kosovo and the EU, and on 2 November 2015, the National Assembly of Kosovo signed it. On 26 January 2016, the European Parliament ratified it as an EU-only agreement that will not need to be ratified by individual member states, using the traditional formula of a mixed agreement, concluded by the EU and its member states. With this formula, the agreement will soon enter into force despite the five member states that do not recognize Kosovo as a state: Cyprus, Greece, Romania, Slovakia, and Spain.[2]

The EU's action in relation to the Stabilisation and Association Agreement has been aimed at transforming Kosovo into a country that would be able to transition into accession, hence its promotion of the incorporation of the EU environmental *acquis* into Kosovo's new policies and legislation, as foreseen in its Article 115:

> The Parties shall develop and strengthen their cooperation in the environmental field with the vital task of halting further degradation and start

[2] This lack of consensus on the status of Kosovo among the member states has led the EU to adopt a special formula to refer to Kosovo in its documents, including the Stabilisation and Association Agreement: 'this designation is without prejudice to positions on status [from the Member States], and is in line with UNSCR 1244/1999 and the ICJ Opinion on the Kosovo declaration of independence' (Fajardo 2015, p. 11).

> improving the environmental situation with the aim of sustainable development in Kosovo. The Parties shall cooperate in the fields of air and water quality (including with regard to radioactive substances in water intended for human consumption), basic safety standards for protection against dangers arising from exposure to ionising radiation, all types of waste management (including responsible and safe management of radioactive waste) and nature protection, monitoring and reducing industrial emissions, ensuring safety at industrial installations, and classification and safe handling of chemicals in Kosovo.
>
> The Parties shall, in particular, establish cooperation with the aim of strengthening Kosovo's administrative structures and procedures to ensure strategic planning of environment issues and coordination between relevant actors and shall focus on gradual approximation of Kosovo's legislation to the EU *acquis* and where appropriate Euratom *acquis*. Cooperation could also centre on the development by Kosovo of strategies to significantly reduce local, regional and trans-boundary air and water pollution, to establish a framework for efficient, clean, sustainable and renewable production and consumption of energy, and to execute environmental impact assessment and strategic environmental assessment. (Council 2015, p. 125)

Nevertheless, the European Commission has recognized that overall 'Kosovo has not progressed beyond the very initial stages of harmonization with the *acquis* in these areas. There has been little progress on new legislation and implementing existing laws' (European Commission 2014, p. 42). However, to enhance future cooperation, better compliance with monitoring and reporting commitments should be requested to document the outcomes of the European investment. Accountability of Kosovo activities is limited as information is not available (European Commission 2013, p. 9). The European Commission has acknowledged that the administrative capacity within environmental and climate sectors is weak in Kosovo, in particular, it considers that the capacity of Kosovar institutions needs to be strengthened to improve their effectiveness. This problem is more acute because the budget of the Ministry of Environment and Spatial Planning (MESP) remains insufficient and the funding for sewage systems, wastewater treatment, and waste treatment and disposal systems remain outside government expenditure plans. So far, Kosovo has failed to establish a mechanism to finance environmental projects, in particular the operating costs of environmental monitoring of institutions and capital investments. So, for example, the green taxes that have been introduced for car registration are not being allocated to any environmental projects. It is of utmost importance that the quality of environmental reporting improves in order to better inform government policies (European Commission 2014). For the European Commission, one of the unresolved issues is that the environment is not yet a government priority.

7.3 Kosovo and Environmental Crime

The UN Security Council Resolution 1244 and the mandate for UNMIK were the legal basis for Kosovo's post-war legal system. Under the UNMIK mandate, the Provisional Institutions of Self-Government adopted a Constitutional Framework, a Criminal Code, and basic environmental laws that after the 2008 independence declaration have been renewed and extensively developed, but enforcement by the new Kosovar institutions remains weak. The weakness and corruption of Kosovo institutions (Morina *et al.* 2011) are considered to be at the root of illegal practices that are openly carried out in most of the territory of Kosovo: illegal logging, illegal hunting, illegal waste management, illegal construction, destruction of cultural heritage of minorities, etc. All these activities would have been designated as environmental crimes if law enforcement agencies had acted. The lack of response to these violations fosters the perception that environmental crimes do not really exist and that impunity reigns due to the failure of law enforcement agencies and the understaffed judiciary to act. In this scenario, environmental crime is the result of the lack of respect for laws or ignorance of their existence, the lack of resources of law enforcement agencies, and, on many occasions, of the high profit made by means of environmental crimes such as illegal logging. However, the problem is compounded if it is considered that these new laws are not rooted in the traditions of this territory but provided by foreign legal experts and committees during the international administration and in its aftermath.

It is not only a problem of laws imported from other legal systems, it is also the failure to turn a territory without its own legal tradition into a law-abiding land.

Ignoring environmental laws harms the environment and should be sanctioned by the administrative and criminal laws and proceedings that constitute the environmental protection legal framework of Kosovo. These comprise a wide range of statutes already in force but not implemented: laws on environmental protection, special protective zones, forests, spatial planning, strategic environment assessment, waste, agricultural land, cultural heritage, construction, hunting, fishing, and the Inspectorate. These main legal instruments have intentionally been created to correspond with EU environmental law and comply with the requirements imposed by the European Commission through the Instrument for Pre-Accession Assistance.[3] As Kryeziu *et al.* argue, 'like any other new country, the laws on paper do not necessarily accompany the proper execution of what is expected of them. Therefore in Kosovo implementation of laws is not fully executed and the few implemented laws are not fully respected' (2012, pp. 14–15). This lacklustre implementation of laws and regulations has not affected the traditional misuse of Kosovo's environment, one of them being deforestation.

However, criminalizing these activities is not possible at this point since the corpus of administrative law is not yet applied, the institutions are not fit for service, and the population is not familiar with the new legal system imposed from above. The inadequacies and loopholes of a legal system created from scratch and one that imports legal traditions alien to the previous system are some of the obstacles that have to be overcome by the new institutions such as the MESP and the Kosovo Environmental Protection Agency (KEPA) that are under-resourced and whose staff lack adequate training and expertise.

In Kosovo, types of conduct that damage the environment can be sanctioned by administrative or criminal laws. A general environmental

[3] See the Instrument for Pre-Accession Assistance (IPA II), Multi-Country Indicative Strategy Paper (2014-2020), adopted on 30/06/2014, available at http://ec.europa.eu/enlargement/pdf/key_documents/2014/20140919-multi-country-strategy-paper.pdf.

law does not exist, but several fragmented administrative laws cover different sectors. The Criminal Code introduces Chapter XXVIII on Criminal Offenses against the Environment, Animals, Plants, and Cultural Objects that is directed to the Kosovo context. The Environmental Inspectorate is the institution that adopts administrative sanctions and initiates criminal proceedings.

An analysis of the legal schema adopted to protect the environment and to sanction the breaches of environmental law shows that Kosovo has a system that combines characteristics of both civil and common law of Europe and the USA. The result has been a convoluted state-building on the part of the international administration. Introducing this new legal schema for environmental protection into Kosovo's less developed legal system strains an already beleaguered administration.[4] Thus, instead of adopting a general law or code for the protection of the environment, Kosovo uses a wide variety of statutes to protect the environment by activities that establish sanctions for their infringement and also refer to criminal proceedings that can be initiated by the administrative authority, that is, the Environment Inspectorate. The hunting law provides an example of this. Inspectors assume a broad mandate that makes enforcement difficult; the statute envisages civil as well as administrative sanctions and the possibility of initiating criminal proceedings.[5] This law also contemplates the seizing of proceeds.[6]

---

[4] The civil law system is characterized by its dependence on administrative law, meaning that criminal law will only intervene when according to the principle of legality, the intensity and seriousness of the breach of administrative law standards of environmental protection requires a criminal sanction. On the other hand, the Common Law relies on an Inspectorate with wide powers to sanction and to decide fines or to initiate criminal procedures (Fajardo 2015).

[5] See Law No. 02/L-53 on Hunting, and in particular, Chapter X on Administrative Sanctions and Article 59 on undertake measures, available at http://www.assembly-kosova.org/common/docs/ligjet/2005_02-L53_en.pdf.

[6] In its Article 62 on Protection measures, the Law on Hunting states: 'Besides the penalty for civil violence from Article 61, the person may be sentenced to the protection measures of seizing the mean item used or meant for committing the civil violence and the protection measure of seizing the property achieve as a result of civil violence or remained as a result of committing the civil violence'.

Kosovar environmental laws are being developed by the government and municipalities monitored by KEPA and enforced by the Inspectorate, which has a broad mandate. However, its full capacity to act will not be developed and operative until the legislature adopts measures to determine special areas of protection or allowed threshold values for standards of emissions when appropriate. Moreover, local authorities have been criticized for their feeble efforts to protect the environment (European Commission 2013, 2014, 2015), especially combating illegal logging and resolving the problems of waste management (Kryeziu *et al.* 2012).

Various reports prepared by institutions and agencies on the field agree on the problem of a lack of commitment of authorities and people. In 2009, the United States Agency for International Development (USAID) clearly laid out the problems of applying environmental sanctions: 'Practically all environmental laws include sanctions for non-compliance. However, they are often broad and general requirements that make it difficult to implement sanctions. It is almost impossible to process violators in the courts' (USAID 2009, p. 15).

In the next section, I introduce three major environmental problems of Kosovo together with their legal framework.

7.3.1 Illegal Waste in Kosovo

The Kosovo Waste Law No. 04/L-060 of 24 May 2012 is an example of how Kosovo's laws lack the capacity to enforce municipal waste management, including both landfill and waste separation (European Commission 2013, p. 39). As the European Commission reported in 2014, 'there are serious challenges to implement[ing] the 2012 law, since the capacity of municipalities, waste and landfill operators and overall funding for investments is still very low. There is no appropriate infrastructure for storing or treating hazardous waste. Therefore, Kosovo either exports its hazardous waste or mixes it with household waste in landfill sites' (European Commission 2014, p. 47). The recent Kosovo Progress Report of the European Commission (2015) offers a depressing picture of the efforts to create the required infrastructure to deal with waste management in the country. Even though the government has approved secondary legislation on waste and on the list of environmental pollutants, basic waste management concepts and definitions need to be developed, including recycling and recovery.

MESP and KEPA have identified more than 400 illegal landfills, but their work did not cover the Serbian municipalities of the north (MESP and KEPA 2014, p. 59). According to the report, 'currently in Kosovo, landfill closure would not be an alternative solution to the problem, because it would consequently create even greater illegal landfills' (MESP and KEPA 2014, p. 30).

On the other hand, and exposing the limits of using a legal definition of environmental crime, no matter how polluting mining and industrial activities are, they cannot be considered environmental crimes if they do not breach a permit, license, or threshold establishing the nature of environmental damage that can be criminally prosecuted. However, most mining and industrial activities in Kosovo cause damage to the environment and human health to such an extent that Kosovo is considered the most polluted country in Europe (World Bank 2013). Article 349 of the Criminal Code criminalizes 'allowing unlawful construction or unlawful operation of plants and installations that pollute the environment'. However, this provision must be further developed in order to concretize the activities and behavior that can be qualified as criminal. Moreover, it requires enforcement and the commitment of public authorities, who up to this point, have been struggling to close, modernize, and restructure obsolete and polluting plants, mines, and industrial complexes.

In Kosovo, no authorities have dealt with the management of waste or pollution produced by industrial and mining activities. Before the war, the mining sector was public, but no legal instruments were in place to develop the adoption and updating of standards of environmental protection and pollution control. This situation has led to serious air pollution, lead poisoning in the water, and uncontrolled dumpsites all over the country. The MESP and KEPA Report on the State of Waste and Chemicals (2014) presents a dramatic situation: 'Almost every industry in the past has inherited landfills or hazardous wastes which have negative effects on the environment. Also, besides these waste disposed in landfills, especially heavy metals, substances of various aggregate forms have remained for a long time without being used in facilities, warehouses, and industrial units' (p. 38). These problems must be solved before new companies take over the mining and industrial sectors. In this regard, MESP and KEPA have recommended that during privatization, the environmental problems inherited from the past should be addressed and the new owners should take responsibility for the rehabilitation of those sites (MESP and KEPA 2014).

Furthermore, addressing the impact of mines and power-generation facilities on air, water, and land represent the most difficult challenges of complying with EU standards. Most energy in Kosovo is supplied by old, unreliable, and inefficient coal power plants. One of them, Kosovo A, is considered to be the most polluting plant in Europe and is scheduled to be closed in 2017 (USAID Kosovo 2012; World Bank 2011). Its awful track record has led the authorities to consider resettling the villages most affected by its pollution. A Draft Law on the Environmentally Endangered Zone of Obiliq and its Surroundings was prepared by the Assembly of Kosovo in 2013 but has not yet been adopted. Article 6.2, dedicated to the adoption of measures to be taken against sources of pollution, envisages the big steps needed to be taken by authorities and companies to deal with pollution. But these measures cannot be adopted at this point due to the lack of resources and legal instruments.

The Trepca Industrial Complex consists of several mines, three ore concentrators with tailings disposal facilities, a lead smelter, a zinc smelter, and several industrial sites and auxiliary facilities (World Bank 2011, p. 49). It was once the largest industry and employer in Kosovo by far, but since 1999 most activities have stopped, and today a marginal level of mining and ore processing remains for maintenance and mine development purposes. Both the lead and zinc smelters have been fully withdrawn from operation. A report by World Bank (2013) found that the mines and concentrators had inadequate environmental controls before 1999 and that this had not changed. So most environmental problems are due to the presence of the past. Mining pollution is mostly the result of environmental emissions—dust as well as discharges to ground and surface water—from mining sites that have not been reopened or decommissioned and has little relationship with current production. Of special concern are mines' tailing ponds and dams/heaps, contaminated dust, erosion, and runoff, seepage, and groundwater contamination (World Bank Report 2013, p. 66).

7.3.2 Illegal Logging in Kosovo

Illegal logging in Kosovo is both a domestic and a transnational problem shared by other Balkan states. Among the driving forces for this illegal activity is a high domestic demand for wood that is four times the production rate. Most of this is used for domestic fuel as there is a lack of an adequate energy supply. Taking into account the social and economic context of this crime, Article 358 of the criminal code allows for an exception for logging destined for household use.[7] Putting aside legal logging for domestic use, illegal logging is one of the most important environmental problems in Kosovo because it causes deforestation and puts ecosystems of flora and fauna at risk. Despite the existing legal framework for forest management, forests are an obvious target for illegal activities, since they cover a large area and it is extremely difficult to ensure their full protection against two major problems: illegal woodcutting and forest fires (Kryeziu *et al.* 2012). Increasing the degree of protection usually involves a significant rise in the cost of forest management, which is often unacceptable for state-owned companies and land

[7] Article 358 of the Criminal Code on Forest Theft: 1. Whoever, with the intent to steal, cuts down trees in a forest and the quantity of the timber cut down exceeds two cubic meters shall be punished by a fine or by imprisonment of up to one (1) year. 2. When the offense provided for in paragraph 1 of this Article is committed with the intent to sell the cut timber; if the quantity of the cut timber exceeds five cubic meters; or, the offense is committed in a protected forest, protected park or any other forest used for a specific purpose, the perpetrator shall be punished by a fine and by imprisonment of three (3) months to three (3) years. 3. An attempt to commit the offense provided for in paragraph 1 of this Article shall be punishable, Code No. 04/L-082 Criminal Code of the Republic of Kosovo, available at http://www.kuvendikosoves.org/common/docs/ligjet/Criminal%20Code.pdf.

owners. High rates of unemployment and low salaries also drive up deforestation.

According to EULEX (2012), 'illegal logging comes in many forms in Kosovo including logging from public forests without permission, logging in protected areas, false declaration of volume of harvested wood and illegal logging from private forests. Smuggling and illegal accounting practices, extend the list further'. Nevertheless, Kosovo Forestry Agency insisted in 2012 that it was stopping needless destruction and that about 8,200 cases of illegal actions concerning Kosovo's forests had been prosecuted in courts; it was also tabulating cases of illegal logging and attacks against foresters or forest guards (Kryeziu *et al.* 2012, p. 11). However, no data on these proceedings is available in the official websites of EULEX or the Kosovar government. The prevalence of illegal logging shows that the current organizational and legal infrastructure is not fully functional, mainly due to the insufficient number of employees in the Kosovo Forest Agency (Markus-Johansson *et al.* 2010, p. 50).

Illegal logging is also a component of transnational organized crime because of Kosovo's undefined and uncontrolled borders. Thus, 'the lack of capacity to protect forests in Kosovo means that publicly and privately owned forests particularly at the border/boundary are vulnerable and a prime target of wood thieves' (EULEX 2012). The geographical situation of Kosovo in the Balkans as well as its uncontrolled and undefined borders have made Kosovo a destination, as well as a transport zone, for illegal wood from Albania and Montenegro. Even though customs authorities control cross-border trade, irregularities in documentation are a problem that has only partly been addressed. No significant amounts of illegal wood have been reported, although there is likely to be a large margin of error (Marcus-Johansson *et al.* 2010, p. 59). Despite the Kosovar authorities cooperating with Serbian border police to prevent illegal trade, irregular practices have been denounced by NGOs that consider northern Kosovo as a 'gangster's paradise' because now 'unlike when UNMIK had a major police presence in the north, the Kosovo Police and EULEX are seldom visible, and Serbs feel that there is no recourse to justice. This can result in odd situations, like armed gangs of Albanians stealing timber from Serbs in the north, with almost no consequences' (Kemp *et al.* 2013, p. 46). Further institutional and practical measures are needed in the border regions to combat trade in illegally logged wood. However, lack of political will and lack of funding and capacity has created a serious obstacle to efficient cross-border cooperation.

7.3.3 Biodiversity and Environmental Crimes

The 2005 Law No. 02/L-18 on Nature Conservation and the 2010 Law No. 03/L-233 on Nature Protection offer clear examples of the problems of depending on criminal law that uses EU environmental legislation as a normative reference to protect the environment. The Law on Nature Protection of 2010 not only seeks to transpose the EU Birds and Habitats Directives, but also refers to them to determine 'species of the Community interest' and 'priority species' according to their annexes.[8] The referral to external instruments could constitute a breach of the principle of legality that must inform criminal law, particularly in a system such as the Kosovar one. The incorporation of the EU environmental law into secondary legislation must be a pre-requisite of its enforcement by criminal law.

The system on ecologically important areas is also firmly linked with EU environmental law and the Natura 2000 Network in which Kosovo is now included. The different nature conservation zones and ecologically important areas must be designated by the national assembly, the government or municipalities. Until the process of designation is achieved, the law cannot be fully enforced. Hitherto, two national laws have been promulgated in 2012 for the national parks of Bjeshket e Nemuna and Sharri, expanding protected area to 10.9 % of the territory of Kosovo (Veselaj and Mustafa 2015). Now a further development of general concepts, such as a conservation status, is also required in order

[8] See Law No. 03/L-233 on Nature Protection, 2010, available at http://www.kuvendikosoves.org/common/docs/ligjet/2010-233-eng.pdf.

to prosecute those activities that cross a threshold of damage that cannot be infringed upon.

The network of legally protected areas was heavily damaged during and after the last war in Kosovo (1998–99; Mustafa *et al.* 2011). However, Mustafa *et al.* (2013) consider most of these protected areas as just 'so-called parks on paper' due to the fact that 'despite having the legal mandate, . . . objectives of management are still on paper, because of the lack of capacities of management authorities to monitor and enforce conservation purposes and objectives' (p. 608). To this day, there is no Red List species for Kosovo (Veselaj and Mustafa 2015). Animal species are without any legal protection and 'hunting laws have not spared even some species that are protected by international conventions and European Union directives (Birds and Habitat Directive)' (Veselaj *et al.* 2012, p. 309).

Kosovo's environment is increasingly strained due to attempts to overcome endemic poverty and relaunch economic activities without including the most basic environmental requirements in the design of public policies and plans. Experts consider that 'in the recent decades, populations of many species in Kosovo are in dramatic decline. This mainly happens due to destruction of natural habitats by humans, with or without being aware of it, for their own survival. Intensification of human activities as a result of growth of industry, energy, transport, agriculture, forestry, tourism, etc., still continues to impact on natural habitats by fragmenting them, leaving but small areas for wild flora and fauna' (Mustafa *et al.* 2011, p. 651). These problems are the main threats to nature in every European country and are also the problems that the EU tries to solve through better implementation of European environmental legislation, using criminal law to enhance compliance with its obligations. The difficulties that the European member states experience when implementing this legislation are magnified in Kosovo.

In 2013, the MESP began measures to combat illegal construction activities in the Sharri National Park. However, the Natura 2000 Network of protected areas has not yet been established and the institutions in this area remain weak in terms of the numbers and skills of civil servants and state inspectors designated for the protection of the environment (European Commission 2014, p. 41).

7.4 The Victims of Environmental Crime

The Constitutional Framework adopted in 2001 by UNMIK under the Security Council mandate of Resolution 1244/99[9] did not foresee a right for information related to the environment. The new Constitution adopted in 2008 introduced a right of information and a duty of responsibility towards the environment in its Article 52 on the Responsibility for the Environment. It states that

1. Nature and biodiversity, the environment, and national inheritance are everyone's responsibility.
2. Everyone should have an opportunity to be heard by public institutions and have their opinions considered on issues that impact the environment in which they live.
3. The impact on the environment shall be considered by public institutions in their decision-making processes.

Paragraph 2 of Article 52 gives constitutional status to the basic general right of information, which is one of the rights envisaged by the Aarhus Convention on access to information, public participation in decision-making, and access to justice in environmental matters. Kosovo has not acceded yet to this convention but has incorporated in its legislation the basic principles of the EU Directive that transposes the convention into EU law.

The basic principles of the EU Directive 'on public access to environmental information' informed the first Law on Environmental Protection of 2003 and specifically were incorporated in the Law on Environmental Protection adopted in 2009. Ever since then, the EU and its member states have promoted public participation and the empowerment of NGOs and citizens to protect the environment in the Balkans.

[9] The Constitutional Framework introduced a Chapter 5 on Responsibilities of the Provisional Institutions of Self-Government that envisaged in its sect. 5.1 that Provisional Institutions of Self-Government shall have responsibilities regarding (i) Environmental Protection. See Constitutional Framework for the Provisional Self-Government of Kosovo, available at http://www.assembly-kosova.org/common/docs/FrameworkPocket_ENG_Dec2002.pdf.

For example, in 2006 the Ministry of Foreign Affairs of the Netherlands financed a regional project on 'Improving Public Participation: Next Steps in Implementing Aarhus Convention in Albania, Bosnia Herzegovina, FYR Macedonia, Serbia and Montenegro and Kosovo', which funded academic research such as Morina's (2006) report on the 'Transposition of the Convention on Access to Information, Public Participation in Decision-Making and Access to Justice in Environmental Matters with the legislation of Kosovo'. In 2013, the European Commission's General Direction on Enlargement organized a workshop in Pristina to showcase EU implementation of the Environmental Information Directive and the Aarhus Convention.[10]

People of all ethnicities suffered the environmental damage caused by the war: the poisoning of wells, the destruction of historical sites, mainly churches and monasteries, and the committing of war crimes have had persistent and long-term effects. Refugees and internally displaced persons have not returned to their homes, and others now occupy the houses and the lands they left behind. Even the UN intervention brought about unexpected and terrible effects; Roma, Askhali, and Egyptian communities were relocated near the Trepca mine where the disposal of hazardous waste in dumpsites has resulted in lead poisoning, seriously affecting the most vulnerable, often the children. These communities so far have not sought compensation or demanded justice from the UN forces that turned a temporary location of 45 days into a permanent home. Their stories have been reported by the European Roma Rights Centre (2005). However, in the area of Mitrovica many others are also affected by this lead poisoning as has been demonstrated in recent reports (Musliu *et al.* 2008).

Nature is also a voiceless victim. From a legal point of view, the concept of victim is conceived restrictively and limited primarily to people exposed to a criminal act as defined by law, while a non-legal definition is broader, including animals and the environment that

[10] See the TAIEX Workshop on the Implementation of the Environmental Information Directive and the Aarhus Convention, available at http://ec.europa.eu/enlargement/taiex/dyn/taiex-events/library/detail_en.jsp?EventID=50080.

have been exposed to harm whether or not by a crime considered illegal. In Kosovo, the environment has been harmed by combatant forces, international intervention, criminals looting resources, and citizens struggling to survive. In this context, the EU has so far played a limited role in protecting the victims of environmental crime. As in other areas of the Balkans, the EU has tried to fund the required infrastructures that can empower civil society. However, this monumental task has started with victims of genocide and war crimes. Raising environmental awareness was not and is not on the top of the agenda of international administration agencies. Nonetheless, special training has been facilitated through EU programs that have financed networks that have temporarily benefitted the population. However, this aid has had only a limited impact up till now. In the Balkans, the EU has funded one of the most important environmental NGOs, the Regional Environmental Center for Central and Eastern Europe, in which Kosovo has participated. It has carried out remarkable work promoting public awareness on environmental problems and on the access to justice under the Aarhus Convention.[11] It succeeded in providing cooperation

[11] REC was established in 1990 by the United States, the European Commission, and Hungary. Today, REC is legally based on a charter signed by the governments of 28 countries and the European Commission, and on an international agreement with the government of Hungary. It defines itself as 'a nonpartisan, non-advocacy, not-for-profit international organisation with a mission to assist in solving environmental problems in Central and Eastern Europe. REC fulfils this mission by promoting cooperation among non-governmental organisations, governments, businesses and other environmental stakeholders, and by supporting the free exchange of information and public participation in environmental decision making'. See REC Mission Statement in its new website available at http://www.rec.org/. REC has an office in Kosovo with the goal of 'empowering citizenship to and support environmentally mainstreamed policy making'. 'The office was established to assist in the development and strengthening of environmental civil society; to support the development and enforcement of appropriate environmental policies; and to ensure that environmental issues are taken into consideration during the process of transition'. The REC office in Kosovo focuses its activities in three main areas: providing support to institutions for efficient environmental management; providing information/education for civil society; development of sustainable communities. See REC Kosovo Office presentation available at http://www.rec.org/office.php?id=9.

tools and training on environmental legislation, but unfortunately, this came to an end when EU support was cut off.

Other international organizations have also tried to promote the protection of environmental victims in Kosovo since the end of the war. In 2001, the United Nations and OSCE prepared an introductory manual on victims of crimes that also targeted environmental harm and environmental victims. Even though the manual is dedicated to human victims, it mentions, albeit briefly, environmental victims. Among its principles on restitution it states that 'in cases of substantial harm to the environment, restitution, if ordered, should include, as far as possible, restoration of the environment, reconstruction of the infrastructure, replacements of community facilities and reimbursement of the expenses of relocation, whenever such harm results in the dislocation of a community' (OSCE 2001, pp. 36–37). However, this principle has not been fulfilled by the very organizations that created the manual, the UN's controversial management of the relocation of internally displaced ethnic groups to dumpsites being a case in point.

7.5 Conclusions

The EU still believes there is a European future for Kosovo, even though it is not paying back in democracy or human rights or environmental protection commitments what Europe was expecting for its assistance. The story of the EU and Kosovo—Europe as giver and Kosovo as recipient—now has another chapter to be written with the Stabilisation and Association Agreement that was finally signed in 2015.

Kosovar environmental law looks fine on paper but law enforcement agencies lack the capacity to ensure compliance, implementation, and enforcement. The lack of enforcement results in crime motivated by large profit and low risk of punishment and the perception that environmental crime is not punished. Thus the environment has and is harmed without those responsible being held accountable for the consequences; in the past it has been combatant forces and peacekeepers, and now it is those who loot and destroy cultural heritage sites and citizens struggling to survive. In this context, of particular gravity is the impunity of criminals who use the permeable borders with Montenegro for illegal logging, associating with organized crime groups willing to incorporate environmental crime into the diverse criminal activities in the area.

The toll to be paid if environmental legislation is ignored is too high: 'in a few years the highly valued zones of nature in Kosovo will lose their values as a result of conversion of land for agricultural purposes, development of infrastructure (unplanned and uncontrolled constructions), fragmentation of habitats (especially by streets and quarries), unsustainable exploitation of forest ecosystems, herbs, certain animals, etc.' (Mustafa *et al.* 2011, pp. 653–654).

The EU has helped to shape Kosovar legal instruments and institutions for the protection of the environment. However, the effectiveness of its assistance is quite limited in terms of positive outcomes; by now weak enforcement constitutes an unresolved problem that is more severe in the Serbian municipalities of Kosovo because of the prevailing circumstances inherited from the war and the international administration.

Current institutions depend on external experts in order to develop secondary legislation and the required toolbox to implement it. This dependency conditions the timing of transposition and enforcement of environmental legislation. Once these institutions are capable of performing the mandate that now is on paper only, they will be able to confront new tasks such as the criminal prosecution of those activities envisaged in administrative and criminal law.

Extreme poverty and high unemployment are the most important economic problems that Kosovo experiences. They drive the political agenda. The incorporation of environmental requirements in the overall economic and political agenda is a necessity, for without taking into account environmental protection the future of Kosovo is being designed with serious gaps: the lack of enforcement of legislation on the administrative and criminal liability of companies is offering a carte blanche to invest without assuming the required measures to cope with pollution, putting in jeopardy future investment and the care of the environment.

References

Bejtullahu, J., & Dobrushi, A. (2005). Alarming facts about roma camps in North Mitrovice/a: Lead poisoning of Romani children. *Roma Rights Quarterly*, Issue 3–4, 53–57.

Blockmans, S., & Wessel, R. (2009). *The European Union and crisis management: Will the Lisbon Treaty make the EU more effective?* CLEER Working Papers 1. The Hague: TMC Asser Institute.

Council of the European Union (2015). Stabilisation and association agreement between the European Union and the European atomic energy community, of the one part, and Kosovo, of the other part, 2 October. http://data.consilium.europa.eu/doc/document/ST-10728-2015-REV-1/en/pdf. Accessed 7 May 2016.

EEAS (2013). Serbia and Kosovo reach landmark deal. 19 April. http://www.eeas.europa.eu/top_stories/2013/190413__eu-facilitated_dialogue_en.htm. Accessed 25 April 2016.

EULEX (2012). Illegal wood-cutting—One of Kosovo's most difficult rule of law issues. *EULEX News*, 17 September 2012. http://www.eulex-kosovo.eu/en/news/000383.phplast. Accessed 14 March 2016.

European Commission (2013). *Kosovo progress report October 2013*. http://ec.europa.eu/enlargement/pdf/key_documents/2013/package/ks_rapport_2013.pdf. Accessed 17 May 2016.

European Commission (2013). TAIEX workshop on the implementation of the environmental information directive and the Aarhus convention. http://ec.europa.eu/enlargement/taiex/dyn/taiex-events/library/detail_en.jsp?EventID=50080. Accessed 17 May 2016.

European Commission (2014). *Kosovo progress report October 2014*. http://ec.europa.eu/enlargement/pdf/key_documents/2014/20141008-kosovo-progress-report_en.pdf. Accessed 17 May 2016.

European Commission (2014). Instrument for pre-accession assistance (IPA II), Multi-Country indicative strategy paper (2014-2020). http://ec.europa.eu/enlargement/pdf/key_documents/2014/20140919-multi-country-strategy-paper.pdf. Accessed 17 May 2016.

European Commission (2015). *Kosovo progress report October 2015*. http://ec.europa.eu/enlargement/pdf/key_documents/2015/20151110_report_kosovo.pdf. Accessed 17 May 2016.

European Council (2015). Stabilisation and association agreement (SAA) between the European Union and Kosovo signed. http://www.consilium.europa.eu/en/press/press-releases/2015/10/27-kosovo-eu-stabilisation-association-agreement/. Accessed 25 April 2016.

European Roma Rights Center (2005). Special issue 'Justice for Kosovo'. *Roma Rights Quarterly* 3 and 4.

Fajardo, T. (2015). *A case study on the EU's promotion of environmental protection through criminal law in Kosovo*, Study in the Framework of the EFFACE Research Project. Granada: University of Granada.

Hay, E. (2014). Internationalized constitutions and peacebuilding. *Leiden Journal of International Law, 27*(1), 141–168.

Kemp, W., Shaw, M., & Boutellis, A. (2013). *The elephant in the room: How can peace operations deal with organised crime.* New York: Publications of the International Peace Institute. https://www.ipinst.org/images/pdfs/ipi_e-pub-elephant_in_the_room.pdf.

Kosovo Code No. 04/L-082, Criminal Code of the Republic of Kosovo. http://www.kuvendikosoves.org/common/docs/ligjet/Criminal%20Code.pdf. Accessed 17 May 2016.

Kosovo Constitutional Framework of the Provisional Institutions of Self-Government of Kosovo. http://www.assembly-kosova.org/common/docs/FrameworkPocket_ENG_Dec2002.pdf. Accessed 17 May 2016.

Kosovo, Constitution of the Republic of Kosovo 2008. http://www.kuvendikosoves.org/common/docs/Constitution1%20of%20the%20Republic%20of%20Kosovo.pdf. Accessed 17 May 2016.

Kosovo Law No. 02/L-18 on Nature Conservation and the Constitutional Framework adopted by the Provisional Institutions of Self-government. http://www.assembly-kosova.org/common/docs/ligjet/2005_02-L18_en.pdf. Accessed 17 May 2016.

Kosovo Law No. 03/L-233 on Nature Protection, 2010. http://www.kuvendikosoves.org/common/docs/ligjet/2010-233-eng.pdf. Accessed 17 May 2016.

Kosovo Law No. 02/L-53 on Hunting. http://www.kuvendikosoves.org/common/docs/ligjet/2005_02-L53_en.pdf. Accessed 17 May 2016.

Kosovo Law No. 04/L-060 on Waste. http://www.kuvendikosoves.org/common/docs/ligjet/Law%20on%20Waste.pdf. Accessed 17 May 2016.

Kosovo Draft-Law on the Environmentally Endangered Zone of Obiliq and its Surroundings, 04-L-231. http://www.kuvendikosoves.org/common/docs/ligjet/04-L-231.pdf. Accessed 17 May 2016.

Kryeziu, R.D., Macula, D., Vllahiu, A., Memija, L., Thaqi, S. (2012). Deforestation in Kosovo: A grave environmental concern. Paper of the American University in Kosovo.

Markus-Johansson, M., Mesquita, B., Nemeth, A., Dimovski, M., Monnier, C., Kiss-Parciu, P. (2010). Illegal Logging in South Eastern Europe, Regional Report. REC Working Paper.

MESP & KEPA (2014). *The state of waste and chemicals report.* Pristina: Ministry of Environmental and Spatial Planning & Kosovo Environmental Protection Agency.

Morina, V. (2006). *The transposition of the convention on access to information, public participation in decision-making and access to justice in environmental matters (The Århus Convention) with the legislation of Kosovo.* Pristina: Regional Environmental Center. kos.rec.org/english/pdf/ReportEng.pdf. Accessed 17 May 2016.

Morina, V. Korenica, F. and Doli, D. (2011) 'The Relationship between International Law and National Law in the Case of Kosovo: A Constitutional Perspective' *International Journal of Constitutional Law* 9 (1) 274–96.

Musliu, A., Vitaku, A., Veseli, B., Strellci, S. (2008). Lead poisoning and blood lead level in mitrovica region, republic of Kosova. *Journal International of Environmental Application & Science, 3*(4), 277–279.

Mustafa, B., Zeqir, V., Hajdari, A., Krasniqib, V. (2011). Management status of protected areas in Kosovo. *Procedia—Social and Behavioral Sciences, 19,* 651–654.

Mustafa, B., Zeqir, V., Hajdari, A., Ibrahimi, H., Beadini, N., Mustafa, N., & Morina, I. (2013). Extension of the national park Sharri boundaries: Significant action for preservation of natural values. *Natura Montenegrina, 12*(3–4), 607–616.

OSCE (2001). *Victim advocacy introductory manual: Working with victims of crime.* http://www.osce.org/kosovo/32001?download=true. Accessed 17 May 2016.

Perriello, T., & Wierda, M. (2006) *Lessons from the deployment of international judges and prosecutors in Kosovo,* Prosecutions Case Study Series. New York: ICTJ.

Regional Environmental Center, REC, Mission Statement. http://www.rec.org/about.php?section=mission. Accessed 17 May 2016.

USAID Kosovo (2009). *Environmental threats and opportunities assessment (ETOA),* pdf.usaid.gov/pdf_docs/Pnads419.pdf. Accessed 17 May 2016.

USAID Kosovo (2012). *Programmatic impact evaluation in the energy sector in Kosovo: Final report.* https://www.usaid.gov/sites/default/files/documents/1863/Programmatic%20Impact%20Evaluation%20in%20the%20Energy%20Sector.pdf. Accessed 17 May 2016.

Veselaj, Z. Mustafa, B., Hajdari, A. and Zenel, K. (2012). Biodiversity conservation status in the republic of Kosovo with focus on biodiversity centres. *Journal of Environmental Biology, 33*, 307–310.

Veselaj, Z., & Mustafa, B. (2015). Overview on nature protection progress in Kosovo. *Landscape Online, 45*, 1–10.

Weber, B., & West, L. (2014), *EULEX—Towards an integrated exit strategy: Strengthening the rule of law through EU-Integration*, Policy Report 05/2014. Berlin: Group for Legal and Political Studies, Prishtina and Democratization Policy Council.

World Bank (2011). *Background paper: Development and evaluation of power supply options for Kosovo.* http://siteresources.worldbank.org/INTENERGY2/Resources/Kosovo_generation_options_report_12312011.pdf. Accessed 17 May 2016.

World Bank (2013). *Kosovo, country environmental analysis: Cost assessment of environmental degradation, institutional review, and public environmental expenditure review.* http://siteresources.worldbank.org/INTKOSOVO/Resources/KosovoCEA.pdf. Accessed 17 May 2016.

Dr. Teresa Fajardo del Castillo is an associate professor in the Department of Public International Law and International Relations in Granada University. She read law at Granada and Poitiers Universities and the Licence Spécial en Droit Européen at the Institut d'Etudes Européennes at the Free University of Brussels. She has spent stages at the Legal Service of the European Commission and has been a visiting researcher at the universities of Florence, Brussels, Geneva, and London King's College. She obtained her Ph.D. with a thesis on the External Policy of the EU in the field of environment. Her research fields are International and European environmental law, international law of the sea and the EU cooperation to development policy. She is engaged in several inter-university and EU projects relating to International and European environmental law. She is currently researching in wildlife crime and illegal, unreported, and unregulated fishing and has published several contributions in these fields.

8

Armenia: A Case Study on Mining

Christoph H. Stefes and Pete Theodoratos

8.1 Introduction

In 1991, following the collapse of the Soviet Union, the former Socialist Soviet Republic of Armenia gained independence. During the first years of its independence, the Republic of Armenia (RA) was embroiled in an ethnic war with Azerbaijan over the Armenian enclave of Nagorno-Karabakh. RA supported the Armenian separatist forces of Nagorno-Karabakh which eventually emerged victorious. In response to RA's support for the separatists, Azerbaijan and its ally Turkey imposed a blockade on RA which remains one of the economy's biggest drains. The political transition from Soviet rule, on the other hand, proceeded relatively smoothly as the Communist Party peacefully negotiated the transfer of political power to the Armenian National Movement under the leadership of RA's first president, Levon Ter-Petrosyan (1991–98).

C.H. Stefes (✉) · P. Theodoratos
Department of Political Science, University of Colorado Denver, Denver, United States

R. Sollund et al. (eds.), *Fighting Environmental Crime in Europe and Beyond*, Palgrave Studies in Green Criminology,
DOI 10.1057/978-1-349-95085-0_8

In later years, the Republican Party became the dominant political force in RA. Robert Kocharyan (1998–2008) and Serzh Sargsyan (2008–) succeeded Ter-Petrosyan in the presidency of RA (Stefes 2006).

According to its constitution, RA is a democracy. In reality, informal practices of authoritarian rule turn the country's formal democratic institutions into a façade. Freedom House, which ranks countries according to the degree of political rights and civil liberties that governments are willing and able to protect, therefore rightly considers RA partially free but not democratic. It is especially the fusion of political power and economic resources that weakens the electoral process and the rule of law more generally. The executive branch routinely ignores the independence of the legislative and judiciary branches that is formally enshrined in the constitution. Moreover, corruption is widespread, further compromising good governance in RA (Freedom House 2014a).

The lack of governmental accountability, bad governance and systemic corruption is a severe threat to the Armenian environment. Environmental protection frequently falls prey to the economic interests of business elites who occupy key positions in the parliament and the executive branch and who bankroll electoral campaigns. It is therefore not surprising that environmental standards in RA are lax. Moreover, environmental laws are frequently violated with impunity as lack of funds and widespread corruption enfeeble law enforcement and adjudication. Yet it would be too short-sighted to focus on just these concrete instances of criminal activities.

From a legal perspective, environmental crime is defined as "an unauthorised act or omission that violates the law and is therefore subject to criminal prosecution and criminal sanctions. This offence harms or endangers people's physical safety or health as well as the environment itself. It serves the interests of either organizations—typically corporations—or individuals" (Yingyi and Emmons 2000, p. 3). It is clear that in RA these acts and omissions do indeed take place. Yet in RA, as in many other countries around the world, behaviour that severely harms the environment might not necessarily violate any existing laws. A non-legal definition might therefore be more apt. For instance, Clifford and Edwards define environmental crime as "an act committed with the intent to harm or with a potential to cause harm to ecological and/or biological systems and for the purpose of securing business or personal advantage" (Clifford and Edwards 1998, p. 24). Definitions found in green criminology literature provide a broader perspective on what constitutes an environmental crime and can help bridge the gap between a narrow legal definition, institutional deficiencies, and insufficient legislation.

However, harm-based definitions might be too broad. After all, humans harm the environment on almost daily basis, by driving cars, flying on planes, and eating fish and meat. It also misses a crucial aspect of environmental crime, that is, the willingness of politicians to provide minimal protection for the environment to foster economic development at any cost and/or to fill their own pockets. We therefore occupy a middle road between narrow legal and broad harm-based definitions of environmental crime.

While we focus on legal processes, we also argue that in RA, environmental crime starts well before the breaking of laws. It begins with the often illicit collusion of political power and economic interests that prevents the passing of more stringent environmental regulations and the allocation of sufficient administrative resources to those government agencies which are formally tasked with the protection of the environment. In other words, the often illegal activities that prevent the passing of stringent environmental legislation should already be considered environmental crime. We define environmental crime as any intentional act or omission that violates the law and thereby prevents the passing of more stringent environmental legislation (e.g. due to corruption), hinders the adequate allocation of resources to public or private agencies charged with protecting the environment, and/or harms the environment. We therefore assume a legal approach, but our point of departure starts before existing laws. Instead, we also look back at the law-making process and emphasize that illegal acts committed at this stage should also be considered environmental crime insofar as they fail to criminalize and detect behaviour that poses a severe threat to the environment. This approach appears to be particularly apt for political systems in which law-making and law-enforcement is literally corrupted due to the collusion between public and private interests.

Nowhere is environmental crime more prevalent and harmful than in RA's mining industry. The country is rich in copper, iron, molybdenum (a refractory element used primarily as an alloying agent in steel, cast-iron, and super-alloys), zinc, gold, and other metals. In addition to base metals, other metals include rhenium, selenium, tellurium, cadmium, indium, and bismuth (Mining Journal 2011). With almost 700 mines in operation, mining is considered an important economic sector in RA, accounting for over half of the country's exports (Ishkanian 2013). The ownership of these mines is often unclear, as many companies are registered offshore. It is clear though that members of RA's political elite have stakes in these companies. Some companies that operate in RA are formally based in the European Union (EU). In general, RA's government attempts to encourage investment in the mining industry through low tax rates as well as lax and ambiguous environmental and labour regulations. Ambiguities in the law are routinely interpreted in ways that benefit the mining industry (Amirkhanian 2013 interview). Moreover, even these weak regulations are frequently violated with impunity. Lack of administrative resources, collusion between private and public interests and the resulting lack of political will and outright corruption are responsible for the lack of enforcement (Aghalaryan et al. 2013 interviews).

The collusion between political power and economic interests at the expense of the environment has manifested itself in the law-making process. For instance, the former Minister for Environmental Protection, Vardan Ayvazyan, purchased about a dozen mines during his tenure at the ministry through a network of businesses owned primarily by members of his family (News.am 2011). Since 2007, Ayvazyan has been in the position to influence mining legislation as a Member of Parliament, including a 2012 piece of legislation that weakened existing regulations related to the selling of mining operations to foreign business and how waste from mining is classified. The most detrimental portion of the legislation in regard to environmental protection was the reclassification of mining tailings from "waste" to "rock piles", which has made prosecuting companies that pollute much more difficult (Iskanian 2013; News.am 2011). This legislation came on the heels of a scandal in which Ayvazyan was implicated in the sale of three mines, for an estimated $24 million, to a Chinese company through a network of subsidiary companies owned by family members and business partners of the minister (HETQ 2011). The pervasiveness of the oligarch's influence throughout the entire process, from the awarding of licenses to the passage of legislation, serves to illustrate the way in which the legislative process in RA facilitates the degradation of the environment. The three mines purchased by the Chinese company have since had the licenses for exploitation reviewed for incomplete or improper environmental impact assessments (EIA) (Ecolur 2011).

The way mining is conducted in RA has disastrous consequences for the country's environment and the well-being of its citizens. Mining has led to widespread deforestation and the destruction of arable land. Moreover, heavily polluted tailings are discarded in ways that contaminate lakes, rivers, and soil. Smelters pollute the air. Mining thereby endangers the health and the subsistence of RA's citizens. Since rivers often cross borders, mining-related pollution endangers the environment and citizens of neighbouring countries as well, namely Georgia and Azerbaijan. In a volatile region of mutually distrusting governments, cross-border pollution is not managed and could further aggravate hostilities between the nations of the South Caucasus (Zarafian, Two Anonymous Mid-Ranking Officials of the RA Government 2013 interviews).

So far, RA's nascent environmental movement has been the only actor able and willing to monitor mining-related environmental destruction, point fingers at the perpetrators, demand stricter environmental regulations and take legal steps, so far, with some success. The EU could strengthen environmental protection in RA by supporting environmental NGOs, assisting the government of RA in the formulation and implementation of stricter environmental regulations and insisting in RA's compliance with domestic laws and international treaties.

The EU and the RA signed a Partnership and Cooperation Agreement (PCA) in 1996 which went into force in 1999 (Eurocentre n.d.). The PCA was meant to spur cooperation in trade, political dialogue, technology, social issues, civil science, investment, economy, culture, and lawmaking (Centre for European Studies). In 2004, RA became a part of the European Neighbourhood Policy (ENP), finalizing its ENP Action Plan in 2006

(Eurocentre n.d.). The ENP is meant to strengthen relations between the RA and the EU through shared dedication to international law and fundamental values (EU External Action n.d. b). The EU Advisory Group provides the RA government with policy advice on a range of issues to spur the implementation of the reform agenda and strengthen its international commitments (EU Advisory Group to the RA n.d.). In July 2013, negotiations on an Association Agreement and a Deep and Comprehensive Free Trade Area (DCFTA) were finalized to deepen the relations between RA and the EU even further. However, only a few months later, the Armenian government declared that it would not join the DCFTA after all, but would become part of a Russian-led Customs Union (Eurasian Economic Union) (EU External Action n.d. a).

Despite RA's recent U-turn, the EU's long-standing assistance programs in the area of environmental protection are likely to continue. The EU and RA have cooperated in this area for years. The two parties are signatories to several bi- and multilateral environmental agreements and treaties, most notably the Aarhus Convention (European Commission n.d.). Moreover, the EU has provided funding for numerous environmental projects in RA. The total EU funding given to current projects and those that were active in the past 12 months amounts to more than 10 million Euros (European Union External Action n.d. e). While these are encouraging steps, the EU needs to step up its efforts to curtail environmental crime in the Armenian mining sector. This report will propose a few steps that the EU could take.

8.2 Overview of the Case

Straddling the Europe-Asia divide, the RA covers an area of almost 28,000 square kilometres, an area slightly smaller than Belgium. A landlocked country, RA is located in the South Caucasus, bordering Georgia and Azerbaijan in the North and East as well as Iran and Turkey in the South and West. Almost 98% of its 3 million citizens are ethnic Armenians (World Factbook 2014). Mining sites are located across the entire country but are concentrated in the Northern and Western parts of the country at its borders with Turkey and Georgia.

To map the political landscape of mining and related (environmental) crime in RA, we start with an overview of the RA governmental institutions at the local, regional, and national level, followed by a summary of the various private actors, profit and non-profit (e.g. companies, environmental NGOs). This overview will also discuss the interests, resources and strategies of the various actors. Furthermore, we identify the relevant international governmental and non-governmental actors that play a role in RA's mining industry. We continue with a cost-benefit analysis of mining in RA, considering economic, environmental, and societal costs and benefits. This section concludes with an assessment of the various national laws and international treaties related to mining in RA, the law implementation process and the probable causes for weak national legislation and even weaker enforcement of national law and international treaties. We will show that in RA, environmental crime begins prior to the law-making stage. A legalistic approach to environmental crime would therefore be too narrow. In other words, environmental laws are undoubtedly violated. Yet the bigger concern is with the lax environmental standards themselves. Environmental crime therefore begins with the illicit processes of drafting and passing these laws, involving the collusion of government officials, parliamentarians, and the country's economic elite. Non-action, of course, should be considered an environmental crime as well. Looking the other way while mining companies destroy Armenia's environment and risk citizens' lives and health is more than just negligence when it is clear that non-action is intentional.

8.3 Government Institutions

As is typical for presidential systems in non-democratic countries, power is heavily concentrated in the presidency.[1] According to RA's constitution, the head of state who is directly elected for a 5-year term with a two-term

[1] At the end of December 2015, a constitutional referendum will be held in Armenia which the voters will most likely approve, turning the regime from a presidential to a parliamentary form of government with power shifting from the president to the prime minister.

limit appoints and dismisses the prime minister and individual members of the cabinet upon recommendation of the prime minister, dissolves the parliament, appoints and dismisses judges and prosecutors, is the commander-in-chief of the armed forces and can issue orders and decrees and declare a state of emergency. The prime minister, as head of government, is primarily responsible for overseeing the implementation of laws and presidential orders and decrees and coordinates the work of the ministries. While prime ministers were frequently appointed and dismissed throughout the 1990s, since 2000, two prime ministers were in office for 6 and 7 years, respectively, indicating a stable working relationship between government and president (Armenian Constitution 1995).

Two ministries are of special importance for RA's mining industry. The Department of Mineral Resources within the Ministry of Energy and Natural Resources issues licenses for the exploration of mining sites and the extraction of mineral resources. It also monitors the operation of mining companies in RA. The Ministry of Nature Protection is responsible for assessing and monitoring the potential and actual environmental impact of mining operations in the country. In the unofficial hierarchy of ministries, the Ministry of Nature Protection ranks very low, which is reflected by the lack of funding the ministry receives; it is notoriously understaffed and underequipped (Barker, Amirkhanian 2013 interviews).

The 131-seat National Assembly is currently dominated by two pro-government parties, the Republican Party of RA whose leader is President Sargsyan and Prosperous Armenia whose leader is one of the richest businessmen in RA. Together, these two parties occupy 106 seats. Some of the richest entrepreneurs in RA occupy a significant number of pro-government seats. Being a member of parliament does not only grant these so-called oligarchs immunity, but also access to important policy-making forums and government agencies (Aghajanian 2012). In contrast, the opposition plays a negligible role in the parliament. Of the opposition parties, the Heritage Party has been an outspoken critique of mining practices in RA (Ishkanian 2013). Yet Heritage only holds 5 seats (Global Security 2013).

The court system is formally independent. However, the authority of the president over the appointment and dismissal of judges limits the independence of the courts. Moreover, judges are notorious for accepting bribes. According to a 2013 report by the Human Rights Ombudsman of RA, "bribe-taking is so rampant in Armenian courts that judges even use an unofficial price list for kickbacks" (Shoghikian and Bulghadarian 2013). In general, corruption is widespread in RA. Transparency International puts RA in 94th place of 175 countries in its widely published Corruption Perception Index (Transparency International 2013).

RA is divided into 11 regional administrations, headed by governors who are appointed by the central government and are tasked with the implementation of the governments' regional policies. Below the regional level, 654 local governments exist whose members are directly elected. The budgets and formal authorities of the regional and local governments are very limited. Moreover, the dominance of the ruling party in the national parliament extends to the local and regional assemblies. Given the dominance of the Republican Party in the regions, limited funds, and their dependence on the central government for the allocation of these funds, local and regional governments play a limited role in regulating RA's mining industry. In general, they have overwhelmingly supported mining projects in their localities (Freedom House 2012).

The Armenian government has been very supportive of expanding mining operations in RA. It considers the mining sector "a key contributor to the national economy." Accounting for over half of the country's exports, it is RA's "most important economic driver." The government lauds RA for being a "mining friendly" country and promises to maintain and enhance legislation that could attract even more investors (Armenia-Canada Chamber of Commerce n.d.). In short, the government argues that mining serves the public interest of RA. This claim will be further investigated below. At this point, it should be emphasized though that the mining industry also serves the pecuniary interests of individual parliamentarians and government officials. As Liana Aghajanian states in *Foreign Policy* magazine:

> Armenia is rich in molybdenum and gold, and that has led to considerable competition among the oligarchs to grab their shares of the resulting profits. National Assembly Chairman Hovik Abrahamyan and member

> of parliament Tigran Arzakantsyan are both shareholders in one leading mining company. One of the most prominent tycoons linked with mining is former Minister of Environmental Protection, Vardan Ayvazyan, who was in charge of regulating large parts of the industry during his stint in government. In September, a U.S. court ordered Ayvazyan to pay $37.5 million in damages to a U.S. mining company that accuses him of corruption relating to his own business interest in the sector. (Aghajanian 2012)

As most interviewees for this study, including the two government representatives, argue, corruption in the mining industry is ubiquitous. Government officials and parliamentarians as well as close relatives have direct stakes in mining companies, most of which are registered offshore to hide the ownership (Aghalaryan, Ayvazyan 2013 interviews). Articles 65 and 88 of the RA constitution explicitly states that members of the government and parliament must not engage in entrepreneurial activities (Armenian Constitution 1995). Moreover, bribes are frequently taken for issuing licenses and determining the tax and fee rates for mining operations, which are by international standards extremely low. This personal stake of public officials in the mining industry seriously compromises its regulation.

8.4 Private Actors

Starting with the for-profit sector, among the dozens of mining companies operating in RA, several are registered in the country, including Meghradzor Gold, Paramount Gold Mining, various companies of the Vallex Group and Multi Group which is owned by the leader of Prosperous Armenia and one of the most influential oligarchs in the country, Gagik Tsarukyan. Many of these companies are, however, either subsidiaries of foreign-owned companies or foreign-owned companies have substantial stakes in these companies. The transnationality of environmental crime becomes obvious here. Tsarukyan is not the only politician who is financially invested in such companies. For instance, Tigran Arzakantsayan of Paramount Gold Mining holds a parliamentary seat for the Republican Party. It is often not clear, though, who has financial interests in these companies as they are often parts of larger conglomerates that are usually registered offshore (e.g. in Lichtenstein and Cyprus), allowing them to hide their true owners. The various links between companies and banks creates an opaque web of subsidiaries, joint ventures, etc. that makes it almost impossible to identify ownerships and assign responsibility (Aghalaryan and Baghdasaryan 2014). This lack of transparency is further exacerbated by the difficulty in assigning specific blame to a perpetrator when an environmental crime is identified. It is often not clear whether an individual or a group of individuals are responsible for an environmental crime and relevant environmental databases do not always contain that information (Lynch and Stretesky 2014, p. 9).

It is generally assumed that any lucrative businesses, including mining companies, cannot operate in RA without close contacts to the government (Ayvazyan and Representative of International Organization 2013 interviews). Like in most post-Soviet countries, the business sector is not well organized. Business owners usually protect their interests through informal contacts to government officials (Stefes 2006). This holds especially true for the companies in the mining sector.

In the non-profit sector, environmental NGOs and grassroots community movements have been in vocal opposition to mining operations throughout the country. The more established and professional as well as better-funded (also accepting foreign donations) NGOs rarely consist of more than a dozen representatives. They have used their resources to undertake studies and inform citizens through public relations campaigns. They are also ready to take formal steps to oppose the mining companies. They lobby the RA government to pass tougher regulations and take companies to court. Among the NGOs most active in monitoring and criticizing mining practices in RA are the Armenian Aarhus Centers which receive support from the Organisation for Security and Cooperation in Europe, the Armenian Women for Health and Healthy Environment, the Acopian Center for the Environment, Ecolur, Armenia's Union of Greens, For Sustainable Human Development Association, and the Helsinki Citizens' Assembly with various offices across RA.

Many Armenians distrust NGOs which they consider elitist and removed from the actual problems that citizens face in their daily lives, especially in the more remote areas of the country. In response to the growing stress that mining operations inflict on Armenians in rural areas, grassroots movements have emerged. These groups are less organized and financially endowed. They mistrust foreign donors and do not take funding from them. They are, however, willing to build coalitions among themselves and often cooperate with Armenian NGOs (Ishkanian 2013, p. 10). The Save Teghut Civic Initiative is probably the most prominent example. It is able to rally hundreds of citizens and enjoys support from individuals and groups in RA and in Western countries (Matosian 2012). Founded in 2007, the goal of Save Teghut is "to stop, by means of a strong civic engagement, execution of the unlawful decision adopted in 2001 by the Armenian Government commissioning exploitation of a copper-molybdenum mine in Teghut. Save Teghut aims at defending the rights of Shnogh and Teghut communities to their property, healthy environment and dignified work" (Save Teghut Civic Initiative 2012). Finally, critical journalists should be mentioned as well. For instance, journalists regularly report about environmental degradation related to the mining industry in RA (Hetq n.d.).

8.5 Foreign and International Actors

As already mentioned, several foreign mining companies are operating in RA. Among these companies are GeoPro Mining (Russia), Global Gold (US), Lydian International (UK), Cronimet (Germany), and FLSmidth (Denmark). As is the case with Armenian mining companies, ownership is not always clear as subsidiaries are frequently registered offshore. It is generally assumed that foreign companies have to maintain friendly relations with high-ranking government officials to receive and maintain business licenses. It is thereby understood that to maintain friendly relations, significant bribes have to be given to these officials (Aghalaryan and Ayvazyan, interviews) (Aghajanian 2012; Aghalaryan and Ayvazyan 2013 interviews).

Among the many international governmental organizations that have offices in RA are the World Bank, the European Bank for Reconstruction and Development (EBRD), the EU, and various organizations of the United Nations such as the United National Development Programme (UNDP) and the United Nations Environment Programme (UNEP). It appears that the international financial organizations in particular have assumed an ambiguous position towards mining. On the one hand, they stress the need for sustainable economic development and mining regulations that are more protective of the environment. On the other hand, their involvement in the most recent revisions of the mining codes has not led to tougher environmental regulations. It should be kept in mind that as large lenders to the RA government, they are interested in the repayment of the loans and mining is still considered one of the few lucrative economic sectors in RA (Amirkhanian 2013).

The EU has also been hesitant to address the mining business in RA. RA and the EU have maintained close economic, social, and diplomatic relations since the mid-1990s. The EU has also sponsored numerous environmental programs in RA. Programs that are currently active or were active in the past 12 months have focused on a variety of topics. The majority of funded projects have addressed issues of biodiversity, climate change adaptation, and safety of nuclear power plant operations. Other projects focus on agricultural land resources, basic drinking water supply and sanitation, waste management and disposal, and environmental education and training. The EU has spent more than 10 million Euros on these projects. It is noteworthy that not a single project has addressed environmental degradation caused by mining (European Union External Action n.d. e).

The diplomatic representations of EU member states and other Western countries have also avoided publicly criticizing the RA government and mining companies. In March of 2014, the RA government and the World Bank, with the support of the International Finance Corporation, EBRD and the embassies of the US, UK, Canada, and Germany, organized a joint conference on "Responsible Mining" in RA. Although it was one of the declared goals of the conference to "explore various perspectives on responsible development of the mining sector in

RA, including improvement of social and environmental management," representatives of the major NGOs and grassroots movements involved in the mining area were not invited (Responsible Mining Conference 2014). In response, these groups staged a protest in front of the conference venue and organized a counter-conference entitled "Irresponsible Mining in Armenia," considering the official conference "an attempt to legitimize the widespread pillage of Armenia's natural resources and an effort to disguise the catastrophic effects of mining on human health and the environment" (Save Teghut Civic Initiative 2014).

In short, an informal pro-mining coalition of government officials, politicians, and oligarchs supports the rapid exploration of mining sites in RA with little respect for the environmental impact, using legal and illegal ways to do so. However, local environmental NGOs and movements, with some support from international actors, have attempted to stop irresponsible mining in RA. International financial organizations as well as Western governments and the EU appear to sit on the fence, publicly condoning environmental groups without putting any pressure on the pro-mining coalition.

8.6 Cost-Benefit Analysis of Mining in Armenia

Mining practices in RA have put considerable stress on the environment. Mining has contributed to rapid deforestation in the country. Between the 1990s and today, the area covered by forests has dropped from 20% to around 7%. The World Bank calculates that at the current rate, RA might lose all of its forests by 2030 (Wallace 2012). In turn, the loss of forests causes the extinction of endangered species and the loss of rare plants. It will also lead to landslides that pose a direct threat to peoples' lives, taking into account that many mining sites and villages are located in close proximity to RA's mountainous areas. Mining also leads to a loss of arable land, depriving many farmers of their means of subsistence. Mining therefore especially hurts the already impoverished population of RA's rural areas (U1+ 2014).

As much as the loss of arable land is regrettable, the mine tailings pose a more direct environmental threat to human and non-human lives as well as valuable ecosystems. Tailings consist of materials that are left over from the processing of ore in which the valuable components are removed. This process involves two stages. During the first stage, rocks are removed to extract the ore. Once the ore is extracted, remaining rock is separated from the valuable ore through the use of pressure, water, and/or chemicals. Mining therefore produces two types of waste—weakly contaminated rocks and the highly contaminated tailings. The latter requires special and expensive treatment in which the material is gathered in insulated ponds that prevent any leaks of the tailings into the environment. In RA, leakages are frequent because the ponds are usually unsafe. Furthermore, ore is often smelted near the extraction site to avoid transportation costs. The smelting of ore releases toxins into the air. Toxins from smelting operations can lead to cardiovascular and kidney problems, complications during pregnancy, cancer, and a myriad of other adverse health effects (United States Environmental Protection Agency 1992). Villages located close to these smelters are hit hardest, as these toxins can be found in high concentrations in the soil that is used for gardening and farming. It therefore requires sophisticated filtering techniques to minimize this air pollution (Mining Facts n.d.). In RA, mining and smelting proceed without any significant environmental precaution. Tailings are dumped into porous and instable ponds. Toxic material therefore regularly leaks into the ground, poisoning the groundwater, rivers, and lakes. Used for irrigation, poisonous water enters the food chain. Moreover, smelters either do not use any advanced filters or do not use any filters at all. Most filters were removed and sold as scrap metal when smelters closed down in the wake of a severe economic recession following the collapse of the Soviet Union. When the smelters were reactivated, no new filters were installed (Siebert 2013). The amount of toxins released into the air, ground, and water is very difficult to assess because the mining companies do not gather and release data. We therefore can only rely on environmental studies that target specific areas in RA. During a research project that the Acopian Center for the Environment, the Blacksmith Institute, and the RA government conducted in 2013, soil samples from 25 mining sites across five regions were gathered. The samples revealed heavy metal concentrations that were well above internationally accepted limits. "Tailing ponds in these mining communities were in a neglected state with no proper fencing and no systematic or adequate monitoring. In addition, these locations had reported many cases of accidents that had resulted in leakage of the toxic pollutants" (Ishkanian 2013).

Since tailings pollute rivers that cross international borders, environmentally unsafe mining practices in RA also negatively affect neighbouring countries, namely Georgia and Azerbaijan. Transboundary pollution adds fuel to the already unstable geopolitical situation in the South Caucasus that has witnessed numerous wars since the disintegration of the Soviet Union in 1991 (Armenia-Canada Chamber of Commerce 2011). Mining-related environmental pollution in RA must therefore be considered a threat to peace and security in the South Caucasus.

The RA government and the mining industry point out that the economic gains from mining are substantial: "In Armenia the mining sector is a key contributor to the national economy. Ore concentrates and metals produced in Armenia account for over half of our country's exports, making the mining industry Armenia's most important economic driver" (Armenia-Canada Chamber of Commerce 2011). Indeed, mining is the biggest recipient of foreign direct investment in RA (USAID 2013). It also creates jobs in impoverished rural areas of the country. At the same time, the economic benefits of mining are not clear-cut. According to official government statistics, mining employs just around 1% of RA's workforce. The reason for this low number is that the ore is usually shipped to Western countries for further processing which is more work-intensive. Mining also accounts for just 3% of RA's GDP. Furthermore, gains from mining in RA are highly concentrated, benefiting primarily foreign companies and Armenian oligarchs (AUA Newsroom 2013). Finally, due to its geographical spread and environmental burden, mining imposes high costs on other economic sectors such as agriculture and tourism. These sectors could potentially contribute to sustainable economic growth, whereas mining relies on finite resources.

The net beneficiaries of mining in RA are foreign companies, Armenian oligarchs and the few thousand people employed in the mining industry. The losers are the people who live in close proximity to the mines and smelters. Environmental pollution directly threatens the health of these people who live primarily in rural communities. Yet the toxic material released by Armenian mines travels beyond this, reaching people hundreds of kilometres away, through the air, water streams, and the food chain. In general, due to its socio-economic and environmental consequences, mining in RA is a threat to domestic and regional security.

8.7 Domestic and International Legislation

Among local experts, it is commonly agreed upon that RA's environmental laws are vague, convoluted, contradictory, and often outdated. They are typically drafted by presidential staffers who have the licit and illicit interests of oligarchs in mind instead of officials of the Ministry of Nature Protection who are better trained and more removed from the economic elite. Add to these shortcomings the fact that presidential decrees and orders occasionally contradict environmental laws which they constitutionally must not do (but are executed nevertheless) and it becomes readily apparent that RA's legislation is inadequate to protect the country's environment (Zarafian, Ayvazyan and Anonymous Representative of International Organization 2013 interviews). The ineffectiveness of laws is especially prevalent in the mining sector.

According to an unpublished study by the Acopian Center for the Environment at the American University of Armenia, several gaps characterize environmental law in RA, especially in the country's mining sector. First, to approve any mining licenses, an EIA is required. However, there are no guidelines as to who should undertake these assessments, which data should be included, and which methodology should be employed (Amirkhanian n.d.). Consequently, the mining companies subcontract these studies to one of their subsidiaries that will always provide favourable assessments. For instance, companies of the Vallex Groups commission the Lernametalurgiai Institute, a subsidiary of Vallex Groups, to write the EIAs for their mining operations including the one in Teghut. Lernametalurgiai Institute is currently the primary author of most EIAs in RA (Ishkanian 2013).

In general, current RA legislation is vague on methodologies that would fairly calculate natural resource and environmental protection fees. Internationally accepted methodologies are omitted. It is therefore unsurprising that RA has among the lowest fees for exploiting natural resources in the world. In RA's new mining code, a natural resource fee has been completely eliminated and replaced with a royalty fees that is very modestly judged by international standards. Yet by imposing fees based only on the proceeds of actual sales, the use of efficient mining technology is discouraged. If the companies would be taxed according to the estimated amount of ore, they would be more inclined to mine more efficiently.

Furthermore, the environmental protection fees for the disposal of mining waste are extremely low. There is no fee for the removal of rocks during the first stage of mining. This waste is wrongly considered non-hazardous and the highly toxic tailings which are the product of the second stage are classified as low-hazardous waste (fourth class, the lowest class, according to RA regulations). The fee is accordingly set at less than three Euros per ton. It should, however, be considered first class hazardous waste for which the fee per ton is almost 100 Euros. Mining companies in RA therefore save millions of Euros each year (Sanasaryan 2008). Moreover, after concluding their operations, mining companies are no longer liable for the sites. Taking care of the rocks and tailings becomes the responsibility of the state of RA, which means that RA taxpayers have to shoulder the financial burden (Amirkhanian n.d.). These regulations provide little incentive for mining companies to conduct their businesses in efficient and environmentally protective ways. Instead, they encourage rapid and inefficient exploration with little consideration for the long-term environmental effects of mining operations. Finally, and this is a telling point, RA law does not include criminal penalties for acts that harm the environment at all.

RA's environmental legislation thereby violates numerous international treaties and conventions that the country has signed since its independence. Article 6 of the RA Constitution and the Article of RA Law on International Agreements clearly state that international treaties trump national law. Environmental advocates routinely point to three international conventions which would, if properly enforced, significantly empower environmental advocacy in RA and thereby improve RA environmental legislation: the Aarhus Convention, the Convention on EIA in a Transboundary Context (Espoo Convention) and the SEA (Kyiv) Protocol (Amirkhanian and Ayvazyan 2013 interviews).

Most notably, the Aarhus Convention requires RA to assure that rights that the Convention grants the public are upheld. These rights include access to environmental information, public participation in environmental decision-making, and access to justice (Aarhus Convention 1998). Currently, RA legislation is not in compliance with the Aarhus Convention. RA's Law on Environmental Impact Expertise (EIE) regulates the organization and implementation of public hearings through which the public can share their opinions on proposed economic activities but according to this law, this public input does not need to be considered in the final decision. Although Paragraph 8 of Article 6 of the Aarhus Convention expressly stipulates that public opinion must be considered in decision-making, the RA government is instead referring to its national legislation in direct violation of the Convention (Amirkhanian n.d.). In respect to access to justice, NGOs filed a lawsuit against the RA government in 2004 for violating the Aarhus Convention and the RA Constitution. The lawsuit was in response to passed legislation which did not seek public participation prior to the legislation being approved. However, the lawsuit was deemed inadmissible because the NGOs lacked jurisdiction to file. Only the president, the government, and the National Assembly could make appeals to the Constitutional Court of RA on the grounds of violations of the RA Constitution (Aarhus Convention Compliance Committee 2006). Additionally, existing legislation does not allow NGOs to go to court in protection of public law which is also in direct violation of the Aarhus Convention. The Mining Code also prevents access to geological data, for example, which is regarded as a commercial secret in violation of the Convention's protection of access to information relevant to the environment (Amirkhanian n.d.). If the Aarhus Convention were fully enforced in RA, these laws would need to be changed, allowing for greater access to information, public participation in the decision-making process, and legal support to combat environmental crime. It is worth noting that international bodies such as the EU can help pressure RA to meet its international obligations.

8.8 Law Enforcement and Adjudication

The Ministry of Environmental Protection is the principal agency to uphold environmental law in RA. For several reasons, it largely fails to do so. First, the ministry is woefully understaffed. As it ranks at the bottom of the ministerial hierarchy, it does not receive the financial means to fulfil its protective role. Budget cuts and political considerations have led to the elimination of several oversight committees in the ministry. For instance, in 2005, the Geology Department's Scientific Council was eliminated. This council was critical in issuing permits for the exploitation of new mines. Regular bureaucrats in the ministry with no scientific training now issue these permits, putting the companies in an advantageous position. The ministry also dissolved a government committee that conducted independent EIAs. In short, the ministry rid itself of the expertise to conduct independent assessments about the environmental harms of proposed mining projects. The ministry is therefore essentially condemned to rubber stamp the EIAs that were conducted by the mining industry such as by the Lernametalurgiai Institute (Ayvazyan and Barker 2013, interviews; Sanasaryan 2008).

Moreover, with the low priority that the RA government ascribes to environmental protection, the Ministry of Environmental Protection is under constant pressure from the presidential apparatus and other ministries to turn a blind eye on environmental issues. As a general rule, the greater the oligarchic influence, the less environmental enforcement there appears to be (Aghalaryan, Barker, Zarafian & Anonymous Representative of International Organization 2013, interviews). Moreover, as the case of the former Minister of Environmental Protection Vartan Ayvazian demonstrates, corruption reaches even the highest levels of the RA government.

Ayvazian revoked a mining license given to a foreign company after the company refused to pay a multi-million dollar bribe to the minister (Hoktanyan 2012). For a bribe or a well-hidden stake in a mining company that is registered offshore, fines and fees are waived or significantly reduced, forest areas are simply declared non-forest areas (in which case mining becomes permissible), and scientific evidence of pollution is ignored (Ayvazyan 2013 interview). For instance, if fish stocks are depleted due to pollution, the ministry calculates the compensation for local villagers based on the market value of the dead fish. It does not consider the long-term costs of severely depleted fish stocks or the costs to the environment that cannot be calculated according to market prices such as the destruction of microorganisms (Anonymous Representative of International Organization 2013 interview).

To assume that courts could hold mining industries and government officials accountable is equally unrealistic. Villagers most affected by mining operations are generally too afraid to go to court. They might lose their jobs and the level of physical intimidation through local thugs is high. Moreover, with their livelihood destroyed due to the pollution of agricultural land, the only way to survive is to take one of the few jobs that mines offer.

Environmental NGOs based in Yerevan have been more willing to take legal action against the mining corporations. However, in violation of international obligations and in contradiction to a ruling by RA's Constitutional Court, lawsuits brought forward by NGOs were thrown out on the grounds that the NGOs' interests were not at stake in these mining operations. Only people directly affected by these operations are legally entitled to take legal action (Amirkhanian n.d.). While it is not clear if illicit payments facilitated these rulings, it would not be surprising. Armenian judges are notorious for taking bribes. Moreover, a remnant of Soviet times still exists, called "telephone justice." It describes the practice of top government officials calling judges to tell them how to rule in cases that affected their political and/or economic interests. Phone calls were used to leave no written traces. The independence of the RA court system is therefore a sham (Aghalaryan 2013 interview; Stefes 2006).

8.9 The EU's Role in Combating Environmental Crime

In addition to strengthening national watchdog organizations, the EU could increase funding opportunities for environmental protection groups and increase EU transparency when negotiating agreements with RA by engaging with the public. Providing more support for organizations which monitor government agencies such as law enforcement and special environmental task forces to assure they are acting in law-abiding ways is another way the EU can help combat environmental crime in RA (Transparency International 2013a).

The EU can use their influence to reinforce current international laws that discourage environmental crime in RA. In 2004, NGOs presented a case to the United Nations Economic Commission for Europe (UNECE) claiming that RA was not compliant with the Aarhus Convention. Upon review, the UNECE agreed and has since pressured RA to take steps to become compliant (Aarhus Convention Compliance Committee 2006). Additionally, the World Bank has been developing a new Convention compliant EIA Law with RA (World Bank 2013). The EU could support international bodies such as the UNECE and World Bank in their efforts to help RA abide by international law while pressuring them to be more receptive to NGO concerns in accordance with the Aarhus Convention and other international treaties.

The EU can use its position as RA's main trading partner and largest import and export market to its advantage when discouraging environmental crime (European Commission 2014b). The EU proposed financial aid to RA for 2014–2017 ranges from €140 to €170 million (European Commission 2014a). RA's closed borders with Turkey and Azerbaijan have limited Armenian economic activity and play a role in RA's heavy dependency on international assistance. In response to past international recommendations, including those given by the EU, to enact anti-corruption measures, RA complied. However, these measures have proved to be mostly symbolic as a means to continue to receive foreign aid. The EU can use its economic position to encourage RA to enact policies that are truly effective in combating environmental crime and compliant with international law as a term of continuing current business relations and financial assistance (Börzel and Pamuk 2011).

There exists a double gap in the RA mining sector which fuels environmental crime in this area. There is a gap between national law and international commitments and a gap between national law and its enforcement and adjudication. In order to mitigate environmental crime in RA, the EU needs to address both gaps. In respect to the first gap, the EU can pressure RA to honour its environmental commitments as well as help it to develop legislation which will be in compliance with these international agreements. Reminding the RA government of its international obligations so that they are enforced in RA will also serve to strengthen the most important pro-environmental actors in RA, namely local movements and NGOs. EU support for these actors in other ways, such as through technical support and funding, can also strengthen their ability to address environmental crimes in their own country. The EU can play a role in addressing the second gap as well. The EU could provide incentives to EU owned companies working in RA's mining sector to operate in environmentally responsible and transparent ways. The EU could further use its civilian and normative power to convince the RA to enforce national and international law as a term of doing business.

8.10 Conclusions and Policy Implications

Though this case study has delved into the relationship between the mining industry and environmental crime in RA, the general characteristics and sources of environmental crime found in this study are not unique to RA. Corruption is a common symptom of mining sectors all over the world which leads to environmental crime that harms the environment and local population, ecosystems, and nonhuman species. In a world still largely fuelled by non-renewable resources, developing countries have an incentive to continue to invest in the mining sector over other industries as a means to increase the pace of their development. For these countries, developing other industries would help to break their dependence on a single sector and the resulting power imbalance and environmental crimes this causes. However, to accomplish this not only in RA but also in countries with similar mining sectors, outside forces such as international institutions and the EU need to incentivize compliance with international agreements and help develop local institutions to enforce both international and national laws. Incentives from outside players to create a mining sector that complies with applicable laws are an important factor to counterbalance the incentives of the mining sector to commit environmental crimes. In this sense, the results of this case study can be applied to mining sectors in other developing countries as well.

References

Aarhus Convention. (1998). 25 June. http://www.unece.org/fileadmin/DAM/env/pp/documents/cep43e.pdf.

Aarhus Convention Compliance Committee. (2006). *Aarhus Convention Compliance Committee Report on the Eleventh Meeting.* United Nations Economic Commission for Europe. Geneva, Switzerland. http://www.unece.org/fileadmin/DAM/env/documents/2006/pp/ece.mp.pp.c.1.2006.2.add.1.e.pdf.

Aghajanian, L. (2012). Breaking the grip of the Oligarchs: How a tragic twist of fate is fuelling a revolt against Armenia's overweening Tycoons. *Foreign Policy.* 5 February. http://www.foreignpolicy.com/articles/2012/11/05/breaking_the_grip_of_the_oligarchs.

Aghalaryan, K., & Baghdasaryan, E. (2014). Teghouts Offshore Labyrinth and Valeri Mejlumyan's Business Empire. *Hetq Investigative Journalists.* 29 April. http://hetq.am/eng/news/54322/teghouts-offshore-labyrinth-and-valeri-mejlumyans-business-empire.html.

Amirkhanian, A. Director of AUA Acopian Center for the Environment. Interviewed by: Stefes, C. 28 November 2013.

Amirkhanian, A. (n.d.) *Review and Gap Analysis of RA Legislation Related to Environmental Protection: Focus on Assessment, Valuation and Economic Instruments.*

Armenia-Canada Chamber of Commerce. (n.d.). *Mining Industry in Armenia 2011.* www.ada.am/files/622/publications/Mining-industry-in-Armenia.pdf.

AUA Newsroom. (2013). AUA study: 'Mining in Armenia Creates Poverty, Income Inequality'. *AUA Newsroom*. 15th April. http://newsroom.aua.am/2013/04/15/aua-study-mining-in-armenia-creates-poverty-income-inequality/.

Ayvazyan, S. Deputy Director of Transparency International Armenia. Interviewed by: Stefes, C. 5 December 2013.

Borzel, T., & Pamuk, Y. (2011). *Europeanization Subverted? The European Union's Promotion of Good Governance and the Fight against Corruption in the Southern Caucasus*. Freie Universität Berlin: KFG the Transformative Power of Europe. http://www.polsoz.fu-berlin.de/en/v/transformeurope/publications/working_paper/WP_26_B__rzel_Pamuk.pdf?1367706588.

Central Intelligence Agency. (2014). *The world factbook-Armenia*. 23 June. https://www.cia.gov/library/publications/the-world-factbook/geos/am.html.

Clifford, M., & Edwards, T.D. (1998). Defining environmental crime. In M. Clifford & T.D. Edwards (Eds.), *Environmental crime. Enforcement, policy, and social responsibility* (pp. 5–30). Aspen Publishers.

COHA. (2014). *Canadian mining in Latin America: Exploitation, inconsistency, and Neglect*. http://www.coha.org/canadian-mining-in-latin-america-exploitation-inconsistency-and-neglect/.

Ecolur. (2013). Chinese didn't know that permitting documents for Hrazden mine development to be Vulnerable. *Ecolur*. 11th April. http://www.ecolur.org/en/news/mining/chinese-didnvt-know-permitting-documents-for-hrazdan-mine-development-to-ve-vulnerable/2278/.

Eurocentre. (n.d.). *EU in Armenia*. http://eucentre.am/eu-in-armenia/#pca.

European Union Advisory Group to the Republic of Armenia. (n.d.). http://www.euadvisorygroup.eu/.

European Commission. (2014a). *Armenia*. Development and Cooperation-Europeaid. http://ec.europa.eu/europeaid/countries/armenia_en?language=bg.

European Commission. (2014b). *Countries and regions*. European Commission. http://ec.europa.eu/trade/policy/countries-and-regions/countries/armenia/.

European Commission (n.d.). *List of treaties by country: Armenia*. European External Action Service Treaties Office Database. http://ec.europa.eu/world/agreements/searchByCountryAndContinent.do?countryId=3858&countryName=Armenia.

European Union External Action. (n.d.,a) *Armenia*. http://eeas.europa.eu/armenia/index_en.htm.

European Union External Action. (n.d.,b). *Eastern Partnership*. European Union External Action. http://eeas.europa.eu/eastern/index_en.htm.

European Union External Action. (n.d.,c). *EU in Armenia | Eucentre*. European Union External Action. http://eeas.europa.eu/eastern/index_en.htm.

European Union External Action. (n.d.,e). *List of projects*. Delegation of the European Union to Armenia. http://eeas.europa.eu/delegations/armenia/projects/list_of_projects/projects_en.htm.

Freedom House. (2012). *Armenia*. https://freedomhouse.org/report/nations-transit/2012/armenia#.VGHXYWNNf-t.

Freedom House. (2014a). *Armenia*. https://freedomhouse.org/report/nations-transit/2014/armenia#.VGCcXIcY1t4.

Freedom House. (2014b). *Nations in Transit: Armenia*. https://www.freedomhouse.org/report/nations-transit/2014/armenia#.VK-ofmMhD0Q.

Global Security. (2013). Armenia- political parties. *Global Security*. 27 March. www.GlobalSecurity.org.

Global Witness. (2014). Gaps in new Afghan mining law pose a threat to stability. *Global Witness*. 19 August. http://www.globalwitness.org/library/gaps-new-afghan-mining-law-pose-threat-stability.

Harutyunyan, S. (2011). *Armenian watchdog sees little action against corruption*. Armenialiberty. http://www.ecoi.net/local_link/199617/318792_de.html.

HETQ. (n.d.). News, Article, Investigations. http://hetq.am/eng/.

HETQ. (2011). 'Who's Minding Armenia's Natural Resources', *HETQ*. 7 February. http://hetq.am/eng/print/628/.

Hoktanyan, V. (2012). *No impunity: Armenian politicians duck justice | Space for transparency*. Transparency International. 26 October. https://blog.transparency.org/2012/10/26/no-impunity-armenian-politicians-duck-justice/.

Human Rights Watch. (2012). *Out of control: Mining, regulatory failures and human rights in India*. Human Rights Watch. http://www.hrw.org/sites/default/files/reports/india0612ForUpload_0.pdf.

Natural Resources Governance Institute. (n.d.). *Indonesia- Transparency Snapshot*. Natural Resources Governance Institute. http://www.resourcegovernance.org/countries/asia-pacific/indonesia/transparency-snapshot.

Ishkanian, A. (2013). *Civil society, development, and environmental activism in Armenia*. London, England: London School of Economics and Political Science (LSE), Department of Social Policy, p. 10. http://eprints.lse.ac.uk/54755/1/Ishkanian_Civil_Society_Development_Enviromental_Activism_America_2013.pdf.

Ishkanian, A. (2013). *Civil society, development and environmental activism in Armenia*. London, England: London School of Economics and Political Science (LSE), Department of Social Policy, p. 10. http://eprints.lse.ac.uk/54755/1/Ishkanian_Civil_Society_Development_Enviromental_Activism_America_2013.pdf.

Lynch, M., & Stretesky, P. (2014). *Exploring green criminology: Toward a green criminological revolution*. Ashgate Publishing Company.

Matosian, M. (2012). Save Teghut' redefines environmental activism in Armenia, *The Armenian Weekly*. 21 February. http://armenianweekly.com/2012/02/21/save-teghut-redefines-environmental-activism-in-armenia/.

Mining Facts. (n.d.). *Mining facts: Resources on mining and mining policy*. Mining Facts. http://www.miningfacts.org/.

Mining Journal. (2011). *Armenia*. Mining Journal Special Publication. June. http://www.miningjournal.com/data/assets/supplement_file_attachment/0004/274972/Armenia_2011scr.pdf.

National Assembly of the Republic of Armenia. (1995). *The constitution of the republic of Armenia (with Amendments)*. 5th July. http://www.parliament.am/parliament.php?id=constitution&lang=eng.

News.am. (2011). Armenia's mining industry became monopoly of state officials. *News.am*. 27 June. http://news.am/eng/news/64720.html.

Newton, J.T. (2007). Case study of transboundary dispute resolution: The Kura-Araks Basin. *Institute for Water and Watersheds at Oregon State University*. http://www.transboundarywaters.orst.edu/research/case_studies/Kura_Arkas_New.htm.

NORAD. (2011). *Joint evaluation of support to anti-Corruption efforts Zambia country report*. Oslo, Norway: Norwegian Agency for Development Cooperation. http://www.oecd.org/countries/tanzania/48912843.pdf.

Responsible Mining Conference. (2014). *Responsible mining conference*. Responsible Mining. http://responsiblemining.am/.

Sanasaryan, H.A. (2008). Armenia must change its mining policy. *Keghart.com*. August. http://www.keghart.com/print/1635.

Shoghikian, H., & Bulghadarian, N. (2013). Armenia's Ombudsman highlights court graft with bribery 'price list'. *Radio Free Europe Radio Liberty*. 11th December. Sec. Armenia. http://www.rferl.org/content/armenia-judicial-corruption-price-list/25197495.html.

Siebert, B. Director at Foundation for the Preservation of Wildlife and Cultural Assets. Interviewed via Skype by: Stefes, C. 19 December 2013.

Save Teghut Civic Initiative (2014). *Alter-conference press release*. Save Teghut Civic Initiative. 28 May. http://teghut.am/en/2014/03/alter-conference-press-release/.

Save Teghut Civic Initiative. (2012). Who we are. *Save Teghut Civic Initiative*. 26 September. http://teghut.am/en/who-we-are/.

Stefes, C. (2006). *Understanding post-soviet transitions: Corruption, collusion, and clientelism*. Euro-Asian Studies. Palgrave Macmillan.

Transparency International. (2013a). *Corruption and the Eastern Partnership*. Transparency International. http://www.transparencyinternational.eu/wp-content/uploads/2013/11/2013-11-27_-Eastern-Partnership-position-paperFINAL.pdf.

Transparency International. (2013b). *Making mining more transparent: Senegal and Ukraine*. Transparency International. 15 November. http://www.transparency.org/news/feature/making_mining_more_transparent_senegal_and_ukraine.

Transparency International Deutschland e.V. (2013). *Tabellarisches ranking*. Transparency International Deutschland. http://www.transparency.de/Tabellarisches-Ranking.2400.0.html.

The European Union and the Republic of Armenia Partnership and Cooperation Agreement. (n.d.). Center for European Studies. http://www.ces.am/images/stories/CESPDF/pca_armenia.pdf.

U1+. (2014). They are now begging the diaspora for money to exploit amulsar mine. *U1+*. 7th November. http://en.a1plus.am/1199767.html.

United Nations. (1991). *Convention on environmental impact assessment in a transboundary context*. Espoo, Finland: United Nations. http://www.unece.org/fileadmin/DAM/env/eia/documents/legaltexts/Espoo_Convention_authentic_ENG.pdf.

United Nations Economic Commission for Europe. (2003). *Protocol on Strategic Environmental Assessment to the Convention on Environmental Impact Assessment in a Transboundary Context*. Kiev: Extraordinary meeting of the Parties to the Espoo Convention. May. http://www.unece.org/fileadmin/DAM/env/eia/documents/legaltexts/protocolenglish.pdf.

United States Environmental Protection Agency. (1992). *Arsenic Compounds-Hazard Summary*. April. http://www.epa.gov/airtoxics/hlthef/arsenic.html.

USAID 1 Armenia. (2013). *Country development cooperation strategy FY 2013-2017*. USAID. August. http://www.usaid.gov/sites/default/files/documents/1863/Armenia-CDCS.pdf.

Wallace, K. (2012). Teghut III—The dangers. *Armenian Environmental Network*. 5 April. http://www.armenia-environment.org/2012/04/05/teghut-iii-the-dangers-2/.

Weber-Fahr, M., Strongman, J.E., Kunanayaga, R., McMahon, G., Heldon, C. (2004). Mining. In Jeni Klugman (Ed.), *A Sourcebook for Poverty Reduction Strategies, 2: Macroeconomic and Sectoral Approaches: 444*. Washington, DC: The World Bank, pp. 5–30.

Weekly Staff. (2013). Commission releases final results, declares Sarkisian victorious. *The Armenian Weekly*. 25 February. http://armenianweekly.com/2013/02/25/commission-releases-final-results-declares-sarkisian-victorious/.

World Bank. (2013). *Discussing the draft law on environmental impact assessment in Armenia*. Discussing the Draft Law on Environmental Impact Assessment in Armenia. http://www.worldbank.org/en/news/feature/2013/06/08/discussing-the-draft-law-on-environmental-impact-assessment-in-armenia.

Yingyi, S., & Emmons, D. (2000). *Environmental crime: The criminal justice system's role in protecting the environment*. Thousand Oaks: Sage.

Zoi Environmental Network (2010). *Mining and environmental in the western Balkans*. United Nations Environmental Programme. http://www.unep.org/pdf/MiningBalkans_screen.pdf.

Interview List

1. Alen Amirkhanian, Director of Acopian Center for the Environment, American University of Armenia, interview by Christoph Stefes, Yerevan, 11 November 2013.
2. Inga Zarafian, President of Ecolur (Armenian environmental NGO), interview by Christoph Stefes, Yerevan, 2 December 2013.
3. Kristine Aghalaryan, journalist, Hetq, Investigative Journalists of Armenia, interview by Christoph Stefes, Yerevan, 3 December 2013.
4. Sona Ayvazyan, Environmental Policy Expert at Transparency International Anti-corruption Center, interview by Christoph Stefes, Yerevan, 5 December 2013.
5. John Barker, International Aid/Cooperation Officer at Delegation of the European Union to Armenia, interview by Christoph Stefes, Yerevan, 4 December 2013.

6. Barbara Siebert, Program Director at Foundation for the Preservation of Wildlife and Cultural Assets, Armenia, interview by Christoph Stefes, Skype, 19 December 2013.
7. Anonymous representative of international organization, interview by Christoph Stefes, Yervan, December 2013.
   Two anonymous mid-ranking officials of the RA government, separate interviews by Christoph Stefes, Yerevan, December 2013.

Dr. Christoph H. Stefes is an associate professor of Comparative European and Post-Soviet Studies at the University of Colorado Denver and a Senior Fellow at Ecologic Institute Berlin. He is the scientific coordinator of the EFFACE project. In his research and teaching, he focuses on comparative politics and teaches classes in comparative environmental governance. His primary focus is on the politics of renewable energy. In recent years, he has published three referred articles on this topic alone. Yet at Ecologic Institute he has also worked on climate change issues and most recently on environmental crime. He has already published one book with Palgrave Macmillan (*Understanding Post-Soviet Transitions*, 2006) and another one, co-edited with Carol Hager, is forthcoming (on Germany's energy transition).

Pete Theodoratos is a graduate student in the Department of Political Science at the University of Colorado Denver. He is interested in international law, environmental policy, and European politics.

9

Summary of Findings and the Way Forward

Christoph H. Stefes and Anna Rita Germani

9.1 Introduction

We conclude this volume by summarizing the main findings of the book's six case studies in order to identify common themes in the cases under investigation, but also to identify differences between them. We focus on a few main issues that the contributors to this volume have addressed such as geographic reach and degree of organization of the environmental crime(s) under investigation; the perpetrators

---

C.H. Stefes (✉)
Department of Political Science, University of Colorado Denver,
Denver, United States
e-mail: christoph.stefes@ucdenver.edu

A.R. Germani
Sapienza University of Rome,
Rome, Italy
e-mail: annarita.germani@uniroma1.it

R. Sollund et al. (eds.), *Fighting Environmental Crime in Europe and Beyond,* Palgrave Studies in Green Criminology,
DOI 10.1057/978-1-349-95085-0_9

and their motives; the victims and their suffering; as well as the efforts made to prevent and prosecute the offenses. Table 9.1 summarizes the main findings of the six case studies.

We conclude this final chapter with recommendations that could help the European Union (EU) and its member states to fight environmental crime more effectively within the borders of the EU and outside of it. We thereby rely on Michael Faure's insightful observations presented in Chap. 2 and additional findings of the EFFACE research project (Faure *et al.* 2016). Among these recommendations are proposals for better and mandatory data gathering and sharing, stricter penalties, confiscation of illegally obtained proceeds, and preventative measures.

9.2 Anatomy of Environmental Crime

Any study should begin with a solid definition of the subject under investigation. Implicitly or explicitly most authors of this volume take a legal approach to define environmental crime, that is, an act that harms the environment and is in breach of a (criminal, civil, or administrative) law or regulation. In short, the law tells us which act is an environmental crime and therefore punishable and which is just pollution that might be frowned upon but is perfectly legal (such as letting your car idle or engage in industrial livestock farming). Jennifer Maher and Ragnhild Sollund (Chap. 5) conceptualize environmental crime in a more comprehensive way, arguing that any act that harms wildlife, many of which result in injury and death, should be considered an environmental crime. The authors thereby acknowledge the inherent rights of animals beyond their utility for humankind (see also Chap. 1).

Christoph Stefes and Pete Theodoratos (Chap. 8) provide a further argument as to why a legal approach might be too narrow to fully grasp the extent of environmental crime. Where economic interests and political authority collude, environmental laws and regulations are usually lax, and resources allocated to law enforcement are often lacking. What might, therefore, be punishable by law in one country is lawful in another. Taking a legal approach to conceptualizing environmental

Table 9.1 Summary of Case Studies

	Land of Fires	IUU Fishery	E-waste Shipment	Wildlife Trafficking	Kosovo	Mining in Armenia
Authors' conceptual approach	Narrow, legal	Narrow, legal; but includes unregulated fishing	Narrow, legal; but recognizes fine line between legality/illegality	Broad, both legal and non-legal acts considered environmental crime	Narrow, legal	Medium; acknowledging environmental crime in law-making process
What is/are the 'crime(s)'?	Illegal disposal and trafficking of toxic wastes	Illegal, unreported, and unregulated fishing	Illegal shipping of electronic waste from EU countries to China	Trafficking of live animals, animal parts, and derivatives	Illegal logging; weakly regulated and illegal mining; illegal waste disposal	Weakly regulated and illegal mining, incl. processing and treatment of refuse
Degree of criminalization	Initially weak (misdemeanour), later stronger (jail sentences)	Weak (mainly fines)	Medium (prison sentences)	Weak (fines and short or suspended prison sentences)	Medium	Weak
Geographic reach	National, regional	Global	Global	Global	National, regional	National, regional

(*continued*)

Table 9.1 (continued)

	Land of Fires	IUU Fishery	E-waste Shipment	Wildlife Trafficking	Kosovo	Mining in Armenia
Organized?	Yes	Sometimes, but also individual vessels	Yes	Often, but also individual and one-time offenders	Sometimes, but also individual offenders	Yes (collusion of economic and political elite)
Who are the offenders?	Mafia groups, businesses, state officials	Fishers, sometimes criminal groups	Organized crime groups; logistics companies; custom officials	Manifold (tourists, crime groups, custom officials, consumers)	Organized crime groups; individuals; state officials	Oligarchs, high-ranking politicians, lower ranking officials
Offenders' motives	Financial rewards and avoidance of costs	Financial rewards	Financial rewards and avoidance of costs	Financial rewards; consumption, status, collections; ignorance	Financial rewards; survival	Financial rewards (profits and bribes)
Who are the victims?	Humans; animals; biodiversity; and ecosystems	Fish, entire species; humans	Humans (primarily Chinese); legal recycling business in Europe	Animals, entire species; humans (secondary)	Wildlife; humans	Humans; wildlife, entire species
Types of victimization	Psychological stress; physical harm (sometimes death);	Physical harm (death), extinction of	Severe physical harm (including death);	Physical harm (often death) deprivation of	Physical harm	Physical harm (sometimes death), economic harm

	release of tox- ins into environment	species; eco- nomic costs	economic harm	freedom, eco- nomic harm		
Facilitating factors	Initially weak laws; weak enforcement; corruption	Difficulty of monitoring; lack of enforcement	Legal loopholes; difficulty of monitoring	Legal loopholes; complexity of CITES treaty; low prioritization	Weak rule of law; corrup- tion; weak state capacity	Weak rule of law; corrup- tion; authori- tarianism
Level of law enforcement	Weak, getting stronger; important role for NGOs	Weak	Weak in Europe; getting stron- ger in China	Varies from country to country; gen- erally low priority, important role for NGOs	Weak	Negligible, key role for NGOs
Crime prevention	Minimal	Potentially strong (rights- based man- agement)	Waste reduc- tion; public campaigns	Reduce demand (currently weak); increase pun- ishment for awareness and deterrence	Minimal	Absent
EU role in fight- ing environ- mental crime	Relatively strong (ECD)	Relatively strong (CFP)	Relatively strong	Currently weak; potentially strong	Potentially strong (Stabilisati- on and Association Agreement)	Limited, unli- kely to increase much (despite ENP)

crime is therefore arbitrary. Stefes and Theodoratos encourage us to take a broader view which directs our attention to the environmentally harmful behaviour that already takes place at the law-making stage. Yet, irrespective of the conceptual approach the authors have taken in their studies for this volume, the case studies primarily focus on environmentally harmful behaviour that is punishable by law.

All instances of environmental crime investigated in this volume from the illegal disposal and trafficking of electronic and hazardous waste to illegal mining cause considerable economic, physical, and psychological harm to humans and wildlife. As several authors point out, environmental crime also often entails a slew of other crimes such as money laundering, theft, and corruption (see, for instance, Chap. 6). It is therefore puzzling how minor the penalties for offenders usually are, ranging from a fine to a few years in prison. Criminals only have to fear tougher penalties if they are convicted of other crimes that are perpetrated in the process of committing an environmental crime. For instance, in every case analysed, organized crime plays a considerable role, which is not surprising taking into account that high profit margins and low risk of detection attract criminal organizations (e.g. Chaps. 3 and 5). In many countries, being convicted of membership in a criminal organization often incurs a lengthy prison sentence. It therefore makes a difference whether the same crime is committed by an individual or a member of a criminal organization.

The extent to which environmental crime is often organized owes much to the fact that environmental crime frequently crosses borders, often many borders. The logistics of transnational environmental crime requires the involvement and coordination of dozens of different actors, ranging from otherwise legal businesses and private citizens to organized crime groups and corrupt officials (see Chap. 5). Of course, environmental crime almost always has a transnational dimension. For instance, air and water pollution crosses borders and foreign companies commit environmental crime in their host countries. Yet, even if we conceive the transnational dimension of environmental crime narrowly—that is, the criminal activity itself crosses borders—it is striking how prevalent transnational environmental crime is. Five of our six case studies indicate a transnational dimension (the exception is the Land of Fires case study) and of those five, three are truly global in scope (IUU fishery, e-waste shipment, and wildlife trafficking).

9.3 Offenders and Their Motives

The case studies show a very diverse group of perpetrators, including natural and legal persons, mafia groups, and elected and appointed officials at various levels of the state hierarchy. Further, some chapters indirectly point to the complicity of ordinary consumers, for example, their contribution to the production of electronic waste and consumption of animals, whether for their products or as food. What seems to connect these various actors are often their motives to engage in environmental crime. Pecuniary gain is the most common driver for criminal behaviour. Gains can thereby range from a few dozen to a few million dollars. The financial gain might be just enough to secure the survival of someone who engages in an environmental crime (e.g. an impoverished animal catcher in Latin America), or the financial gain might be substantial, albeit indirect, through the avoidance of costs that proper waste disposal incurs, securing the survival of a company. In many cases, environmental crime creates the income for lavish life styles and the ability to edge out economic competitors that 'foolishly' adhere to the law. Environmental crime, therefore, does not just entail environmental injustice but also social, economic, and ecologic injustice.

However, not all drivers are economic; in some cases (notably in the case of wildlife trafficking, Chap. 5) the motives are multifaceted and go beyond financial gains. For instance, religion and traditions might motivate the killing or abuse of animals. Finally, perpetrators do not even know that they are committing a crime. Tourists who bring products from rare species back home from their vacation might not think that these animals are protected by international treaties. This example also hints at the different levels at which offenders are aware of the consequences of their doing and feelings of guilt and responsibility. For instance, if environmental crime is widespread, as is the case in Italy's 'Land of Fires' (Chap. 3) and in Kosovo where illegal logging is part of daily household heating (Chap. 7), individuals' sense of wrongdoing might not be very well developed. Moreover, a lack of appreciation of the extent of damage that environmental crime causes will certainly facilitate engagement in environmentally harmful behaviour.

A fisherman who brings in another undocumented catch of a few tons might not think that his action contributes to the irreversible depletion of fish stocks.

Looking at the types of actors, their motives, and level of organization, we can identify specific groups. At the most basic level, individuals commit environmental crime either for minimal gains (or just survival) or because they are simply ignorant of relevant laws and regulations. In these cases, information campaigns and smaller administrative fines might suffice as deterrents. In the case of companies, the damage done and the profits reaped are much higher. Companies might collude with organized crime groups and/or with state officials to illegally dispose, for instance, large amounts of toxic waste. Depending on the extent of organization and damage done, administrative fines would have to be very high to serve as a deterrent. Prison sentences might be added. Very importantly, companies should be sentenced to pay appropriate restitution. Finally, as several case studies show, organized crime groups and corrupt state officials often facilitate and cover up environmental crime. For these actors, only lengthy prison sentences will work as deterrence. The illegal proceeds (profits and bribes) should be confiscated as well.

9.4 Victims and Harms Suffered

The victims in our cases studies are humans and wildlife alike. The psychological (see especially Chap. 3) and physical harm inflicted on humans and animals alike can be severe. In the case of animals, illegal fishing and poaching/trafficking has already led to the extinction of entire species. Furthermore, environmental crime might not only deprive animals of their habitat but also humans of their anthroposphere. Less severe, but still economically harmful, is environmental crime that deprives people of their sources of income. For instance, the Armenian mining industry destroys pristine environments, leading to a decline in tourism (Chap. 8). Yet many instances of environmental crime cause more than just material damages. They lead to ailment and even deaths, as humans are exposed to toxic material in soil, air, and water. As the case study of e-waste shipments from Europe to China shows (Chap. 5), it is often disenfranchised groups that suffer most from environmental crime in addition to the discrimination they already experience due their social, ethnic, religious, or other distinguishing status.

As Eileen Skinnider (2013, p. 1) argues, victims of environmental harm are not widely recognized as victims of crime. In part this is due to the perception of environmental crime as 'victimless' (Korsell 2001) but also because environmental harm does 'not always produce an immediate consequence and the harm may be diffused or go undetected for a lengthy period of time' (Skinnider 2011, p. 2) and because governments, industry, and in some cases, particular communities and society as a whole condone environmentally harmful activities (White 2015). The effects of a single offense may not appear severe in the short-term, but the cumulative impact of repeated violations in the long run can be irreparable, such as the exploitation of resources from mining and the extinction of species. This implies that society is often unaware of its victims, especially if their voices are not heard (animals, disadvantaged groups, children). Moreover, regulators may not set levels of enforcement effort and compensation properly.

9.5 Law Enforcement and Crime Prevention

The case studies show that environmental crime is facilitated by numerous factors that allow criminals to reap huge gains at low risk. Among these factors, weak laws and regulations full of loopholes and lenient penalties figure prominently (see Chaps. 3, 5, and 6). In addition, rigid law enforcement is often non-existent either due to corruption, weak state capacity, the absence of a rule of law culture (e.g. in Kosovo and Armenia), or because environmental crime is not made a political priority, which leads to minimal funding and training for law enforcement agencies (e.g. in the case of e-waste shipping and wildlife trafficking). Finally, environmental crime is sometimes difficult to detect and requires specific expertise. Wildlife trafficking serves as a telling example, as law enforcement officers are often unable to detect protected species (Chap. 5).

Given these facilitating factors, it is not surprising that law enforcement is often lacking. While we see some encouraging developments in Italy and China, the overall record of law enforcement is unimpressive. If the state largely fails to fight environmental crime, the role of victims and their organizations becomes even more important. If victims of environmental crime are recognized and protected as such, they are more likely to organize in the fight against environmental crime and join forces with state agencies. If they are not, the criminal justice system loses important evidence and the enforcement of laws against criminals becomes less effective. Three case studies clearly demonstrate the critical role that victims and nongovernmental organizations are able to assume in pushing for stricter laws, monitoring criminal activities, calling out the perpetrators and their stooges in state and government, and increasing the public's awareness of pollution and threats to biodiversity (Chap. 3, 7, and 8).

The contributors to this volume also examine ways to prevent environmental crime. Maher and Sollund, for instance, point out that wildlife trafficking is driven by consumer demand, and information campaigns against wildlife trafficking might reduce the demand for animals and animal parts (Chap. 5). As far as the illegal shipping of e-waste is concerned, what drives this crime is the tremendous amount of e-waste produced in the global north. Stricter regulations that would reduce the amount of waste produced would help mitigate this push factor (Chap. 5). A small, but good, example is the introduction of standard chargers for (almost) all cell phones in the EU. Finally, rights-based management helps to overcome the Tragedy of the Commons in the fishing industry and allow owners of fishing fleets to buy fishing permits if there are underutilized vessels. This will reduce incentives for illegal fishing.

The role of the EU in helping its member states and other states with which the EU maintains close political and economic ties to prevent and combat environmental crime is potentially huge. By passing the European Crime Directive and the Waste Framework Directive, the EU has already clearly articulated its willingness to combat environmental crime. Through the Common Fisheries Policy, it can directly control illegal fishing. Moreover, the EU has signed several international treaties that oblige the EU and its member states to fight, for instance, wildlife trafficking (one being CITES). Finally, through its European Neighbourhood Policy and the Stabilisation and Association Agreement, the EU can support non-EU member states to combat environmental crime more effectively. Yet in the end, the EU lacks a strong executive branch. It has to rely on national governments to implement its directives, regulations, and programs. In the case of Armenia, its leverage is undermined by the strong presence of Russia in the region. In Kosovo, it has to deal with weak state capacity. And even its own member states show a woefully inconsistent willingness and capacity to enforce environmental laws. While this all does not bode well for the fight against environmental crime, several measures with the potential to make the fight a bit easier can still be taken. The concluding section of this chapter will summarize some of these measures.

9.6 The Way Forward

It would be easy to conclude that environmental crime could simply be fought by introducing environmentally harmful behaviour in the penal codes of EU member states and punishing such behaviour with stiff penalties (i.e. lengthy prison sentences). To some degree, this is indeed a recommendation of the EFFACE research project. For instance, EFFACE recommends that 'higher sanctions [should be imposed] when the environmental crime occurs in the context of organised crime' (Faure *et al.* 2016, p. 12). As our case studies indicate, whenever organized crime is behind environmental crime, numerous other crimes are committed at the same time. For reasons of deterrence, the imposition of stricter penalties therefore seems obvious, despite the well-known harmful effects of prisons (Christie 2007).

However, as Faure points out in Chap. 2 of this volume, the EU and its member states have already come a long way from largely neglecting environmental crime and relegating it to administrative law (though with added criminal provisions) to introducing environmental crime in penal codes, partially due to the EU's passing of the Environmental Crime Directive in 2008. Yet as he also convincingly argues, there is some value in linking administrative law and criminal law, as it allows prosecutors and judges to choose from an array of penalties, ranging from administrative fines and payment of damages to lengthy prison sentences. Prosecuting environmental crime merely through the penal code is expensive and therefore leads to low conviction rates, which ultimately fail to deter would-be criminals. Prosecuting environmental crime also through administrative and civil law might therefore be more effective.

Taking into account how lucrative environmental crime can be, it seems appropriate to hit perpetrators hardest where it hurts them most—in their pockets. EFFACE, therefore, recommends that 'rules on the confiscation and forfeiture of the proceeds of environmental crime should be adopted at the EU level' (Faure *et al.* 2016, p. 12). Restoration of harms means that environmental crime will not pay (i.e. if detected). Hence, not just criminal sanctions can provide the 'effective, dissuasive and proportional' sanctions that the Environmental Crime Directive demands; financial penalties might be effective as well (Faure *et al.* 2016, p. 14). There is accordingly room to apply the EU's Environmental Liability Directive to cases of environmental crime (Faure *et al.* 2016, p. 15).

Nevertheless, any talk about appropriate penalties is premature if the prosecution of environmental crimes is lacking. The case studies show that prosecution rates vary significantly across EU member states. The variance owes much to loopholes and convoluted legal provisions in the member states. Clarifying environmental laws would be a first step towards more effective prosecution. Furthermore, environmental crime should receive the political priority and financial resources it deserves. The creation of specialized agencies for the prosecution and adjudication of environmental crimes—so far lacking in most member states—would then be possible (Faure *et al.* 2016, p. 23). In addition, prosecution would be much improved if victims of environmental crime and their NGOs would have formal recognition and public support. As the case studies demonstrate, NGOs have played a pivotal role in raising public and political awareness and calling out perpetrators of environmental crime. In countries outside of the EU (see the Armenian and Kosovo case studies), they are often the only effective guardians of the environment.

Outside of the EU, the EU and its member states should assume a strong role as advocates for stricter international treaties on environmental crime and help signatories to these treaties fulfil their international obligations by providing legal, financial, and technical support (Faure *et al.* 2016, pp. 27–8.). It would help as well if the EU reprimanded those signatories to already existing treaties that are in violation of their international obligations. The weight of the EU's assessment is of course enhanced if these countries have also signed bilateral treaties with the EU. Armenia's frequent disregard of the Aarhus Convention is not a trivial offense. It is a violation of Armenia's constitution and severely undermines the role of environmental NGOs (see Chap. 8).

What has not been discussed much within the EFFACE project is the ability and need to remove the incentives for environmentally harmful behaviour. The case studies show that environmental crime is driven by economic incentives which are partially related to the unnecessary demand for environmentally harmful goods such as electronics and ivory. That is not to say that the world should do without computers and smart phones (although it could definitely do without ivory products and the killing or capturing of endangered species), but the production of these electronics must take place with the goal of producing as little toxic and other waste materials as possible (see Chap. 6). Furthermore, awareness campaigns should help consumers to make more sustainable choices. In short, environmental policies should be rethought, going beyond the simple increase of criminal enforcement and stiffer penalties, by addressing, where possible, the dynamics behind the demand and the supply sides of both the legal and the illegal markets (Hayman and Brack 2002). Moreover, the introduction of market institutions that internalize the external costs of environmental crimes and overcome the Tragedy of the Commons might help to discourage environmentally harmful behaviour. The introduction of rights-based management systems, as discussed in Chap. 4, might be a step in the right direction.

Environmental crime has only in recent years entered the political discourse in the EU and its member states. Hence, much of the debate proceeds without a solid empirical foundation, which suggests that policy recommendations must be made with a grain of salt. The EFFACE project and this volume have tried to close some of the empirical gaps in the debate. Yet, the editors and contributors are humble enough to acknowledge that our contribution is a small one. We therefore conclude with our other colleagues of the EFFACE project that European authorities must do a better job gathering empirical evidence about environmental crime and sharing it with their colleagues, policy analysts, and the academic community (Faure *et al.* 2016, pp. 13–4). The fight against environmental crime is a vital one. It can only succeed with consolidated and profound knowledge of the subject matter.

References

Christie, N. (2007). *Limits to pain: The role of punishment in penal policy.* Eugene OR: Wipf and Stock.

Faure, M. *et al.* (2016). Conclusions and recommendations. *EFFACE.* Berlin: Ecologic Institute. http://efface.eu/sites/default/files/publications/EFFACE_Conclusions_recommendations.pdf. Accessed 13 May 2016.

Hayman, G., & Brack, D. (2002). *International environmental crime: The nature and control of environmental black markets.* London: The Royal Institute of International Affairs.

Korsell, L.E. (2001). Big stick, little stick: Strategies for combating environmental crime. *Journal of Scandinavian Studies in Criminology and Crime, 127*, 127–148.

Skinnider, E. (2011). *Victims of Environmental Crime–Mapping the Issue,* Research Report, The International Centre for Criminal Law Reform and Criminal Justice Policy, Vancouver, BC, http://www.academia.edu/3679107/Victims_of_Environmental_Crimes_-_Mapping_the_Issues. Accessed 19 May 2016.

Skinnider, E. (2013). Effect, issues and challenges for victims of crimes that have a significant impact on the environment. http://icclr.law.ubc.ca/sites/icclr.law.ubc.ca/files/publications/pdfs/Final%20Paper%20-%20Effect%20Issues%20and%20Challenges%20for%20victims%20of%20Environmental%20Crime.pdf. Accessed 19 May 2016.

White, R. (2015). Environmental victimology and ecological justice. In D. Wilson & S. Ross (Eds.), *Crime, victims and policy: International contexts, local experiences* (pp. 33–52). London: Palgrave Macmillan.

Dr. Christoph H. Stefes is an associate professor of Comparative European and Post-Soviet Studies at the University of Colorado Denver and a Senior Fellow at Ecologic Institute Berlin. He is the scientific coordinator of the EFFACE project. In his research and teaching, he focuses on comparative politics and teaches classes in comparative environmental governance. His primary focus is on the politics of renewable energy. In recent years, he has published three referred articles on this topic alone. Yet at Ecologic Institute he has also worked on climate change issues and most recently on environmental crime. He has already published one book with Palgrave Macmillan (*Understanding Post-Soviet Transitions*, 2006) and another one, co-edited with Carol Hager, is forthcoming (on Germany's energy transition).

Anna Rita Germani (PhD, MSc) is Aggregate Professor in Economics in the Department of Law, Philosophy and Economic Studies (Faculty of Law) at the University of Rome 'La Sapienza' where she teaches International Economics and Economics of Public Procurement. Her main research interests focus on environmental law and economics issues, such as public enforcement of environmental laws and judicial and prosecutorial discretion in prosecuting environmental crimes. She has published referred empirical articles on environmental justice and illegal trafficking of waste and, most recently, she is working on environmental crime and victims issues.

Index

R. Sollund et al. (eds.), *Fighting Environmental Crime in Europe and Beyond,* Palgrave Studies in Green Criminology,
DOI 10.1057/978-1-349-95085-0

MIX
Papier aus verantwortungsvollen Quellen
Paper from responsible sources
FSC® C105338

Printed by Books on Demand, Germany

MIX
Papier aus verantwortungsvollen Quellen
Paper from responsible sources
FSC® C105338

Printed by Books on Demand, Germany